STAR GAZING

Feminists have argued that cinema spectatorship is a gendered process. But what is at stake when female spectators look at female stars? *Star Gazing* puts spectators themselves back into theories of spectatorship in a historical investigation of the pleasures of cinema. Jackie Stacey combines film theory with a rich body of ethnographic material to investigate how female spectators understood Hollywood stars in the heyday of film culture, the 1940s and 1950s.

Drawing on letters and questionnaires from over three hundred keen cinema-goers, *Star Gazing* investigates the significance of certain Hollywood stars, for women in wartime and postwar Britain. Three key processes of spectatorship – escapism, identification and consumption – are explored in detail in terms of their multiple and changing meanings for female spectators.

Stacey's work challenges the universalism of psychoanalytic theories of female spectatorship which have dominated the feminist agenda within film studies for over two decades and, by demonstrating the importance of cultural and national location for the meanings of female spectatorship, *Star Gazing* gives a new direction to questions of popular culture and female desire.

Jackie Stacey lectures in Film Studies and Women's Studies in the Sociology Department at Lancaster University; she conducted the research for this book while at the Department of Cultural Studies at the University of Birmingham. She is co-editor, with Hilary Hinds and Ann Phoenix, of *Working Out: New Directions for Women's Studies* and, with Sarah Franklin and Celia Lury, of *Off-Centre: Feminism and Cultural Studies*.

STAR GAZING

Hollywood cinema and female spectatorship

Jackie Stacey

London and New York

First published 1994
by Routledge
11 New Fetter Lane, London EC4P 4EE

Simultaneously published in the USA and Canada
by Routledge
29 West 35th Street, New York, NY 10001

© 1994 Jackie Stacey

Typeset in Times by
Florencetype Ltd, Kewstoke, Avon
Printed and bound in Great Britain by
Biddles Ltd, Guildford
Printed on acid free paper

British Library Cataloguing in Publication Data
A catalogue record for this book is available from the British Library

Library of Congress Cataloging in Publication Data
Stacey, Jackie.
Star gazing: Hollywood cinema and female spectatorship/Jackie Stacey.
p. cm. Includes bibliographical references and index.
1. Women in motion pictures.   2. Motion picture audiences.
3. Feminism and motion pictures.   I. Title.
PN1995.9.W6S7   1993
791.43′082 – dc20   93-10970
CIP

ISBN 0-415-09178-0 (hbk)
ISBN 0-415-09179-9 (pbk)

*This book is dedicated to all the women who wrote
to me with their memories of Hollywood stars of
the 1940s and 1950s.*

CONTENTS

ILLUSTRATIONS

FIGURES

TABLES

ACKNOWLEDGEMENTS

The research for this book was funded by the Economic and Social Research Council, and conducted at the Centre for Contemporary Cultural Studies (now Department of Cultural Studies), at the University of Birmingham. The final stages of this book were completed in the Department of Sociology at Lancaster University. I am grateful to both those institutions for their support during this period.

So many friends and colleagues have contributed in different ways to the production of this book. Sarah Franklin inspired me to undertake this research and, indeed, to believe that feminist scholarship could make a difference. I shall remain indebted to her for sharing with me her intellectual and other energies. Richard Dyer's friendship and professional support has been a delight throughout the last six years, and his enthusiasm for my work has been greatly encouraging. Celia Lury has been a remarkable friend and colleague and has offered intellectual insight and emotional support during the writing of this project. More recently, Lynne Pearce has engaged with this research on all levels with a keen sense of clarity and with infectious conviction.

My deepest gratitude goes to Maureen McNeil and Richard Johnson, with whom I worked in the Department of Cultural Studies at the University of Birmingham where the research for this book was conducted. Richard's intellectual pleasure in discussing this, and other, research was a constant incentive, and his capacity to situate and to synthesise were greatly appreciated. Maureen offered me an intellectual rigour which has pushed me towards greater clarity and sharper argument in this book. As a friend and a supervisor, Maureen has shown me enormous generosity and kindness.

I would like to thank all those who commented on earlier drafts of this work. The 'Women Thesis Writers Group' was a great source of support during the first few years of this research and I am grateful to everyone who shared their ideas and work during that period, especially Michele Fuirer, Janet Newman, Jayne Warburton, Diane Hamer, Mieke Bernink and Klaatje Schwarzer. In addition to those mentioned above, Angela Lloyd and Debbie Steinberg kindly proofread later drafts. I would also like to thank Dorothy Sheridan at the Mass Observation Archive, Sussex University, for her help.

Finally, I would like to thank Hilary Hinds for her support, guidance and unfailing patience. Through transitions and traumas her resilience has been remarkable. Her intellectual precision has been invaluable (as has been her knowledge of punctuation). For her help throughout the writing of this book I am touched and deeply grateful.

I would like to thank all the women who corresponded with me about the female stars of 1940s and 1950s Hollywood cinema. I am extremely grateful for all the material they so kindly sent me. They include: Kathleen Abbott, Barbara Acton, G. D. Adams, Peggy Adams, Elizabeth Allan, Betty Allen, Margaret Angell, Rene Arter, Ruth Atkins, D. Atkinson, J. Bainborough, Gina Baker, Pamela Ball, Barbara, Vera Barford, Kay Barker, M. A. Barlow, Eva Barnes, Jean Barrett, K. Bates, Audrey Bealer, Peggy Bellamy, Dorothy Bennett, B. Benson, Nanette Bidgood, Brenda Biggs, P. Bingham, Joyce Blackburn, Brenda Blackman, P. Blackwell, B. I. Booth, L. Bradley, Naomi Brannan, Muriel Breach, Mavis Bridger, Judy Broadley, J. Brockett, J. L. Bromhead, Joan Brown, R. Brown, Diana Browning, Edna Buckland, Marie Burgess, Edna Burland, Marian Burton, Gwendoline Cadman, B. Campbell, Maisie Caplin, M. P. Carney, Joan Carter, Vera Carter, Jennifer Caves, Valerie Channell, D. V. Chivers, Dorothy Clarke, Sarah Clarke, D. M. Clarke-Smith, Marinne Claydon, Joan Clifford, Mabel Cluton, June Coates, Vera Cochran, Betty Cole, Margaret Coneys, Sylvia Cooke, Maureen Cooper, Brenda Court, Mona Cowell, Helen Cox, J. Crabtree, Mary Crabtree, Geraldine Crick, Cleone Critchlow, L. Crossman, Betty Cruse, Diana Crutwell, Constance Culley, Betty Cunningham, Mary Cuthbert, Mary Dainty, Marjory David, Jean Davis, L. Davis, Jean Davison, D. Delves, Margaret Denne, Sheila Dennison, Christine Didcock, S. Donavan, Pamela Done, Eilish Doran, Joan Draper, Edna Dukes, W. Eden, Evelyn Elliott, Elizabeth Elrick, Jean Fearn, Avril Feltham, M. Figg, Gladys Fisher, J. A. Fletcher, Judith Ford, Mary Ford, Barbara Forshaw, Jean Forshaw, Iris Foster, Victoria Foster, Betty Forsyth, Molly Frost, June Fuller, Margaret Gair, Doreen Gibson, Charlotte Gilchrist, Pat Gildea, J. Gittins, Peggy Glew, Brenda Goatham, R. Goddard, Frances Goon, June Gough, Sheila Gough, Doris Graham, Pam Gray, R. M. Ground, Sheila Hackett, Dorothy Hackwell, A. Hall, Jill Hall, E. M. Harris, E.M. Haskell, Heather Hawkes, Lilian Hayward, Shirley Hedderman, Dawn Hellmann, Gwen Hemsworth, P. Hicklenton, Ursula Hill Male, Dorothy Hilton, Margaret Hobb, Daphne Hobbs, Brenda Hodgson, Marion Hoffe, Violet Holland, A. Holt, Janet Hooper, M. L. Houseman, Margaret Hoyte, Josephine Hulland, Margaret

ACKNOWLEDGEMENTS

Humphries, Elsie Jacobs, Eileen Jenkins, R. Jepson, Brenda Johnson, J. E. Johnson, Jean Johnston, Gwyneth Jones, Jo Keen, June Kelly, Josephine Kemp, Pauline Kemp, Christine Kennedy, Joan Kiely, Phyllis Knight, Rita Laundon, Audrey Lay, Carole Lethbridge, Joyce Lewis, Pamela Light, Joyce Littler, Mary Looker, Joyce Lucas, Kathleen Lucas, Margaret McCaig, D. F. McCarthy, Joyce McCarthy, Pat McDonald, Hilda McFarlane, Elizabeth McIntyre, Anne McKinlay, Mrs McNorton, June McTaggart, Barbara McWhirter, A. Mahoney, P. K. Malcolmson, Barbara Mann, Jean Manuel, Kathleen March, G. E. Marks, Mary Marshall, I. Masters, Joyce Masters, Ella Matthews, I. O. Matthews, Brenda May, Mary May, Peggy Meek, Joyce Merry, Winifred Miklaucich, Veronica Millen, Julie Miller, Violet Miller, Millie Mills, Ivy Monk, Joan Mooney, Edith Moor, Sara Moore, Betty Morgan, Cynthia Mulliner, Lilian Naylor, Shirley Newing, Mrs Newman, Sonia Nimmo, Barbara Noble, Margaret Norton, May Nuckley, Christena O'Donnell, Verena O'Donnell, Ellen O'Flynn, Patricia Ogden, Yvonne Oliver, Doreen Oram, Pauline O'Shea, Sally Paine, M. Palln, Brenda Paterson, Maud Patterson, S. L. Paul, Sarah Paul, E. R. Peckham, Daphne Pedder, Shirley Phillips, Beatrice Povey, K. Price, Phyllis Pugh, R. C. Railton, Betty Ramsay, Georgina Rapley, Joan Rawlings, Sharon Reed, Annie Renak, Phyllis Reynolds, Christine Rice-Garwood, D. Richardson, Joy Roberts, Patricia Robinson, Sonja Robinson, Dorothy Rogers, Elizabeth Rogers, Barbara Rolston, May Ross, June Rothery, S. Rowark, Mrs Rumsey, Mary Russell, Pamela Ryan, Thora Savage, Evelyn Schen, Catriona Scott, Dorothy Scott, J. Scott Warren, Dorothy Seaman, Isabella Selley, J. Sheppard, D.K. Shilvock, M. Siggers, Patricia Simonis, Kathleen Sines, Betty Slater, Jean Smith, Margaret Smith, Queenie Smith, P. Snow, Winifred Spooner, Daphne Stacey, Selma Stanley, Stella Startup, Phyllis Stent, Muriel Stevens, Margaret Stokes, G. Stollery, Joan Strafford, O. Straw, Mabel Stringfellow, Mary Suggett, T. Sullivan, Lily Sumner, Jean Taylor, Sheila Tester, June Thomas, R. Thomas, Juliet Thompson, Shirley Thompson, Rita Titchener, Mary Tomkinson, E. Tonge, M. Topham, Muriel Towers, Joyce Townsend, E. Turner, Norah Turner, Margaret Twycross, Irene Valentine, J. Valken-Stephenson, Dorothy Vanson, Mary de Ville, K. Wadey, Joyce Wakeman, W. Wane, Doris Warren, Gwyneth Wathen, S. M. Watkinson, Diana Watts, J. West, Audrey Westgarth, Violet Whitcher, Jean Whittern, J. R. Whittle, Mary Williams, Sheila Willis, Mary Willmot, Barbara Wilson, Mary Wilson, Mary Windsor, Ena Wood, E. M. Worrall, E. Wright, Sheila Wright, Joy Yalden, Kathleen Yaxley.

I am also grateful to the men who corresponded with me, although I have not used their material in this particular research project: Eric Burns, G. H. Edge, Max Howlett, David Gold, John Greaves, Dave Iredale, John Kemp, Arthur Kennedy, John Ludlow, J. Merry, Derek Metheurgham,

Wilfred Milburn, J. Millward, Frank Read, M. S. Rogers, Fred Shipgood, Harry Statham, Frank Warren, Dennis Weller, John Whittingham, John Wilmshurst, R. W. Wilson.

I would like to acknowledge the BFI Stills Library for the stills reproduced in Chapters 4, 5 and 6.

1

HOW DO I LOOK?

THREE PICTURES

Picture 1: happy days?

The scene (Fig. 1.1) is a 1950s party held in the 1970s. Full dresses, long-jacketed suits, 'American' teenagers and barbecued hot dogs. The snap-shot is posed and attention is drawn to the presence of the photographer by the person on the right tipping the hat of the 'teddy-boy' of the teenage couple and grinning directly at the camera.

I am standing on the left dressed in a borrowed outfit. All my clothes (including the appropriate undergarments) were borrowed from my mother who was in her twenties during the 1950s, and who, I was always told, had a waist measurement of twenty-two (or was it twenty-four?) inches. Why was it, I always wondered, that women's waists were so much smaller in those days? The aim that evening was to produce an image: 1950s glamour. This party gave me the chance to try to be glamorous, but, at the same time, to deny my investment in producing such an image, since it was done in the spirit of the party's theme.

In this photo (shown here in black and white) I achieved something of the glamour I had longed to feel that evening. This is partly because of the way my face is photographed: it is close enough to be recognised as me, and yet far enough away for the particular details that teenage girls dislike about their faces to be concealed. The features are clearly lit, but the quality of the skin, every teenager's obsessive concern, is not. The dark rings under my rather deep-set eyes cannot be noticed. There is a 'flatness' to the face, my skin glows at a distance, and blemishes cannot be detected. It produces a kind of anonymity in so far as it is the features, almost in isolation, that are seen to stand out from a rather neutral facial back-ground.[1] In other words, the photo offers an image which is pleasingly more glamorous than my memory of how I felt that evening.

The key features of feminine glamour are highlighted: the eyes and the mouth. Both are emphasised by the way the light has fallen on my face: the

1

Figure 1.1 Snapshot

sparkle in the eyes, and the glistening of the pink lipstick and nail varnish all suggest the glow and luxury of 1950s Hollywood glamour. The angle of the photo, too, is pleasing: there is no hint of profile, the full-face shot satisfying my desire to play down the angularity of my face, which I then perceived as 'unfeminine' and definitely 'unglamorous'.

The focus on the face is extended to the body by the light falling on the naked neck and shoulders. This light creates shadows above the collar-bones, emphasising the hollows above, hinting at slenderness and elegance. The all-in-one strapless corselette under the dress went from hips to bust, pulling in the stomach, and fastening at the back with dozens of hooks and eyes. The white cotton dress was tight-waisted and full-skirted, with stiffened petticoats; it had a whaleboned bodice. The body could be safely displayed since the tight underwear held tummy in place and pushed breasts upwards in a vain attempt to imitate 1950s fullness.

The borrowed pearls and pink woollen stole, which were also my mother's, counter the hints of American 'brashness' or even 'sexual availability'. All other accessories, including the frosted pink lipstick and nail varnish, the drop pearl earrings, and the gold bracelet and rings, were mine. The combination of these accessories and the dress produce a particularly middle-class British version of glamour. The full skirt and ostentatious petticoats are sobered by the pearls and the pink woollen stole. The whiteness of the dress invokes an innocence, a sexual (and, perhaps, racial) purity; this complements the pink of the lips, the nails and the stole, a colour with associations of feminine passivity, gentleness and softness. The image here rests as a bid for glamour tempered by British, middle-class restraint and respectability.

Picture 2: eternally feminine

This advertisement (Fig. 1.2) is taken from a 1955 copy of the film weekly *Picturegoer*. The Hollywood star, Susan Hayward, is photographed looking at a sculpture embodying her own idealised image. The mock Greek sculpture suggests the existence of an eternal, quintessential feminine beauty, constant through the ages. The Hollywood star gazes up at the classical ideal of herself; the emphasis on the neck and shoulders of the sculpted bust is replicated by the display of those parts of the star's body. She looks at an image of herself 'as the sculptor saw her'; thus the female star becomes a spectator, examining an image of herself represented through someone else's imagination. Her expression is one of awe and wonder, echoing processes of female spectatorship, in which feminine ideals are on display to be admired by women in the cinema audience.

The sculpture looks like marble, but also like soap. Marble has connotations of high art, of permanence, of beauty, of appreciating value and of wealth. Soap, in contrast, is an everyday commodity. It is cheap; it is functional; it is dissolvable and therefore temporary; and it is replaceable. However, the implication is that the use of this particular commodity, Lux Toilet Soap, can enable the female consumer to approach the marble ideal. The name 'Lux', an obvious derivation of luxury, contradicts the associations with the everydayness of the product. Thus a chain of feminine consumptions is set into play: the spectator/consumer looks to the star who looks to the classical ideal of herself. The link between all three, the advertisement tells us, is the soap.

Both the marble and the soap are white and the whiteness is emphasised throughout the wording of the advertisement: the word 'white' is, in fact, used four times. Susan's skin remains constant, despite the variety of her film roles, we are told, because 'she's never wavered in her choice of the

whitest soap'. Whiteness is associated here with purity: 'It's the snowy, white look of Lux Toilet Soap that tells you worlds about its *purity*'. The connotations of sexual and racial purity intermingle. The use of a classical styled sculpture connects this Hollywood star to an ancient European high culture associated with 'civilisation' and 'world domination'. Thus whiteness suggests purity, cleanliness, beauty and civilised culture. Its opposite, though unspoken, is significant: blackness suggests impurity, dirtiness, ugliness and uncivilised culture.[2]

The caption at the top of the advertisement, 'How do you see Susan?', has an ambiguous address: it asks the female reader/consumer, the film star herself and, perhaps, the sculptor, the same question. The 'Susan' refers both to the film star and the image produced by the sculptor. The caption has no direct connection to the product being advertised; it does not refer to the softness of her skin, or the glow of her freshly washed cheeks, for example. Instead, the star is defined in terms of how she looks, and how she is seen by others. Looking and being looked at are both of significance here; the star is caught observing an image of herself, and the female spectator is addressed as a consumer of images of feminine beauty, and thus as an observer of other women, but also of herself.

Picture 3: image as identity

A woman poses for the camera in a full-length, silk, skin-coloured undergarment, shown here in black and white (Fig. 1.3). Her facial expression is coy, and slightly embarrassed, undermining the glamorous, if exaggerated, pout of the open mouth. The uneven colouring of the face reinforces the childlike quality of the expression, suggesting unfinished make-up. The costume exposes naked arms, neck and shoulders (collar-bones highlighted) within the conventions of the pin-up photograph, and yet her posture is timid and awkward, leg bent forward half-heartedly and hand covering crotch bashfully (hiding the camera cable?), refusing the viewer the usual pleasures of sexual objectification.

The undergarment, a highly fetishistic garment with its many lace ties and firm conical cups, draws attention to breasts, waist and ankles. But the cups are not filled and have been poked in to highlight the discrepancy between body and costume. Thus the pattern of the evenly stitched concentric circles on the cups, culminating in pointed perfection, is disrupted and parodied. Like a child dressing up in her mother's clothes which are too big for her, the model's discomfort in this luxurious and glamorous costume draws our attention to its artifice.

The backdrop of large white and pinkish-brown flowers on a sky-blue background is made of shiny silk material and suggests a type of 1950s American 'garishness'. The creases on the backdrop emphasise its function as prop, and thus draw attention to the mechanisms of image-making. The

5

Figure 1.3 Cindy Sherman, no. 131, 1983; (Sherman, 1991: 41). With permission of
the artist/Metro Pictures, New York

framing further dislocates any desire for visual pleasure in the way the head and feet are cut off and the completeness of the female form denied. There is a staginess to the whole photograph which militates against the pleasures of sexual display for the spectator.

The model and the photographer are Cindy Sherman, a feminist who has used herself in a host of different disguises and poses to produce playful masquerades. Using herself as her own model, and a delayed shutter release technique, Sherman has parodied visual styles and iconography from classical portrait painting to Hollywood cinema. In her earlier black and white 'Untitled film stills' she imitated Hollywood styles to explore particular narrativised femininities. Playing with our familiarity with Hitchcock's heroines, or the classic pin-up, Sherman encourages her spectators to make sense of the images and yet simultaneously forces us to retrace our own steps. Thus, the conventional visual pleasures of classic icons of femininity are both constructed and deconstructed at the same time.

In this photograph, Sherman becomes the classic pin-up for the male gaze, offering exposure of the female body, fetishistic costume, and a sexual pout, yet also ridiculing its visual conventions and indeed its consumers. Such parody highlights the emptiness of role-playing and the centrality of image to the constructions of femininity. Here, it is not a case of Sherman challenging images of women, but of questioning women's role as image.

THE POWER OF THE LOOK

All three images, the 1970s snapshot, the 1950s Lux advert and the 1980s feminist avant-garde photograph, raise questions about gender, power and the pleasure of looking; all these are of central concern in this book. Who looks and who is looked at are not neutral phenomena, but rather are cultural practices involving power relations. It has long been recognised that men and women in this culture have a different relationship to the division of *looking* and *being looked at*. As long ago as 1972, John Berger highlighted the connections between looking and possession, offering a critique of the 'ways of seeing' through which men control women. In his much-quoted analysis, he claimed that:

> *men act* and *women appear*. Men look at women. Women watch themselves being looked at. This determines not only most relations between men and women but also the relation of women to themselves. The surveyor of woman in herself is male: the surveyed female. Thus she turns herself into an object – and most particularly an object of vision: a sight.
>
> (Berger, 1972: 47)

The production of the feminine self as object of desire is the subject of all three images discussed above. The female body is on display and is made pleasurable for the approval of the male surveyor. In this 'society of the spectacle' (see Debord, 1977) it is women's bodies that have become the ultimate sexual spectacle for the pleasure of the male gaze. Indeed this split, between being a subject and object, referred to by Berger, has been seen as a key characteristic of female sexuality within this society. According to Catherine MacKinnon, female sexuality is 'that which is most one's own, yet most taken away' (MacKinnon, 1982: 515). In other words, women's sense of themselves as sexual subjects cannot exist without their awareness of themselves as sexual objects.

In each case-study above, femininity is not a natural, biological phenomenon, but rather an effect which has had to be worked hard at to achieve. The work of femininity (see Winship, 1981) involves continually producing oneself, indeed one's body, for the pleasure and approval of others. This work on the body can be seen in each of the above examples in which the production of self as image is central to the meaning of femininity. Writing about the work of Cindy Sherman, Judith Williamson argues that: 'Sherman's pictures force upon the viewer that elision of image and identity which women experience all the time: as if the sexy black dress made you *be* a femme fatale, whereas "femme fatale" is, precisely, an image, it needs a viewer to function at all' (Williamson, 1986b: 91–2). Williamson goes on to highlight how: 'Sherman's work is more than either a witty parody of media images of women, or a series of self-portraits in a search for identity. The two are completely mixed up, as are the imagery and experience of femininity for all of us' (Williamson, 1986b: 112). Thus, for women, the perception of self, and the perception of self by others, are typically bound up in a complex, even inextricable, way.

Identity, image and feminine ideals are connected through the sale of commodities in a consumer society. Placed in a film magazine, the Lux soap advertisement addresses female readers as spectators and consumers simultaneously: details of Susan Hayward's next film are given at the bottom of the advertisement for Lux soap. It is not only through the purchasing of consumer items, such as soap, however, that women are linked to commodity exchange. In the same way that women are both subjects and objects of relations of looking, they can also be seen as both products and consumers of commodity exchange. In the Lux advertisement, for example, the boundaries between products and consumers are blurred. The star image is a product of the Hollywood film industry and of the Lux advertisement, and thus, like the soap, is sold to the female spectator as a commodity, but the star herself is also, supposedly, a consumer (of Lux soap). The sculpture of the star is made from a material which resembles soap, the product being advertised, thus uniting consumable feminine ideal with consumable product. Finally, the soap is defined

8

in terms of its appearance, paralleling definitions of femininity as 'there to be looked at': 'When 9 out of 10 film stars use it, you can be sure that pure, white Lux Toilet Soap lives up to its appearance!' The work of femininity, then, requires the consumption of commodities. However, it not only involves consumption, both of images and of products, but also the negotiation of a feminine identity in a culture where women are both subjects and objects of commodity exchange.

FEMININITY AND STARDOM

Hollywood cinema has been a key source of idealised images of femininity in this culture. The cinema combines the exchange of looks with the display of commodities, and as such, has been of interest to feminists challenging conventional definitions of femininity. As Mary Ann Doane has argued: 'The cinematic image for the woman is both shop window and mirror, the one simply a means of access to the other' (Doane, 1989a: 31). What is puzzling, however, is that feminist work on Hollywood cinema has paid little attention to stars. This is striking since female stars seem to be an obvious focus in the analysis of the construction of idealised femininities within patriarchal culture. Attention to genre (especially melodrama, the woman's film and *film noir*) and to narratives (especially those reproducing the oedipal drama) and to forms of looking (especially voyeurism and fetishism) have tended to dominate the feminist agendas of the last ten years.[3] There remains, then, surprisingly little feminist work on Hollywood stars.[4]

In addition to the relative lack of feminist analysis of Hollywood stars, there has been even less interest in how *women* look at images of femininity on the cinema screen. If the images we see on the cinema screen are produced for the 'male gaze', how do female spectators relate to such representations (see Chapter 2)? The arguments about women's place as objects of the male gaze and of commodity exchange focus exclusively on cultural texts to draw their conclusions about female spectatorship. Be it oil paintings (Berger, 1972), photographs (Williamson, 1986b) or advertisements (my own analysis above), the subject of scrutiny has not been the women who look at these texts, but rather the texts themselves. How might our understanding of female spectatorship be transformed by accounts of its processes offered by women in the cinema audience? Why have feminist film critics shown so little interest in such accounts?

In the work which has been produced on Hollywood stars, for example, feminist film theorists have tended to reproduce a *textual* analysis. Despite the very different theoretical perspectives within feminist film criticism, the analysis of stars has shared this limited focus. The two key perspectives, which are usually contrasted with each other in the typical account of developments within feminist film theory, the 'images of women'

9

approach, typified by Haskell (1973), and the 'woman as image' approach, typified by Mulvey (1975), have nonetheless shared a common reliance on textual analysis, ignoring the question of how female spectators make sense of such representations.

Molly Haskell, for example, discusses the female stars in Hollywood cinema in terms of stereotypes which limit and control definitions of femininity in a male-dominated culture. The typical female of the 1940s was the 'treacherous woman', associated with stars such as Rita Hayworth in *Gilda* (1946, Charles Vidor) and *The Lady from Shanghai* (1948, Orson Welles), or the 'superfemale', such as Bette Davis in *Jezebel* (1938, William Wyler), the woman who, 'while exceedingly "feminine" and flirtatious, is too ambitious and intelligent for the docile role society has decreed she play' (Haskell 1973: 214). The other side to this construction of women as dangerous or rebellious, thus justifying the punishing narratives, is the 'sweet and innocent' type: 'For every hard-boiled dame there was a soft-boiled sweetheart' (Haskell, 1973: 194). Stars associated with this feminine stereotype included June Allyson, Olivia de Havilland and Deanna Durbin.

Haskell's extremely comprehensive analysis criticises these representations of women and situates their constructions within the domain of collective male fantasy. These stereotypes, she claims, are damaging, unrepresentative and negative images of women based on men's versions of femininity. Although her analysis refers outside the film texts to feminine stereotypes more generally, and to the patriarchal culture in whose interest they are perpetuated, Haskell's discussion of the stars themselves is restricted to the characters portrayed and their narrative treatment in the films.

A very different approach to stars within feminist film criticism has been the investigation of female stars as objects of the 'male' gaze. Rejecting the images of women approach for its problematic 'reflectionism',[5] Laura Mulvey focuses instead on how the cinematic language of Hollywood constructs female stars. Mulvey analyses Sternberg's use of Dietrich as the 'ultimate fetish' in her well-known essay 'Visual pleasure and narrative cinema':

> The beauty of the woman as object and the screen space coalesce; she is no longer the bearer of guilt but a perfect product, whose body, stylised and fragmented by close-ups, is the content of the film and the direct recipient of the spectator's look.
>
> (Mulvey, 1989: 22)

This fetishisation of the female star within Hollywood cinema is a form of scopophilia (or pleasure in looking) for the spectator. The other source of pleasure is the objectification of the female star for the voyeuristic gaze of the spectator. To illustrate this process, Mulvey discusses the heroines of

Hitchcock's films who are constructed as passive objects of the sadistic controlling voyeurism of the male protagonist, and, by extension, the spectator: 'The power to subject another person to the will sadistically or to the gaze voyeuristically is turned onto the woman as the object of both' (Mulvey 1989: 23).

LOOKING AT FEMALE SPECTATORS

Little attention, then, has been paid to female stars by feminist film theorists except in terms of how the stars function within the film text. With a few notable recent exceptions, however, the small amount of feminist work which *does* exist on stars has barely begun to address the question of the relationship between stars and spectators.[6] My aim in this book, then, is twofold: first, to contribute to the emerging body of feminist work on Hollywood stars, and second, to build upon the very small amount of work on cinema audiences through an analysis of the relationship between female spectators and female stars. How do women look at their Hollywood ideals on the cinema screen? What pleasures can they gain from the feminine images produced for the male gaze? What readings do female spectators make of the female Hollywood stars produced by a male-dominated film industry?

The feminist work addressing these questions within film studies has been done mainly within psychoanalytic and semiotic frameworks. The focus of these studies has been the ways in which Hollywood pleasures reproduce certain patterns of the 'patriarchal unconscious'. This work is discussed in Chapter 2 of this book. Offering an account of the enormous impact of Mulvey's theories of the male gaze, I consider the subsequent responses to her challenge, and then assess the usefulness of psycho-analytic frameworks for the analysis of visual pleasure, sexual difference and cinematic spectatorship generally.

A rather different set of answers to the questions set out above can be found within cultural work on television (and video) audiences. This work typically uses ethnographic approaches (including interviews with, or let-ters from, audiences) to analyse the consumption of popular cultural forms.[7] What is analysed in these studies of how male and female specta-tors watch differently is thus not the unconscious pleasures of the viewing process, but the audience's own accounts of their readings of programmes, and of their viewing practices more generally. Highlighting the contrasts between these two bodies of work, I offer an analysis of the ethnographic work on gender and spectatorship in the second half of Chapter 2.

Studies of audiences in cultural studies have traditionally given a voice to what particular groups of people have to say about the media and what they mean in their everyday lives. This is not to say that they have all remained crudely empiricist, as many who are critical of this tradition have

11

claimed. Rather, it has meant taking the audience seriously in an attempt to counter both the popular and, indeed, the critical assumption that audiences (especially female ones!) are 'passive dupes' who are easily manipulated by the media.

What, then, are the reasons for the reluctance on the part of feminist film theorists to venture into the area of audience research? Theoretical anxieties concerning 'crude' empiricism apart (see Chapter 2), there are methodological, and perhaps 'ethical', issues that have prevented feminist researchers from investigating cinema audiences. First, the ease of conducting textual analysis certainly compares favourably with the uncertainties and practical problems of audience research: in my experience, the former is more straightforward, less time-consuming and more manageable. The film text is a discrete object of study which is *usually* easily accessible, in contrast to spectators who have to be selected, contacted, and whose tastes, opinions and feelings have to be collected before any analysis can even begin. Studying cinema spectators from past decades adds further problems to questions of 'access' and additionally complicates interpretative strategies because of the questions of how processes of memory structure spectators' accounts of their viewing practices.

In addition, the political and ethical questions of the relationship of feminist researcher to female audiences have not had to be dealt with directly when 'texts' rather than 'spectators' are under scrutiny. It is certainly less controversial within the politics of feminist research to make critical judgements about film texts than about the female spectators who enjoy them.[8] This has been consistently true of feminist film criticisim in which Hollywood cinema has been condemned so vehemently for reproducing patriarchal ideology, and its pleasures rejected for operating in accordance with masculine fantasies about women. Typical of much feminist analysis, the earlier phases of feminist film criticism displayed a tendency to see patriarchal cinema as monolithic. Within such a framework it has been easier to condemn the dominant cinematic institutions and the films they produce, rather than to analyse the women in the cinema audience to whom Hollywood may have meant so much. Such a critical analysis of women in the cinema audience would have raised all kinds of issues about the relationship between the feminist researcher and female spectators more generally which can be somewhat skirted around by focusing on film text. Hence, the study of women audiences has been more common in cultural studies where an emphasis on resistant and oppositional cultures has always been maintained. In accordance with this emphasis, the active role of the audience in the production of cultural meanings has been foregrounded (see Chapter 2); thus female spectatorship might be seen as a process of negotiating the dominant meanings of Hollywood cinema, rather than one of being passively positioned by it.

My own approach to the questions of gender and spectatorship discussed so far combines elements from the work analysed in Chapter 2: my questions about feminine identities, pleasure and cultural ideals are prompted by feminist psychoanalytic criticism, but answered through a study of a particular group of female spectators, rather than analysis of film texts. Both engaging with, and yet also somewhat at odds with, psychoanalytic theory, then, my approach in this book straddles two very different traditions.

My original interest in this research was largely generated by the psychoanalytic debates about sexual difference, cinematic spectatorship and visual pleasure. The psychoanalytic questions about the construction of feminine subjectivity in a culture where women are exchanged between men as objects were central ones informing my desire to do research on Hollywood stars. However, I have also sought to highlight the limits of psychoanalysis and to question many of its universalistic claims by offering a historicised account of spectator/star relations. This necessitated broadening the scope of the study to include an analysis of historical discourses, institutional changes and the social relations of spectatorship. This investigation of femininity, spectatorship and Hollywood stars aims to demonstrate the importance of situating female spectatorship within specific cultural and historical locations. What I hope is distinctive about this research, then, is this attention to location and specificity. It is not only that the significance of cultural images needs to be understood in relation to its spectators, as I argue in Chapter 2, but also that the meanings of films and stars necessarily vary across time and place.

The appeal of 'whiteness' and of 'Americanness', discussed in relation to the three images above, for example, changes within specific contexts. The obsession with whiteness evident in the Lux advertisement would have had a particular symbolic significance in Britain in the 1950s where the magazine was published. In 1950s Britain the importation of black workers from Asian and Caribbean countries meant that considerable anxiety was expressed among white people about their continuing supremacy, and about the boundaries between black and white, and between Britain and the colonised countries. The 1950s saw the emergence of particular discourses about 'race', 'difference' and cultural identity which necessarily informed the appeal of white female stars to specific cinema audiences at that time.[9]

The appeal of Americanness similarly had a changing significance in 1940s and 1950s Britain. The snapshot of the 1950s discussed above demonstrates the clear association of Americanness with the decade of the 1950s: I am shown eating a hot dog, the stereotypical American snack; my '1950s' outfit is clearly an attempt to replicate a kind of Hollywood glamour. Indeed, the image I achieved was clearly based on the idea of the 'American teenager' – the two words seeming inseparable in this period. The suggestion here is that by the end of the 1950s American culture had become an integral part of British culture in ways that were not possible in prewar Britain.

My aim, then, in this book is to investigate female spectatorship in terms of its historical and national specificity. My particular focus is 1940s and 1950s Britain. There are several reasons for this choice of period. One of them is my own personal interest in Hollywood cinema at this time. My own love of Hollywood stars developed when I watched films on television with my mother. The Sunday matinée remains a 'treasured memory' for me (see Chapter 3), particularly in contrast to watching 'the football' to which we were otherwise subjected. Many of these were 1940s and 1950s films; my mother had, of course, grown up seeing them for the first time 'at the pictures'.

There are more conventionally academic justifications for this focus, and these are twofold: first, the 1940s and 1950s have been seen as a period of immense change for women in Britain. Since one of my aims here is to challenge the universalism of much psychoanalytic work on female spectatorship, it made sense to concentrate on a specific historical period containing strongly contrasting characteristics.

The 1940s and 1950s have been heavily mythologised in contemporary British culture, which some would say is still characterised by its 'make do and mend' mentality and obsession with the Second World War. Within feminist history, this period has also been mythologised as representing a particular kind of change. Women's changing roles at this time have been important in demonstrating that the sexual division of labour is indeed socially constructed, rather than biologically determined: how else was it possible for women suddenly to do 'men's' jobs, and for children to be perfectly well looked after by state nurseries? The image of woman as 'Rosie the Riveter' enjoying factory work and the company of other women in the 1940s, and becoming a wife and mother, busy with her own appearance, interior design and childcare in the 1950s, has become the typical version of these two decades. This rather stereotyped representation is based upon the experiences of some white, middle-class women at this time, and has been generalised in rather problematic ways that ignore both class and ethnic differences among women, as well as the fact that many women continued in paid employment after the war. Indeed, this 'reserve army of labour' theory of women being pulled in and out of the labour market according to the needs of capital has been discredited in more recent feminist writing on paid employment (Walby, 1986, 1990; Beechey, 1987).

Nevertheless, the 1940s and 1950s were undoubtedly a time of profound change for many women in Britain. These changes were indeed connected with the Second World War and women's entry into particular areas of paid employment from which they had traditionally been excluded.[10] The postwar period was also a period of rapid change in which *some* women were forced back into the home and encouraged to become wives and mothers again, instead of workers. The 'consumer boom' in mid to late

1950s Britain encouraged women to spend time and money on their own appearances and that of their domestic interiors. Some women were, of course, more able to do this than others. However, there was a general shift in discourses of gender, glamour and commodification which accompanied the expansion of consumer markets and impacted upon spectator/ star relations at this time.

In particular, the shifts for many women from relative austerity to relative affluence, and the expansion of consumer markets aimed at women, had a significant impact on definitions of femininity. The relationships between female spectators and Hollywood stars are investigated in this book within the historical specificity of such changes. What does it mean, for example, to watch the ideals of femininity embodied by the Hollywood stars in the context of the 1940s wartime austerity? How might this have a different significance to spectators in the consumer boom of the 1950s, the so-called age of affluence?

The second reason for the focus on the 1940s and 1950s is that much feminist film theory has been produced in relation to popular Hollywood films of this period. The *films noirs* and thrillers of the 1940s and the melodramas of the 1950s have been central to the developments within feminist film criticism.[11] Although the period of 'classic' Hollywood dates back to the 1930s, I was keen to focus the analysis as sharply as possible; and since my primary interest was to investigate female spectatorship and historical change, the 1940s and 1950s offered an obvious, and useful, boundary. In addition, aiming to contact female spectators of a specified period, I knew that significantly fewer women from the 1930s audiences would still be alive.

In order to provide geographical specificity, this study concentrates on female spectators in Britain. This focus was partly determined by convenience: it would have been time-consuming and expensive to contact women outside Britain. However, it was also decided upon because of my desire to challenge the rather over-generalised accounts of gender, visual pleasure and the power of the look discussed above. Instead, the central aim here is to analyse the specificities of how British women look at Hollywood stars on the screen. Thus national, as well as historical, location is of central concern to this investigation of female spectatorship and Hollywood stars.

Studying 'actual' spectators, instead of films texts, presents a multitude of methodological problems. Who to study, how to collect the material, what methods of interpretation to use, and how generalisable the conclusions are – all these questions need careful consideration. This may be one reason why the ethnographic work on audiences shows a preoccupation with methodological questions, in stark contrast to the psychoanalytic work, in which there is rarely any reflection upon methodology.[12] In addition to the difficulties of doing 'ethnographic' work with contemporary audiences, my interest in analysing spectators' readings of Hollywood stars in the 1940s and 1950s presents further complexities. What are the possible sources of material in the historical study of cinematic spectatorship? What might be the status of these sources? How might the passage of time have transformed their meaning? Instead of making the research processes of decision making and selection invisible, which is so often the case in the interests of academic 'tidiness', I have included a discussion of these processes in Chapter 3. This chapter thus retells the research narrative and analyses the particular methodological issues raised in doing this kind of audience research.

The focus of this research eventually became female spectators' memories of Hollywood stars in 1940s and 1950s Britain. More specifically, this book offers an analysis of the material I received in response to an advertisement I placed in two popular women's magazines (see Appendix 1). This material took the form of letters and, subsequently, questionnaires. The particular methodological issues about the status of this material, the forms of its production, the processes of memory formation, as well as the issues at stake in its interpretation, are also discussed in Chapter 3.

One further aim of this research is to address a gap in the literature by looking at relations between femininities in patriarchal culture. So much work in film studies has hitherto been concerned with questions of sexual difference, and the ways in which femininity is the object of masculine desire; instead, my interest is how women look at feminine ideals on the cinema screen.[13] Thus, my focus here is on the relationships between *female* stars and *female* spectators. To my surprise, a handful of men also responded to my advertisement, but I have not included analysis of this material here.[14] It seems to me better suited for another project at a later date. Furthermore, some women did mention male stars, and others wrote of their frustration at not being asked about male stars. Again, and for similar reasons, this would have been a different project and may be the subject of future research.

My respondents came from a relatively homogeneous group, all being readers of the same two women's magazines. Any research has to make selections in order to limit its focus and these selections will necessarily determine the kind of results produced. This research is no exception. My respondents were all white, typically came from the same class backgrounds (C1, C2 and D, see Appendix 3) and were mostly 60 years of age or over. Thus the arguments I have made in this book relate to a particular group of women. This homogeneity is clearly a result of the corresponding homogeneity of the readership of the two magazines, *Woman's Realm* and *Woman's Weekly*. Indeed, these two were chosen because of their appeal to women in the age range who would have memories of the cinema in the 1940s and 1950s.

This is thus a study of white British women's fantasies about glamour, about Americanness and about themselves. The conclusions are inevitably determined by this focus. Furthermore it is a study of women's memories of Hollywood stardom produced by a group of women belonging to similar class positions.[15] Thus the cinematic 'tastes' expressed are those of a specific group at a particular historical time. Studies of stardom conducted with a different group of spectators, in terms of class, ethnicity or nationality would no doubt produce a very different set of materials. These issues raised by the specificities of this research, together with the methodological issues they generate, are analysed more fully in Chapter 3.

The chapters which follow (Chapters 4, 5 and 6) provide the analysis of the material I collected in response to my advertisements for recollections of female Hollywood stars during the 1940s and 1950s. The first of these offers a brief analysis of cinema-going practices in Britain at that time. It then goes on to analyse spectators' memories of Hollywood cinema and its stars in relation to the notion of 'escapism', a rather neglected question within analyses of popular culture. Here its gendered dimensions are discussed within the context of wartime Britain.

Whereas Chapter 4 deals with the question of why women went to the cinema, Chapter 5 offers an analysis of the processes of spectatorship operating both inside and outside the cinema, resulting from the viewing of a particular film, or star. This chapter is particularly concerned with the relationship between the star images on the screen and the feminine identities of the spectators at that time. Taking the much-debated question of 'identification' as its starting point, this chapter investigates how female spectators remember their relationship to their Hollywood ideals at this time.

As I have already argued, one way in which spectators are connected to Hollywood stars is through commodity consumption. Chapter 6 looks at the role of consumption in spectator/star relations in 1940s and 1950s Britain. It extends the debates about woman's place as subject and object of the cinematic gaze, reassessed in Chapter 5, to look at the specific question of commodity exchange. Do Hollywood stars simply encourage female spectators to buy commodities in order to produce themselves as commodities for others? What other meanings and practices are revealed by spectators' own accounts of this relationship? How might women's pleasure in such forms of consumption be theorised and understood? These three 'ethnographic' chapters, then, analyse the memories of why women went to the cinema, their viewing practices in the cinema and what they consumed in connection with the cinema.

In the final chapter, Chapter 7, I consider some of the general issues about female spectatorship to have emerged from the study. In particular, I consider how the changes in spectator/star relations might be conceptualised. In an attempt to combine an analysis of the psychic transformations with one of the broader cultural changes in 1940s and 1950s Britain, this final chapter draws together some conclusions about a shift in the cinematic modes of perception in this context. It suggests that the nostalgic longing for a time when 'stars were really stars' articulates a desire for a time when stardom signified something very different from what it does today, and highlights a change in the cinematic mode of perception which began during the 1950s.

2

FROM THE MALE GAZE TO THE FEMALE SPECTATOR

In publishing new research it is customary to situate it in relation to existing debates within the field. Without such an outline of academic context, research questions and findings can seem idiosyncratic or inaccessible to readers unfamiliar with the area of study. In addition, offering an assessment of existing debates serves to establish the precise theoretical, methodological and political interests of the author and to construct and limit the specific field within which she seeks to place her contribution.

The problem with such a task in interdisciplinary work such as this is the breadth of academic debate which could be covered in order to put the reader 'in the picture': film studies, feminist theory, history, sociology and cultural studies all contain scholarship of importance to this project. Since an account of all these fields would constitute a book in itself, I shall restrict my analysis to two key areas which particularly inform this research – theories of spectatorship within feminist film criticism, and work on gender and audiences in cultural studies. It is a central aim of this book to begin to combine aspects of these two fields and to bridge the gap which has developed between them. It is thus necessary to set out in this chapter the arguments from each field within their own specific histories, before I attempt to combine them in my own work in the rest of this book.

> The magic of the Hollywood style at its best . . . arose, not exclusively, but in one important aspect, from its skilled and satisfying manipulation of visual pleasure.
>
> (Mulvey, 1975: 8)

For almost two decades now feminists have been debating the 'peculiar power and pleasure of the cinema' (Williams, 1989: 335). Central to this debate has been a critique of the forms of visual pleasure offered by Hollywood cinema, and of the ways in which these visual pleasures address a masculine spectator. Laura Mulvey's critique of the 'male gaze' and its visual pleasures for the cinema spectator has been the springboard for much feminist film criticism since 1975. Her article provoked an explosion of responses many of which rejected her pessimistic conclusions about the place, or lack of one, of 'woman' in dominant narrative cinema. Mulvey's significance cannot be overestimated; feminist film criticism has shown a continuing preoccupation with the questions of pleasure, spectatorship and gender identity foregrounded in her work. Although they offer critiques of Mulvey's position, many of these responses have nevertheless continued to address the kinds of questions she posed, demonstrating the enormous significance of her contribution. Thus, despite the fact that her arguments have been fully debated elsewhere,[1] I shall begin with a brief discussion of Mulvey's early work, since, without it, many of the theoretical debates which have followed would lack an intellectual context, and furthermore, the paradigmatic significance of her contribution would be denied.

Mulvey's article on visual pleasure and narrative cinema (1975) offered an analysis of the deep-rootedness of the structures of the patriarchal unconscious in the pleasures of popular cinema. It presented an important challenge to those engaged in psychoanalytic film theory by insisting on the centrality of the meanings of masculinity and femininity to the pleasures of popular cinema.[2] Additionally, it challenged feminists working with visual representation to move outside the conventions of Hollywood pleasures to produce a radical address to cinema spectators.

Its widespread impact might be accounted for in two contradictory, yet mutually dependent, ways: first, it gave feminists systematic 'evidence' of the patriarchal nature of popular cinema which validated their criticisms of it; and second, almost inevitably, it constructed a *monolithic* system in which the cinematic apparatus was saturated with patriarchal needs and desires.[3] This produced responses from feminist critics (including Mulvey herself) who have challenged such a model by exploring the cracks and fissures in this apparatus in an attempt to rescue women from total silence and victimhood. Thus, the reason for the success of Mulvey's challenge was also perhaps, paradoxically, the same reason it received so much criticism.

MULVEY'S MALE GAZE

Mulvey's analysis of the pleasures of Hollywood cinema led her to conclude that the spectator position offered is a 'masculine' one. According to Mulvey, there are three looks within the dominant mode of Hollywood cinema. First, there is the look of the camera(man), the director and the editor, who, while apparently representing a scene in a 'neutral' way, make a particular selection of shots, close-ups, angles and so on; the realist conventions of classic narrative cinema which make us believe the fictional world of the film is 'actually' occurring obscure the selection process that limits and controls how we look at a particular scene.[4] Second, there is the look within the film, which refers to the look between the actors within the film; the male characters objectify the female ones through their active, desiring and powerful look. Third, there is the spectator's look; this is determined by the above two. The spectator identifies with the powerful look of the male character on the screen, and his position in relation to it is produced by the camera(man)'s/director's look. In popular cinema point-of-view shots and shot/reverse-shot editing techniques are used to achieve the effect of seeing the female characters as objects of desire through the eyes of the male characters.[5] The conventions of Hollywood narrative cinema construct a particular spectator position, then, whilst carefully covering up the ways in which this is achieved.

The structures of looking in the cinema which produce voyeuristic pleasures are dependent upon precisely such an illusion. The spectator has the privilege of 'invisibility', looking without being looked at. The look of the 'camera' and the spectator seem subordinate to that of the characters (Mulvey, 1975: 18). In the dominant patriarchal system of visual represen-tation, sexual difference demarcates the active/passive, looking/looked-at split. Mulvey considers how the woman is constituted as object of the male gaze by the structures of the look in the cinema: 'Going far beyond highlighting the women's to-be-looked-at-ness, cinema builds the way she is to be looked at into the spectacle itself' (*ibid.*: 17).

Using Freudian psychoanalysis Mulvey explores the ways in which popu-lar cinema offers the spectator not only voyeuristic, but also fetishistic pleasures. Accepting the Freudian model of the boy and the girl child's 'discovery' of sexual difference which involves their different movements through the oedipal and castration complexes, Mulvey argues that the resulting fears and desires in the spectator's unconscious are played upon in particular ways by popular cinematic forms.[6] As well as controlling the woman as image through the pleasurable fantasy of power evoked by voyeurism, then, fetishistic looking enables the spectator to disavow the threat of castration by denying the difference the woman signifies.

According to Mulvey, the visual pleasures of narrative film are built around two contradictory processes: the first involves objectification of the image and the second identification with it. The first process depends upon 'the scopophilic[7] contact with the female form displayed for the spectator's pleasure' (Mulvey, 1975: 13): here the spectator's look is active and feels powerful. This form of pleasure necessitates the separation of the 'erotic identity of the subject from the object on the screen' (*ibid.*: 10). This 'distance' between spectator and screen contributes to the voyeuristic pleasure of looking in on a private world. The second form of pleasure Mulvey discusses depends upon the opposite process: identification with the image on the screen, which 'is developed through narcissism and the constitution of the ego' (*ibid.*: 10).

Mulvey's argument here is drawing on the work of Jacques Lacan, who placed psychoanalysis within a structuralist approach. She refers here particularly to Lacan's theory of 'the mirror phase' (Lacan, 1977). Lacan offers an account of the unconscious origins of pleasure in identification.

He describes how a child's initial recognition of itself as separate from the external world, as a subject, is a vital step in the constitution of the ego. Lacan uses a mirror to illustrate his point but the process might also occur in relation to the mother, for example. The child's image 'reflected' back to itself is gratifyingly unified, yet the child is still physically uncoordinated. The sense of unity in the image is pleasing to the child since it does not experience such a feeling in its own body. This initial recognition of self in an image is, then, simultaneously a misrecognition. Lacan argued that the child will continue to make such identifications as it grows up and that this is how the ego will be constituted. As Mulvey argues: 'It is the birth of a long love affair/despair between the image and self image which has found such intensity of expression in film and such joyous recognition in the cinema audience' (Mulvey, 1975: 10).

FEMALE SPECTATORSHIP

If feminist film criticism in the 1970s was characterised by debates about the male gaze, debates in the 1980s were characterised by their emphasis on female spectatorship.[8] Largely in response to Mulvey's critique, feminists began to explore the possible meanings of spectatorship for women. As Rosemary Betterton asks, given that images of female sexuality in this culture 'are multiplied endlessly as a spectacle for male pleasure . . . what kinds of pleasure are offered to women spectators within the forms of representation . . . which have been made mainly by men, for men?' (Betterton, 1985: 4).

However, as a special issue of *Camera Obscura* (20/21, 1989) demonstrates, there continues to be little consensus amongst feminists about the reference of the term 'female spectator'. Barbara Creed highlights four different definitions operating within feminist film criticism: the diegetic (the woman on the screen), the imaginary (construction of patriarchal ideology), the theorised (in feminist film criticism) and the woman in the audience (Creed, 1989: 133). Creed's separation of these four definitions is unusual. The more typical dichotomy conceptualises the female spectator either as 'an effect of discourse, a position, a hypothetical site of address of the filmic discourse' (Bruno, 1989: 105), or as the woman in the audience who brings to the film her particular history and social identity.

Within psychoanalytic models, which arguably still predominate in feminist film criticism, spectatorship is generally conceptualised within the former formulation: 'What seems determining is the textual production of sexual difference, that is, the way in which a film constructs sexual difference for its narrative and characters and through narration, for the spectator' (Cowie, 1989: 129). This construction of the textual spectator often occurs in strong opposition to the so-called empirical spectator: the woman in the audience. Mary Ann Doane, for example, asserts:

I have never thought of the female spectator as synonymous with the woman sitting in front of the screen, munching her popcorn. . . . It is a concept which is totally foreign to the epistemological framework of the new ethnographic analysis of audiences. . . . The female spectator is a concept, not a person.

(Doane, 1989b: 142)

Similarly, Guiliana Bruno states:

I am not interested in an empirical analysis of the phenomenon of female spectatorship. . . . I cannot get over an old semiotic diffidence for any notion of empirical 'truth' or 'reality', which I find very problematic. There are ways in which for me the phantasmatic level is more real than reality itself, or the so-called reality of facts.

(Bruno, 1989: 106)

Typical of much feminist psychoanalytic film criticism, both writers dismiss the question of how women in the audience watch films as uninteresting or irrelevant to debates about female spectatorship. Mary Ann Doane's claim that the female spectator is 'a concept and not a person' suggests a rather troubling division between film theory and cinema audiences. Similarly, Guiliana Bruno's claim that she finds 'the phantasmatic level more real than reality itself' suggests that actual cinema audiences are necessarily uninteresting to the feminist film critic.

The dichotomy of the 'textual' versus the 'empirical' spectator, or the 'diegetic' versus the 'cinematic' spectator, is often used as a shorthand to characterise the difference between the psychoanalytic model in film studies and ethnographic approaches to female spectatorship which have characterised cultural studies work. As can be seen from the discussion that follows, the model of spectatorship predominantly employed within feminist film criticism is the psychoanalytic, 'textual' one. Much of the ethnographic work has remained within the study of television, and, more recently, video. This work has drawn primarily on the field of cultural studies which has a long-standing concern with audiences and questions of cultural consumption. In contrast, film audiences have been of remarkably little interest to feminist film critics, who have remained sceptical about the empiricism of such studies. Such scepticism has resulted in a rather crude, blanket dismissal of women in the cinema audience, as if any study which involves people who attend cinemas must necessarily fall into the negative traps of empiricism. These different conceptualisations of the 'female spectator' could be schematically summed up as shown in Table 2.1.

In the rest of this chapter these two, very different, approaches to the question of female spectatorship will be discussed. Prompted by the provocative gaps in Mulvey's original attack on 'the male gaze', female

Table 2.1 Contrasting paradigms: film studies and cultural studies

Film studies	Cultural studies
Spectator positioning	Audience readings
Textual analysis	Ethnographic methods
Meaning as production-led	Meaning as consumption-led
Passive viewer	Active viewer
Unconscious	Conscious
Pessimistic	Optimistic

spectatorship has been a central, if contested, question within feminist analysis of the visual media. My reconstruction of these debates deals first with the responses to Mulvey within feminist film theory and second with the ethnographically based studies of female spectators, informed by cultural studies. Whilst acknowledging the significant differences between these two bodies of work, I shall endeavour to highlight the increasing importance of areas of overlap and exchange within feminist cultural criticism in the 1990s.

FEMININITY AND TEXTUAL DESIRES: MASOCHISM, MOBILITY OR MASQUERADE?

To return first, then, to the critiques of Mulvey's attack on the visual pleasures of Hollywood cinema. Two questions emerge directly from her analysis: first, how might the male body on the screen be the source of erotic pleasure;[9] and second: 'where is the place of the feminine subject?' (Rodowick, 1982: 8). Several possible answers to this important question have been offered within feminist film theory in the last decade. The first has been to explore the different gendered positions from which a film can be read and enjoyed. This problematises the model of Hollywood cinema as a monolithic apparatus producing unified and masculinised spectators. It offers an explanation of the pleasure of Hollywood cinema based on sexual difference. What this 'difference' signifies, however, in terms of the cinematic pleasures of spectatorship, has proved highly contestable.

This approach has tended to claim a space for female desire in the cinema based on a psychoanalytic understanding of the meaning of sexual difference. Raymond Bellour's work is one such example. He has explored the way the look is organised to create filmic discourse through detailed analyses of the system of enunciation in Hitchcock's films.[10] The mechanisms for eliminating the threat of sexual difference represented by the figure of the woman, he argues, are built into the apparatus of the cinema. However, the version of female desire that emerges is a very pessimistic one; woman's desire only appears on the screen to be punished and controlled by assimilation to the desire of the male character. Bellour thus insists upon the masochistic nature of the female spectator's pleasure in Hollywood film (Bellour, 1979: 97). Bellour, then, *does* provide an account of the feminine subject and women's spectatorship that offers a different position from the masculine one set up by Mulvey. However, he fixes these positions within a rigid dichotomy that assumes a biologically determined equivalence between male/female and the masculine/feminine, sadistic/ masochistic positions he believes to be set up by the cinematic apparatus. The cinema here is seen as a deterministic apparatus, controlling the meaning produced by a film text unproblematically. As Bergstrom points out: 'the resulting picture of the classical cinema is even more totalistic and deterministic than Mulvey's. Bellour sees it as a logically consistent, complete closed system' (Bergstrom, 1979: 57).

The problem here is common to much structuralist analysis: subjectivity is only conceptualised as an effect of textual polarities. There is little possibility here of the female spectator reading Hollywood films 'against the grain', of seeing more than one meaning in a film text, or indeed of understanding masculinity and femininity as fluid aspects of spectators' identities. In other words, the textual meaning is fixed and the sexed subjectivities of cinema spectators are read off across a binaristic determinism.

A second rethinking of the 'male gaze' offers a more mobile model of cinematic spectatorship. For example, in her 'Afterthoughts' article (1981) on visual pleasure, Mulvey herself addresses many of the problems raised so far about female spectatorship. In an attempt to develop a more 'mobile' position for the female spectator, she turns to Freud's theories of the difficulties in the attainment of so-called mature heterosexual femininity (Mulvey, 1981: 12–15). Required, unlike men, to relinquish phallic activity and the female object of infancy, women, it is argued, oscillate between masculine and feminine narrative identifications. To demonstrate this oscillation between positions, Mulvey cites Pearl Chavez's ambivalence in *Duel in the Sun* (1946, King Vidor), the splitting of her desire (to be Jesse's 'lady' or Lewt's tomboy lover), a splitting which also extends to the female spectator.

Mulvey's revision is important for two reasons: it displaces the notion of the fixity of the spectator positions produced by the text; and it focuses on the gaps and contradictions within patriarchal signification, thus opening up crucial questions of resistance and diversity. However, the binary model of sexual difference used still reinforces the somewhat problematic notion that fantasies of action 'can only find expression . . . through the metaphor of masculinity' (Mulvey, 1981: 15). In order to identify with active desire, the female spectator must assume a masculine position: 'the female spectator's phantasy of masculinisation is always to some extent at cross purposes with itself, restless in its transvestite clothes' (*ibid.*: 15). How, then, might we conceptualise the identity of the female spectator who actively desires – is masculinity really the only option?

The specificity of the female spectator is extended further in recent feminist work on popular cinema. This model of mobility, specific to the female spectator position, is developed further, for example, by Teresa de Lauretis in her exploration of these debates specifically in relation to narrative structures, both psychic and filmic. De Lauretis argues for an understanding of the *double identification* of the female spectator who, she argues, is involved in a twofold process: identification with the active masculine gaze and with the passive feminine image. This second identification 'consists of the double identification with the figure of narrative movement, the mythical subject, and with the figure of narrative closure, the narrative image' (de Lauretis, 1984: 144). Thus de Lauretis extends debates about the gaze within film theory to the important question of how spectators are narratively, as well as visually, inscribed by film texts.

A third theorisation that differs from Mulvey's model of the masculinised female spectator is the view of femininity as self-referentially commenting upon its status as image. For example, Mary Ann Doane's theory of femininity as 'masquerade' (1982) explores the difference in the female spectator's relationship to the dominant patriarchal structures of cinematic looking organised around voyeurism and fetishism. Doane argues that femininity is constructed differently in relation to the voyeuristic and fetishistic drives of the masculine subject/spectator.

Drawing on theories of female specificity in terms of 'spatial proximity' (see Irigaray, 1985) Doane argues that the gap between the image and the self necessary for voyeurism and fetishism is not part of the dominant construction of femininity. Thus, the female spectator cannot be a straightforward voyeur, since: 'For the female spectator, there's a certain overpresence of the image – she is the image' (Doane, 1982: 78). Similarly, the female spectator has a problematic relationship to the fetishistic gaze in the cinema, since: 'The boy, unlike the girl in Freud's description, is capable of a revision. This gap between the visible and the knowable, the very possibility of disowning what is seen, prepares the ground for fetishism' (*ibid.*: 80). Due to the definition of femininity as image resulting in a certain 'overidentification' with the image of the woman on the screen: 'the female spectator's desire can be described only in terms of a kind of narcissism – the female look demands a becoming' (*ibid.*: 78).

According to Doane, however, a distance between image and feminine subject might be achievable in terms of an understanding of femininity as itself a 'masquerade' (see Riviere, 1986). Unlike the 'trans-sex identification' of Mulvey's later model of the female spectator position as one of transvestite mobility, moving between the masculine and the feminine (Mulvey, 1981: 13), Doane introduces the notion of masquerade to describe an 'excess of femininity', a 'flaunting of femininity' in order to achieve the distance lacking in its dominant construction: 'The masquerade's resistance to patriarchal positioning would therefore lie in its denial of the production of femininity as closeness, as presence-to-itself, as, precisely, imagistic' (Doane, 1982: 81–2).

These accounts of female spectatorship in the 1980s provide important contributions to understanding the pleasures of Hollywood cinema beyond the rigidity of the model of the voyeuristic and fetishistic gaze of the masculine spectator. They extend and challenge the Mulveyian model of the male gaze in ways that open up the meanings of sexual difference and the pleasures of cinematic spectatorship.

Their use of psychoanalytic models, however, remains problematic in so far as they theorise identification and object choice within a framework of binary oppositions (masculinity/femininity: activity/passivity) that necessarily masculinise active female desire. This is largely due to the use of psychoanalytic frameworks which collapse gender and sexuality into a totalistic binarism of masculinity and femininity. Thus a consideration of 'bisexuality' within these debates tends to refer to the adoption of masculine and feminine positions of identification, leaving uncontested the assumption of heterosexuality in the processes of cinematic spectatorship. When, for example, Doane (1982: 81) argues: 'As both Freud and Cixous point out, the woman seems to be *more* bisexual than the man', the implication is *not* that she desires both women and men, but that she moves between masculinity and femininity. Thus the object of desire is ignored in favour of a consideration of the active or passive *nature of that desire*.

FEMALE SPECTATORSHIP AND HOMOEROTIC DESIRE

Typical of much psychoanalytic work, feminist film criticism has, on the whole, failed to address the possible homoerotic pleasures for the female spectator. Presented with desirable images of femininity on the screen, the possibility of homoerotic pleasure for the female spectator would seem to be an obvious absence from the multiple variations of desire and identification explored above. When homoeroticism is mentioned within these debates the limits of such a framework, which can only consider woman's desire for another woman in terms of masculinity, become clear. Doane's analysis of the first scene in the film *Caught* (Max Ophuls, 1948) demonstrates the problems with the psychoanalytic binarism perfectly:

> The woman's sexuality as spectator must undergo a constant process of transformation. She must look, as if she were a man with the phallic power of the gaze, at a woman who would attract that gaze, in order to be that woman. . . . The convolutions involved here are analogous to those described by Julia Kristeva as 'the double or triple twists of what we commonly call female homosexuality. . . . I am

looking, as a man would, for a woman; or else, I submit myself as if I were a man, who thought he was a woman, to a woman who thinks she is a man'.

(Doane, 1981–2: 77)

Female homoeroticism is thus seen in terms of masculinity since it can only be conceptualised within the binarism of masculinity and femininity, ignoring any specificity to such forms of pleasure and desire between women.

I have argued elsewhere that this problematic is particularly well demonstrated in relation to films concerning one woman's obsessive fascination with another, since the dynamic between the two female characters on screen reproduces that between female film stars and female spectators: a fascination with an idealised other which could not be reduced to male desire or female identification within the available psychoanalytic dichotomies, but rather necessitated a rethinking of the specificities of forms of feminine attachment.[11] I argue that *one* element of cinematic pleasure for female spectators might be a kind of homoeroticism evoked within such fascinations. Ironically, psychoanalytic theory often suggests such a general availability, since it claims that homoerotic desire forms some part in all our psychosexual developments, be it on conscious or unconscious levels. However, because of its rigid adherence to the binarism of masculinity and femininity discussed above, the specificity of any such desire between women is almost unthinkable.

My previous attempts to introduce this problematic onto the feminist film theory agenda received responses which precisely demonstrated the problematic I sought to address. Both Mandy Merck (1987) and Teresa de Lauretis (1991) return to Freudian binarisms to respond to my argument. The reply to my critique of the limited binarisms of psychoanalytic theory was thus made in exactly the psychoanalytic terms I challenged. My appeal to move outside this framework to address feminine desires more broadly, or to rethink narcissism in relation to the feminine other, is ignored and instead Freud is called upon to refix the binarism I attempted to disrupt. A circular argument is thus established: the critique of Freudian binarisms is misplaced because Freudian theory can demonstrate the validity of such a binarism.

Not surprisingly, the specificity I sought to address at once disappears and instead of female homoeroticism we are once again left with the Freudian definition of female narcissism. Merck argues that the fascination with the power and sophistication of another woman, which I suggest might characterise the relationship between female stars and female spectators, 'conforms to Freud's third example of the narcissist's love objects: "what he himself [*sic*] would like to be"' (Merck, 1987: 6). Similarly, de Lauretis claims that my analysis confuses desire with identification and that, in fact, the 'fascination' I describe 'is still a form of identification with

28

the image of woman, if a powerful and attractive womanhood, a feminine role model or ego ideal, and a quintessentially heterosexual one; it is not desire between women but indeed "intra-feminine", self-directed, narcissistic "fascinations"' (de Lauretis, 1991: 262). Indeed, she concludes by claiming that 'for Stacey [as for Sedgwick] desire between women is not sexual' and that I suggest that 'sex, "real sex" only happens with men' (*ibid*.: 262). Thus the dichotomy of 'desire' and 'identification' are re-affirmed in de Lauretis's argument which returns to Freud for validation of this rigid distinction.

My concern with the possibility of homoeroticism in the forms of fascination between women available to *all* women in the cinema audience assumes that pleasures of spectatorship work on unconscious, as well as conscious, levels. This does not mean that there is not further room for important enquiry into such questions as the specificity of lesbian desire, nor does it mean that I believe 'desire between women is not sexual'. Rather my argument has the opposite implication from de Lauretis's unlikely claims; I am not de-eroticising desire, but rather eroticising identification. I suggest that identification between femininities contains forms of homoerotic pleasure which have yet to be explored. This is not to argue that identification is the same as desire, or *only* contains desire, but rather to try to open up the meanings of both categories to enable a fuller understanding of the pleasures of the cinema for female spectators. To avoid further confusion, let me restate that my intention is to broaden the definition of desire but not to deny its erotic meanings, and to explore the ways in which female identification contains forms of desire which include, though not exclusively, homoerotic pleasure.

Reflecting upon these exchanges, I now believe that much of the confusion results from the refusal to address the 'actual' spectators in the cinema. If 'spectatorship' is simply a textual position, then there may only be a masculine or a feminine option; however, if spectatorship refers to members of the cinema audience, surely the possible positionings multiply. The reluctance to engage with questions of cinema audiences, for fear of dirtying one's hands with empirical material, has led to an inability to think about active female desire beyond the limits of masculine positionings.[12] By introducing the female spectator (in the cinema) into the equation, I would argue that there are cultural meanings associated with women looking at glamorous feminine ideals that differ from those ascribed to men. Given the saturation of this culture with images of attractive femininity, what might be the specificity of women's relationship to such desirable images beyond the psychoanalytic options of masculinisation or narcissism?

In Chapter 5 I challenge the Freudian separation between 'object libido' and 'narcissistic or ego libido', the one having 'to do with desire, wanting to have (the object), the other is desexualised and has to do with narcissistic identification, wanting to be or to be like or seeing oneself as (the object)' (de Lauretis, 1991: 260). Indeed, I would agree that such a dichotomy: '"ignores the fundamental narcissistic nature of all object relations", if they begin with the child's fascination with its own image' (Merck, 1987: 6, quoting Penley, 1985). My argument is that narcissism is not just love of self, but always involves an image of the other. Feminine narcissism, however, takes on a specific meaning in cultures where women are so consistently defined as both subject and object of the gaze. Thus 'wanting to be like' does not *necessarily* exclude an erotic component. Indeed, narcissism, as Lynne Pearce (1991) has pointed out, may be closely connected to forms of homoeroticism: the self-adoration implying a worship of femininity in general (*ibid.*: 19). Like Pearce, I would argue that such fascination with femininity continues beyond the 'adolescent' phase, dismissed by Freud as a stage on the way to mature heterosexual femininity, and indeed may continue to inform women's pleasure in images of femininity throughout adult life. Thus, female identification, I would argue, involves a more complex set of cultural meanings than is suggested by the psychoanalytic model.

FORMATIONS OF FANTASY – OUT OF THE IMPASSE?

One significant shift within feminist film theory has been from the rejection of the possibility of identification as positive for the female spectator, typical of work in the 1970s and early 1980s, to the more recent analysis of the flexibility of the spectator's subject positioning in fantasy. Confounding the usual coupling of anti-identification and pro-psychoanalysis, on the one hand, and pro-identification and anti-psychoanalysis, on the other, Elizabeth Cowie has argued for the multiple positions of cross-gender identification available to both sexes.

Cowie (1989) argues for the need to retheorise the scopophilic pleasures of voyeurism and fetishism which have dominated the feminist agenda for some years now. Drawing on the work of Laplanche and Pontalis, Cowie (1984) proposes instead an analysis of the place of fantasy in cinematic spectatorship and its pleasures. Fantasy generally signifies the world of the imagination, the inner world of idealised scenarios and wish-fulfilment and is opposed to the so-called world of 'reality'. Cowie's emphasis here is on the psychoanalytic interpretation of fantasy not in terms of content, but as a 'structure: fantasy as the *mise-en-scène* of desire, the putting into a scene or staging of desire' (Cowie, 1984: 71), in which the fictional pleasures offered to the subject are not gender specific.

Conceptualised as a scene, rather than simply as a set of wishes, fantasy can be closely linked to filmic representation. The same formations which are structured in the Lacanian imaginary are seen to exist in public forms of fantasy such as film. Of the three modes of fantasy – primal, unconscious and conscious daydreams – it is only in the latter that the 'I' of the story, the subject, is stable, Cowie argues. In the former two, the subject takes up a variety of subject positions and thus is not fixed. Cowie extends Lacan's argument with regard both to daydreaming and to fictional narrative film where such de-subjectivisation takes place. The cinema, Cowie argues, offers the specularisation of fantasy in which the spectator takes up several subject positionings (Cowie, 1984: 102).

Through this more flexible model of fantasy, Cowie explores the multiple identifications offered to the spectator by a film text and the interchangeability of different subject positions for the spectator (Greig, 1987: 40). Thus rather than being constrained by the negative construction of feminine identification discussed earlier, female spectators, like male spectators, are likely to make multiple identifications across gender boundaries. As a result, the feminine spectators may, or may not, be women, or only women (see Penley, 1989: 256).

'SOMETHING FOR EVERYONE': FANTASIA AND FEMINISM

This recent work on fantasy may have moved the debates on from the restrictive 'Althusserian spectator',[13] helplessly postioned as a subject by the film text, which influenced so many of the earlier arguments about the construction of passive female spectators, but it raises some fundamental problems for feminist film criticism. Most notably, if gender identifications are no longer thought to be connected to the gender of the spectator, and all spectators are similarly free-floating and autonomous, the investigation of the different psychic investments of women and men in the cinema becomes impossible. As Mary Ann Doane argues, if the exploration of the notion of fantasy reveals 'the psychical instability which thwarts the fixing of identity and the constant slippage between various textual positions' then such an unfixing of sexual difference would surely mean that 'there is no need for feminist criticism' (Doane 1989b: 145). Similarly, Jacqueline Rose, whilst acknowledging the need 'to recognise the instability of unconscious fantasy and the range of identifications offered by any one spectator', cautions against this leading to 'an idealisation of psychic processes and cinema at one and the same time' which results in an analysis of the cinema where there is 'something for everyone both in the unconscious and on the screen' (Rose, 1989: 275). In other words, this more flexible model of spectatorship suggests that sexual difference is so fluid as to have little determining significance in cinematic spectatorship.

How, then, are the meanings of sexual difference fixed, if temporarily, in relation to the pleasures of spectatorship? My argument is that, as well as analysing the unconscious processes of spectatorship, feminist film criticism needs to develop a theorisation of how identities are fixed through

31

particular social and historical discourses and representational practices, outside, as well as inside, the cinema. The exclusive focus on the unconscious processes of spectatorship has been unable to explain precisely how such meanings are fixed.

One problem with Cowie's analysis, which takes film texts as evidence for the workings of the unconscious and vice versa, is that the specificities of the two processes are ignored. Since both the film and the psyche are considered texts they are treated as analogous in often rather confusing and misleading ways. But how analogous are these processes and are the specificities of each lost in such analyses? Despite the apparent interest in specifically cinematic pleasures, through the focus on visual pleasure, for example, much of this work tends to read these pleasures through an understanding of early psychic formations which actually pays little attention to the *cinematic* context of those pleasures. What is left out of such theories of spectatorship is cinema spectators and the formation of their social identities, which will shape the kind of readings made of films.

A central problem with many theories of female spectatorship, then, concerns the implications for the place, or the lack of one, for the social identities of spectators. Instead of looking at the relationship between material and psychic reality, Cowie argues: '[W]hat Freud shows is that it is irrelevant to consider whether the event was fantasised or real, or whether the woman wishes it to be real, for the fantasy refers not to physical reality but to psychical reality' (Cowie, 1984: 76). Cowie's emphasis here typifies her more general reluctance to engage with questions of social identity in relation to spectatorship. The conclusion to be drawn from the reading of fantasy as the location of free-floating, sexually undifferentiated, multiple subject positionings would seem to reinforce the separation of unconscious processes from 'the rest' of subjectivity. Thus, rather than exploring the relationship between the psychic and the social, this particular reading refuses such questions. As Annette Kuhn has argued:

> Theories which emphasize sexual difference would mostly have us believe that subjectivity is formed through unconscious operations. But how, if we are talking about feminine/female subjectivity, is it possible in these terms to deal with such representations as 'lived experience' and 'memory'? . . . How might 'social forces' be negotiated, be represented, in lived experience, in memory or indeed in unconscious processes?
>
> (Kuhn, 1989: 215)

LOCATING SPECTATORSHIP

Processes such as desire and identification involve conscious and unconscious formations of subjectivity. The social formation of such processes

within particular discourses has remained a marginal interest within feminist film criticism, in favour of approaches which privilege the 'psychic
reality' of the female spectator. In attempting to broaden the debate about
cinematic spectatorship, E. Ann Kaplan discusses the importance of the
desire to identify with screen characters in terms of the emotional connection that identifying involves; this needs to be understood, she argues, as 'a
socialized urge towards identifying' (Kaplan, 1989: 198).[14]

In addition to the lack of consideration of sociality in many psychoanalytic accounts of spectatorship, the historical specificity of the cinematic
spectator has also been ignored. The reluctance by many feminists working
within a psychoanalytic model to deal with actual members of the cinema
audience has been accompanied by a refusal to deal with the historicity of
spectatorship. Feminists such as Patrice Petro (1989), Miriam Hansen
(1989) and Carol Flinn (1989), on the other hand, have integrated textual
analysis with a historical approach to spectatorship and have attempted to
theorise the relationship between the psychic and the social subject. Carol
Flinn argues against the position typified by Doane in the introduction to
this chapter, which sees the question of the female spectator exclusively as
a theoretical one: '[I]f the female spectator were only a theoretical construct, unrelated to the empirical audience – [we would have to] assume
that theory transcends history' (Flinn, 1989: 152).

Similarly, Miriam Hansen's argument challenges the dichotomy between
the textually constructed spectator and the individual movie-goer, which
she sees as symptomatic of the troubling, but increasing, division of labour
between film theory and film history:

> Not only do we need to conceptualise spectatorship as a process that
> mediates between the two levels, as a historically constituted and
> variable matrix; we also need to complicate the issue with a third
> term – one that accounts for the social, collective, experiential dimen-
> sion of collective cinematic reception.
>
> (Hansen, 1989: 169)

Until recently, the values embedded in reception have thus been ignored
by many feminists concerned with questions of spectatorship in favour of
the study of the values embedded in production (see Citron *et al.*, 1978:
93). The social discourses and historical locations of particular female
spectators watching films in different contexts have only recently been put
more centrally on the agenda. I would argue that it is only by combining
theories of the psychic dimensions of cinematic spectatorship with analyses
that are socially located that the full complexity of the pleasures of the
cinema can be understood. The analysis of female spectators' accounts of
the cinema may open up multiple or contradictory readings, depending on
variables such as context, company, mood, or differences amongst female
spectators: *Now Voyager* (1942, Irving Rapper) may mean different things

to a young woman watching it with a friend and fellow Bette Davis fan in the cinema in the 1940s, to an older woman watching it on television with her daughters on a rainy Sunday afternoon in the 1970s, and to a film student watching it in a lecture theatre with a hundred other students in the 1990s.

Feminist work generally in the late 1980s and early 1990s has been increasingly concerned with 'the politics of location';[15] historical situations, and social differences between women, have been placed firmly on the agenda in opposition to the rather universalising theories of the 1970s.[16] Within feminist film criticism, the politics of location is also making its mark: increasingly issues of ethnicity, class, sexuality and nationality are being placed on the agenda.[17] However, despite these political and theoretical challenges to the psychoanalytic textual model of spectatorship, the basic methodology has largely remained intact – 'other' categories have simply been added into the textual analysis. Very little feminist work has moved beyond the text to look at how women in cinema audiences make sense of popular films.

Two notable exceptions to this are Helen Taylor (1989) and Jacqueline Bobo (1988). Rather than offering *one* reading of *Gone With The Wind* (1939, Victor Fleming, George Cukor and Sam Wood) based on textual analysis, Taylor investigates the meaning of *Gone With The Wind* as a cultural phenomenon. Taylor analyses:

> how *GWTW* lives in the imaginations, memories and experiences of individuals and groups – that is, through the eyes of its fans, who, to judge by the statistics of book sales, film and television viewing figures and a wealth of memorabilia and popular references, come from many nations, classes, races, generations and life experiences.
>
> (Taylor, 1989: 18)

What is distinctive about Taylor's approach is the way in which she manages to combine analyses of production, text, historical context and audiences' accounts of the significance of the film in their lives. Taylor thus successfully highlights the limits of the textual approach which posits a single position for the female spectator: 'women's voices have spoken of the varied and contradictory ways in which this one work has accumulated significance in their lives, making the notion of a *single GWTW* impossible' (Taylor, 1989: 232). Instead, Taylor demonstrates the importance of the changing historical context to the pleasures of popular films for female spectators. Thus female spectatorship, rather than being a single, unified theoretical category, with little or no connection to history or to women in the cinema audience, can be understood here as a changing, dynamic and historically specific category.

Like Taylor, Bobo attempts to introduce a specificity to the question of pleasure, female spectatorship and popular cinema. Jacqueline Bobo's work (1988) on *The Color Purple* (1985, Steven Spielberg) uses interviews with black female spectators. Bobo argues that *The Color Purple* has a specific set of significations for black women which escaped the white feminist academics who criticised it so harshly. Bobo's work also draws upon cultural studies approaches to explore the question of the cultural reception of popular film. Like Bobo, I would advocate the use of some aspects of cultural studies approaches in order to develop an understanding of female spectatorship which moves beyond the universal and the textual assumptions of much of the feminist film theory discussed so far in this chapter.

BEYOND TEXTUAL DETERMINISM

In contrast to the lack of interest in actual cinema spectators in film studies, a plethora of research on this topic has been produced within cultural studies. This work has been centrally concerned with television audiences and, to a lesser extent, more recently with the domestic consumption of videos (Gray, 1987, 1992). Since the early 1980s, cultural studies work on television audiences has been developing rapidly, and in recent years 'audience studies' have become a definite 'boom area'. Indeed, audience studies have become *so* popular that Charlotte Brunsdon has felt it necessary to appeal for the retention of 'the notion of text as an analytical category' (Brunsdon, 1989: 120). Unlike film theory, then, in which the text has typically tended to be privileged over context, television studies have tended to privilege the context over the text (Gray, 1987: 45).

The television audience is different from the cinema audience in a number of important ways: their different regimes of representation and reception have been documented more fully elsewhere (Ellis, 1982: 162). However, these differences do not account for the striking discrepancy between the vast amount of academic study of television audiences compared with the minimal interest in the cinema audience. This discrepancy might be partly accounted for by the fact that the study of television audiences emerged largely within 'cultural studies', or at least drawing on approaches developed within this field. Two tendencies in cultural studies are significant here: first, cultural studies has had a strong tradition of interest in 'unrepresented' groups (Hoggart, 1958, and Williams 1965, 1977), initially in terms of class, and later in terms of ethnicity and gender. Second, and perhaps consequently, cultural studies has had a long-standing commitment to understanding popular culture in terms of consumption. In addition, its association with radical politics of resistance in the 1970s and 1980s, together with the influence of the Gramscian model of power which emphasised negotiation and struggle, rather than entirely successful domination, may have made cultural studies particularly receptive to the study of how consumers, rather than producers, make cultural meanings.

As I argued above, the female spectator in film studies has predominantly been a textual one. Devoid of sociality and historicity, the spectator has often been seen to be a subject position produced by the visual and narrative conventions of a film text and assumed to respond to it in particular ways due to the universal workings of the female psyche. The women in the cinema audience have been virtually absent from consideration within much feminist film theory and the model of female spectatorship so produced has been criticised for its ahistoricism and lack of attention to contextual specificities.

It is in the work on audiences/readers in cultural studies that we find some of the analysis I have suggested is lacking within feminist theories of cinematic spectatorship: here researchers have been keen to find out about what actual audiences think and feel about the programmes they watch, or the books they read, and to analyse the particular contexts in which cultural meanings are made. In many of these studies the audience or reader is seen to take an active role in meaning production, and thus a more optimistic reading of popular culture often emerges in which audiences negotiate meanings and thus dominant ideologies are not necessarily seen to be totally successful.

In audience studies, the interaction between text and reader, programme and viewer, has been foregrounded in order to look at the meanings produced in specific contexts. These studies have therefore focused on actual audiences, and have employed a variety of more ethnographic methods,[18] such as interviews, analyses of letters, questionnaires and so on, to investigate the processes of cultural consumption. Cultural studies approaches, then, have argued that cultural meaning does not reside exclusively within the text, but rather that: '[T]he content of any message, whether textual or behavioural, is not simply found in that message but is constructed by an audience interacting with that message' (Radway, 1986: 96).

In addition to the general interest in how people make sense of popular culture, cultural studies work has emphasised the significance of the context of consumption. The focus on the viewing context has been important in so far as audiences, rather than being ahistorical fixed positions in texts, have been considered as people with social lives and domestic habits, whose readings of particular programmes would be shaped and influenced by social identities and cultural differences, such as gender, race and class.

ACTIVE AUDIENCES

Cultural studies work on audiences has attempted to develop a model of audiences as active participants in the production of meaning, but to situate this process within a set of power relations. In his influential work on encoding and decoding, Stuart Hall (1980) argued that meanings do not reside in texts, but rather in the negotiation between reader and text which may produce one of three possible decodings: dominant, negotiated or oppositional. Thus a more diverse range of meanings was seen to be produced by a text depending on the particular viewer and the particular context (*ibid.*). Resistance to dominant cultural meanings could thus be theorised within this method of cultural analysis, challenging the rather gloomy and deterministic model of the textual spectator employed in film studies.

David Morley's study of *The 'Nationwide' Audience* (1980) marked an important shift towards a critical interest in ethnographic audience study. Extending Hall's claims about negotiated meanings further, Morley offers an analysis of the processes of decoding by a particular audience. Morley's study argues strongly against the notion of the textual spectator being elaborated in the journal *Screen* at this time, and proposes instead a more complex model of the interaction between text and reader dependent upon the discursive context of reading. Decoding, then, was argued to be a struggle over the meaning of a text in which the audience actively engages with a programme, rather than being passively positioned by it. Television viewing was thus seen as a practice in which viewers played an active role (*ibid.*).

This challenge from cultural studies to the presumed passivity within the textual model of spectatorship is especially significant in terms of investigating women's role as cultural consumer. Women are typically ascribed the place of passivity within patriarchal culture, and this has been reinforced within the textual model of spectatorship. Thus there has been a political imperative to challenge such a presumption of double passivity, and to look at the ways in which women negotiate media meanings through active processes (Gledhill, 1988).

This challenge has had particular significance in terms of considering women as cultural consumers. David Morley has argued that the 'television zombies' of the 'effects' model of audience analysis are always 'other people' (Morley, 1989: 16). In addition to this, it has been argued that 'these "other" people helpless before the television set are implicitly feminine. Women are the ones responsible for maintaining psychic and social well-being through the institution of the family – the very things television is so often thought to destroy' (Seiter *et al.*, 1989: 1). This general association of women with the damaging effects of television on society is further compounded by the particular connection between women viewers and the 'worst' kind of television programmes; the popular forms with which women are conventionally associated, such as soap operas or romance narratives, are precisely those which have been most forcefully condemned as 'mindless nonsense', 'escapist rubbish' and 'the trashiest trash' (Brunsdon, 1986a). In addition, feminists have consistently challenged the cultural ascription of women to the position of passivity more generally, an ascription which has been reinforced by the notion of the passive viewer within television discourses.

'THE SUPREMACY OF THE AUDIENCE'

Feminist work on women audiences, then, has been doubly motivated to reclaim the audience from a discourse which presumes their mindless passivity. Much work has focused on how women watch or read particular popular genres such as soap opera or romance fiction. One of the first contributions to this debate was Dorothy Hobson's study *'Crossroads': The Drama of a Soap Opera*. In terms of where she locates the cultural production of meaning, her study is one of the first to take the audience and their viewing context seriously. Her central questions in this study explicitly highlight the active participation of the *Crossroads* audience.

In her analysis Dorothy Hobson demonstrates how much cultural knowledge the audience bring to the text and thus emphasises the *activity* of the viewing process. The reading of the programme, she argues, extends far beyond the text itself and depends upon knowledge and experience outside the viewing situation. This knowledge comes from their experience of being women, mostly working-class women, whose lives are often divided by the dual pressures of family and work, constrained by economic pressures, and concerned with the 'personal' areas of kinship and interpersonal relationships. Furthermore, she goes on to argue, the audience extend their reading of the programme beyond what is actually represented (Hobson, 1982: 132). These meanings could not be ascertained from the signifying practices within the text, or from an analysis of the spectator position constructed by it. Rather, they depend on a model of the audience that takes into account the social knowledges and historical contexts, defined by class and gender, and which therefore produces diverse readings. According to this approach, then, an analysis of the construction of social identities is crucial to an understanding of how an audience makes a reading of a particular programme.

However, in challenging the myth of the passive viewer, and replacing it with an active, more creative, and diverse model, Hobson argues for the 'supremacy of the audience's own perception of the reality of the programme' (Hobson, 1982: 134). Over-compensating for previous textual determinism, she claims that: 'To try to say what *Crossroads* says to its audience is impossible for there is no single *Crossroads*, there are as many different *Crossroads* as there are viewers. Tonight twelve million, tomorrow thirteen million: with thirteen million possible understandings of the programme' (*ibid.*: 136).

The mind boggles at the task before the media critic if this is truly the case! Hobson's claims here, perhaps with polemical intent, exaggerate the sovereignty of the viewer. The challenge to the notion of the passive female viewer overemphasises the supremacy of the audience in meaning production, and produces the kind of populism typical of some cultural studies work, which embraces the pleasure of the viewer as unproblematically positive.[19] In her enthusiasm for challenging textual determinism and its resulting condemnation of women who enjoy soap operas, Dorothy Hobson produces a rather unmanageable model of subjective relativism.

VIEWING PRACTICES AND THE SOCIAL RELATIONS OF CONSUMPTION

The investigation of context in television viewing practices is continued in David Morley's ethnographic study *Family Television: Cultural Power and Domestic Leisure* (1986) in which he extends the earlier work on audiences in three specific ways. First, the study looks at television viewers in their domestic sphere, and analyses viewing practices within specific family contexts. This shift is, in fact, a result of David Morley's criticism of his earlier audience studies which 'extracted' the viewer from her/his viewing context, as he himself did in his *Nationwide* study. Second, and resulting directly from the first point, this study introduces the importance of the social relations of television watching. David Morley argues against earlier, limited analyses that treated 'watching TV' as if it were something separate from social relations. He thus avoids the pitfalls of the rather individualistic and idiosyncratic model of spectatorship asserted by Hobson (1982). Instead he analyses viewers in relation to each other, and viewing practices within the social relations of the family. The study thus highlights issues of power and control in relation to the sexual division of labour, patriarchal authority, and gendered viewing practices.

The final extension of previous models of television watching is Morley's attempt to bring together questions of interpretation of the media with questions of its use. Television, then, is analysed here as an integral part of the patriarchal social relations of the family; it is used to produce conflict, as well as to avoid it, to start conversations, as well as to kill them. The viewers are seen not only to play an active role in producing the meaning of a media text, but also to *use* the television in their familial interactions, thus extending the 'meaning' of television beyond the actual representations it produces.

By interviewing the viewer within a particular set of social relations, David Morley's study manages, in some respects, to investigate the 'social subject' as proposed by Charlotte Brunsdon in her attempt to resolve the 'text/context dichotomy' (Brunsdon, 1981, see also Kuhn, 1984). His analysis constructs the viewer as a social subject with a sense of agency. The various formations of subjectivity, and unequal degrees of agency, differ particularly according to gender divisions within the family. Thus social identities such as gender are analysed within a specific set of familial practices, and the consumption of media forms is seen as integral to these processes.

However, the results of this study raise a more general problem in audience research about the extent to which gendered patterns of viewing might have been predicted without the research. Morley concludes that: 'Women tend to do other activities whilst watching TV' whereas 'men do nothing else'; 'women's viewing is scattered' whereas 'men watch more TV in uninterrupted blocks of time'; men, not women, tend to operate the remote control; women prefer comedy, fiction programmes, men prefer factual programmes (Morley, 1986: 146–72). These results offer a rather unsurprising set of gender divisions around television viewing practices. In fact, Morley does not find evidence of the more flexible model of subjectivity he advocates in his introduction and there remains a substantial discrepancy between his theoretical claims about subjectivity and his rather dualistic conclusions about gender differences.

The question of the social relations of media consumption is also addressed by Ann Gray in her study of women and the domestic use of VCRs (1987, 1992). Using an ethnographic approach to investigate the specific meanings of VCRs within the home, Gray argues that any understanding of television and video audiences must include an analysis of the determining factors shaping the consumption of these media within the domestic environment. According to Gray, 'new technology in the home has to be understood within the context of structures of power and authority relationships between household members, with gender emerging as one of the most significant differentiations' (Gray, 1987: 38).

Women's television viewing practices are described by some of those interviewed in Gray's study as integral to their domestic routines: a daytime soap opera may be watched as a reward for the successful completion of particular domestic tasks (Gray, 1987: 48). Similar to the female readers of Mills and Boon romances in the United States in Janice Radway's study (1984) discussed later in this chapter, some women in Gray's study used soaps to signify a breathing space from the demands of others. Some watched with other women, and these 'women-only' viewing contexts meant that films, such as romances, could be enjoyed without the heckling of male partners who considered such videos trivial and who ridiculed women for watching them. Thus, the patriarchal power relations of the family determine not only who chooses the videos watched in the mixed or 'family' viewing situation, or who controls the remote button, or who understands the time-set mechanism on the video, but also how some genres are defined as serious and others as trivial. Women audience's pleasure in soaps and romances can frequently be felt to be embarrassing or foolish by the women themselves who have had to defend their taste against male derision (Gray, 1987; Taylor, 1989).

Both Morley (1986) and Gray (1987), then, argue convincingly for the importance of the social relations of consumption in understanding gendered audiences. The viewing context, in each of these cases a domestic one, is demonstrated to have a determining role in the meanings produced by male and female audiences. This argument could be usefully investigated in relation to the cinema within film studies, where the social relations of cinema-going has been virtually ignored. Many audience studies (my own included) retain the primary focus on the audience's accounts of the media. Very few successfully rise to Charlotte Brunsdon's challenge of exploring the 'interplay of social reader and social text' (Brunsdon, 1981). One of the few examples of work on the consumption of visual media which addresses this set of interactions is Valerie Walkerdine's study of video watching.

THE 'MAGIC CONVERGENCE'

In her article 'Video replay; families, films and fantasy' (1986), Valerie Walkerdine offers an analysis of the viewing of the video *Rocky II* (1979, Stallone) by the Coles, a working-class family, in their domestic context. This analysis is combined with a critique of the role of the academic researcher as 'spectator' within this process. Like the studies of television audiences discussed so far, Walkerdine's study is a challenge to models of textual spectatorship and an attack on the 'universalism of meaning, reading and interpretation' (*ibid.*: 182) characteristic of theories of signification which situate meaning exclusively within the media text. Additionally, Walkerdine criticises the more sociological audience studies in which audiences are interviewed about their responses to a programme. Many of these studies, she argues, ignore the politics of representation, and merely reproduce audience responses as if they spoke for themselves. The researcher remains a structuring absence, as if the role were a 'neutral' or 'objective' one. In opposition to this view, Walkerdine highlights precisely the investment of the researcher in the project.

Drawing on textual analysis, discourse theory, ethnography and psycho-analysis, she analyses the relationship between filmic and lived discourses of 'fighting'. In addition, her analysis of Mr Cole's working-class masculinity, as a socially constructed spectator, offers an examination of the intersection of discourses of social differences in the historical subject. Walkerdine argues that films such as the *Rocky* series and *Rambo* can be read as fantasies of 'omnipotence, heroism and salvation. They can thus be understood as a counterpoint to the experience of oppression and power-lessness' (Walkerdine, 1986: 172). She therefore analyses Mr Cole's reading of *Rocky II* in terms of discourses of fighting which intersect with discourses in the rest of his life, particularly in his domestic context, as a working-class father. Thus, texts should be seen as a set of significations produced by the processes of reading within a given context: '[R]ather the

41

viewing constitutes a point of dynamic intersection, the production of a new sign articulated through the plays of significance of the film and those which already articulate the subject' (*ibid.*: 189).

Trying to avoid a kind of simple functional determinism, she argues that each reading produces a new sign: 'The magic convergence, therefore, is an act of signification, the fusion of signifier and signified to produce a new sign, a new place' (Walkerdine, 1986: 171). By introducing the term 'discourse' into her analysis, Walkerdine avoids some of the pitfalls of crude textual or social determinism. Instead, she argues, the consumption of popular culture should be understood as a set of interrelating discourses: in this case, the textual discourse of fighting, the lived discourses in the family, the psychic discourses of the masculine subject inscribed within a historical moment. In some important ways, then, Valerie Walkerdine's study moves the challenge to textual determinism into a new and exciting area of investigation. Her study offers an investigation of the 'interplay of social reader and social text' (Kuhn, 1984: 26) in a way that previous studies have been unable to.

Despite advocating such an interactive model, however, it is significant that in Walkerdine's own analysis the actual investigation of the text is soon forgotten. Although *Rocky II* is analysed as a popular myth of power and success, offering the pleasures of a fantasy of individual achievement to a male spectator excluded from such possibilities in his working-class life, the film text is used primarily as a means of exploring formations of working-class masculinity. Certainly, the visual mechanisms of the film are virtually ignored in this study, which is surprising given the claim that boxing is a spectacle of working-class masculinity. Processes of identification with the hero are unproblematically asserted, ignoring possible contradictions in the text. What also remains somewhat unelaborated is the question of *how* textual, social and subjective formations interact. Thus cultural consumption does, to some extent, remain a 'magic convergence'!

Whatever the limits of Walkerdine's study, however, its methodological combination of text, reader, researcher and context remains impressive. Studies that draw on psychoanalytic theory to analyse gendered readings tend to be those least able to address the social, cultural and historical context. Walkerdine's combination of ethnography with psychoanalytic theory marks an important break with the existing dichotomies of psychic versus social readers, and a departure for audience studies which have typically ignored questions of the unconscious.[20]

THE PLEASURE OF POPULAR CULTURE

A central concern within feminist work on the relationship between particular audiences/readers and specific genres, such as the romance or the soap opera, has been the pleasure of these popular forms for women. How and why these particular forms are popular with women has been analysed in a variety of ways that challenge the usual dismissal of these pleasures as 'foolish escapism'. Instead, women's pleasures have been located in the relationship between the patterns of narrative and of scheduling, and the sexual division of labour and resulting social organisation of women's lives. Women's pleasures, for example, have been situated in the match between the forms of feminine cultural competence and the thematic focus on inter-personal relationships in soap operas (Brunsdon, 1981). In addition, the narrative structure of American daytime soap operas has been paralleled with the structure of women's domestic work: both are cyclical and full of interruptions: in other words, neither a woman's work, nor a soap opera story 'is ever done' (Modleski, 1982).

A significant contribution to this re-evaluation of popular pleasure and feminine subjectivity is Tania Modleski's study of three popular feminine forms: Harlequin Romance, the Gothic novel and daytime soaps (1982). Modleski's work challenges feminist criticisms of popular culture as necess-arily bad for women, the Frankfurt School's rejection of popular culture as merely reproductive of the dominant ideology,[21] and the typical dismissal of 'feminine' forms as insignificant, trivial and unworthy of critical analysis. Instead of adopting these rather patronising and/or pessimistic approaches to popular culture, Modleski analyses what forms of pleasure these texts offer women and asks: can any of these pleasures be seen as resistant to patriarchal authority, and what are the contradictory forms of feminine subjectivity constructed within these texts?

Modleski analyses the pleasures of romance novels in the light of psychoanalytic theories of 'hysteria' which describe a duality, or 'double conscience' in female patients.[22] Romance narratives require a separation of 'the "informed reader"', who knows the formulaic patterns of this popular narrative form, and 'the necessarily innocent heroine' of the story (Modleski, 1982: 32). The Gothic novel is analysed in terms of the elements of the female oedipal trajectory it reproduces. These narratives, she argues, articulate fears and phobias specific to the contradictions of feminine subjectivity (*ibid*.: 33). Finally, the pleasures of daytime soap operas are analysed in terms of the construction of the female spectator as a kind of ideal mother, trying to have her family happy and united, but continually thwarted by the arrival of new traumas. Although she argues that soap operas construct an extreme form of feminine selfless-ness, Modleski nevertheless emphasises the centrality of intense emotions such as anger, envy and admiration to the meaning of these feminine texts.

Modleski's study, however, retains many of the problems of the textual model of spectatorship employed within film criticism. The uniformity of the trajectories of feminine subjectivity, based on the universal feminine psyche, leaves little room for a diversity of positions of readership/

viewership. A kind of reflectionism operates in Modleski's matching of psychic positions with textual ones which relies on mere analogy of structure (narrative and psyche). The conclusions thus once again cannot tell us anything about how these texts are read differently by specific groups of women. Seiter *et al.*, for example, challenge Modleski's conclusions about the soap-opera viewer as ideal mother: 'one of the problems with the spectator position described by Modleski is that the "ideal mother" implies a specific social identity – that of a middle-class woman, most likely with a husband who earns a family wage' (Seiter *et al.*, 1989: 241). The international study of readings of *Dallas* (Katz and Liebes, 1985) further highlights the importance of context for understanding the meanings made of soap operas.

In an important shift towards situating the pleasures of the popular within a specific context, Radway's ethnographic exploration of women's pleasure in reading romances (Radway, 1984) marked a new direction within feminist analysis of popular culture. Like Modleski, Radway is unwilling to dismiss the readers as necessarily being as conservative as the forms they enjoy. Radway argues for an analysis of the pleasures of romance within the broader social meanings of the genre to the women readers. Instead of criticising their pleasures in terms of their 'false consciousness' which is evidence of their complicity with their own subordination under patriarchy, Radway attempts to accept their defininitons of their desires, fears and needs and to situate them within the context of their daily lives.

By analysing reading as a practice within the social context of a particular group of women's lives, Radway is able to highlight an important contradiction in the pleasures of romance reading for women: 'The act of romance reading is oppositional because it allows the women to refuse momentarily their self-abnegating social role . . . [but] the romance narrative structure embodies a simple recapitulation and recommendation of patriarchy and its constituent social practices and ideologies' (Radway, 1984: 210). The practice of reading, Radway concludes from her ethnography, is, indeed, a way for women to assert their much-prized autonomy, normally undermined by their roles within households in which they are so frequently defined as being there for others. Thus despite the content of the romance novel, which defines women as ultimately dependent on men, the assertion of independence nevertheless takes place through the act of reading itself.

The question of the gendered pleasures of consumption is investigated in Ien Ang's study *Watching Dallas: Soap Opera and the Melodramatic Imagination* (1985) in which she attempts to analyse the diversity and contradictions of women's readings of *Dallas*. By challenging explanations of the appeal of *Dallas* either as American imperialism, or as unique and miraculous, Ang aims to produce a social analysis of pleasure based on her reading of viewers' accounts of why they enjoyed watching this 'Hollywood soap'.

The female audience in this study is shown as active and selective, rather than as passively positioned by the text. However, in contrast to much audience research which simply treats what people say as the truth about the media, Ang analyses the letters she receives as texts, looking at the gaps and contradictions as signs of negotiation with dominant ideology. Ang draws upon Pierre Bourdieu's work on patterns of taste and sources of pleasure in consumption practices of contemporary culture (Bourdieu, 1980). She highlights his emphasis on the pleasures of recognition in popular forms of consumption. According to Bourdieu, Ang argues, popular pleasure:

> is characterised by an immediate emotional or sensual involvement in the object of pleasure. What matters is the possibility of identifying oneself with it in some way or another to integrate it into everyday life. In other words, popular pleasure is first and foremost a pleasure of recognition.
>
> (Ang, 1985: 20)[23]

A central question for Ang then is: what do female audiences recognise in *Dallas* and how and why is this a pleasurable process? The pleasures of a desirable lifestyle, of abundance, glamour and power are combined in *Dallas* with the emotional realism of soaps generally, Ang argues. It is 'the structure of feeling' in *Dallas* which many women recognise and take pleasure in: 'Many letter-writers contend that the pleasures of *Dallas* come from the "lifelike" character of the serial . . . what is experienced as "real" indicates above all a certain structure of feeling which is aroused by watching the programme: the tragic structure of feeling' (Ang, 1985: 47). Women viewers of *Dallas* can identify with this structure of feeling from their everyday lives: 'the pleasures of *Dallas* consist in the recognition of ideas that fit in with the viewer's imaginative world. They can "lose" themselves in *Dallas* because the programme symbolizes a structure of feeling which connects up with the ways in which they encounter life' (*ibid.*: 83).

An important theme explored by Ang, ignored by many others working in this area, is the question of fantasy. Confounding the usual dichotomy of fantasy versus reality, Ang argues that the pleasure of popular culture for women as 'a flight into a fictional fantasy world': 'is not so much a denial of reality as playing with it. A game that enables one to place the limits of the fictional and the real under discussion and make them fluid' (Ang, 1985: 49). In exploring the question of fantasy, Ang raises the crucial question of the relationship between the feminist critic and women in her study:[24] 'A new antagonism is constructed here: that between the fantasies of powerlessness inscribed in the tragic structure of feeling, and the fantasies of protest and liberation inscribed in the feminist imagination' (*ibid*.: 132).

In challenging earlier feminist criticisms of popular culture, Ang argues that 'a serious theoretical problem arises here. This has to do with the danger of an overpoliticizing of pleasure' (Ang, 1985: 132). This position on women's pleasure in popular forms could not be more different from Mulvey's challenge to feminists to destroy popular pleasure, with which I began this chapter. These studies of women audiences/readers within cultural studies are typical of what Charlotte Brunsdon has called 'redemptive readings': 'academic analysis of popular texts and pastimes which sought to discredit both the left-pessimistic despair over, and the high cultural dismissal of, mass and popular culture' (Brunsdon, 1989: 121).

Yet some feminists continue to disagree with Ang's caution and argue instead that the study of women's pleasures in popular culture has swung too far the other way. Indeed, the exploration of pleasure by cultural critics has been condemned for its virtual endorsement of the industries producing it. In the shift in feminist research from 'bad' text to 'good' audience (Brunsdon, 1989: 125), it has been argued that important political questions have been lost: as Seiter *et al.* (1989: 5) argue 'there is nothing inherently radical about pleasure'. Judith Williamson (1986a) and Tania Modleski (1986b) both caution against the dangers of embracing the pleasures of the popular too readily: according to Modleski critics may 'unwittingly wind up writing apologies for mass culture and embracing its ideology' (*ibid*.: xi).

Within much cultural studies work, pleasure and activity have been further conflated. The resulting assumption has been that women's pleasure in a text can be equated with their activity as audiences, and activity is necessarily resistant, being the opposite of passivity, which is assumed to mean collusion. It may be that this is wishful thinking on the part of the feminist critic who wishes to justify her own pleasure in texts which might be considered politically conservative or patriarchal. Indeed, one could take the opposite view and argue that, in fact, being an active female spectator of Hollywood stars, for example, one is colluding more deeply with patriarchal cinema than a passive spectator would be. Or, alternatively, the activity of the female spectator may involve 'displeasure' and rejection or derision of the popular text she has viewed.

In other words, it seems crucial to be clear about the value of the active, rather than the passive, model of the female spectator within feminist criticism. Furthermore, the questions of pleasure and of activity need to be specified more rigorously, rather than always being assumed to stand in for one another. I would argue that the need to understand popularity and pleasure does not necessarily result in an endorsement of the texts producing it, nor a condemnation of the female spectators watching it. As this book will go on to show, the female spectator's pleasure in a given text needs to be situated within the specific viewing context in order for its meaning to be fully understood. The point of feminist analysis of popular culture is not to condemn or to champion individual women, but rather to analyse its pleasures in order to understand them and to situate those individual viewing practices within a broader context.

CONCLUSION

My theoretical interests in this research thus draw upon both feminist film theory and cultural studies audience research. Indeed, like some recent work discussed in this chapter, such as Walkerdine (1986), Radway (1984) and Ang (1985), it aims to combine elements from each of these bodies of work which have historically been set in antagonism to each other. I have argued that recent work in cultural studies has helped to promote a sense of female agency through its work with audiences which has shown the need for an interactive model of text/audience/context to account for the complexity of the viewing process. Instead of the textual spectator within feminist theory, much recent cultural studies work has argued for a model of the spectator as a social subject, who is herself inscribed by various and competing discursive formations (such as gender, class, ethnicity and sexuality).

Still lacking in this complex equation, however, is an adequate notion of the historical specificity of the cinema spectator, and one of my aims here is to develop a notion of the spectator as an 'historical subject' in such a way that the cultural locations of the text–audience encounter are understood. Thus the 'active' role of the female reader or viewer, it has been argued, has been an important corrective to those early models of audiences as passive dupes. However, pleasure and activity should not simply be celebrated in the name of a naive kind of populism. 'Activity' in and of itself is not a form of resistance: women may be active viewers in the sense of *actively* investing in oppressive ideologies. I would argue for the need to understand popularity and pleasure as historically located in order to theorise the full complexity of female spectators' relationships to popular culture.

The difference here between the study of film and television is again striking. Whilst it may be time for feminists looking at television to pause and caution against the abandonment of the text in favour of audience, in feminist film criticism the exploration of women as cinema spectators has barely begun, with the exception of the two studies discussed (Bobo, 1988; Taylor, 1989). Many of the insights in the work analysed above require further development in the study of film audiences. Theories of spectatorship need to begin to produce analyses of female spectators situated within particular viewing contexts. In the same way that the 'social subject' has been mobilised within cultural studies as a way of combining textual with contextual readings, so my aim is to offer an elaboration of the 'historical spectator' in relation to Hollywood cinema as a way of combining historical and cultural location with psychoanalytic accounts of subjectivity.

My approach could be summed up as follows: holding on to some crucial questions from the psychoanalytically informed feminist film theory, I move beyond the confines of its textual methodology in order to answer them. Thus, although Freudian and Lacanian theories of the unconscious are not central subjects of my investigation, questions of pleasure, fantasy, identification and desire in female spectatorship, which have been so central to those theories, form a crucial part of my analysis. But what are the implications of combining theories and methods from these two schools of thought, so often elaborated in opposition to each other? In answering this question I was struck by the fact that there are so few debates within feminist film theory about methodology, and so many about 'theory'. There is a striking absence of methodological consideration in feminist film theory, as there is in film studies more generally. This is, no doubt, in part, due to adoption of textual analysis from 'literary studies', which itself has rarely debated methodological questions; and in part due to a deliberate strategy of differentiation from the empiricism of media sociology.[25] In contrast to audience research, feminist film theory rarely offers debate about the suitability of psychoanalytic models, or the appropriateness of textual analysis as a method. In an attempt to open up such a debate, the particular methodological considerations of an analysis of the historical female spectator are the subject of the next chapter.

3

THE LOST AUDIENCE
Researching cinema history and the history of the research

Except for the legendary viewers who dove under their seats at the sight of Lumiere's train coming into the station; the countless immigrants to the U.S. who, we are told, learned American values in the sawdust-floored nickleodeons of the Lower East Side; and those who, to a person it would seem, applauded Al Jolson's 'You ain't seen nothing yet' in 1927; film history had been written as if films had no audiences or were seen by everyone in the same way, or as if however they were viewed and by whomever, the history of 'films' was distinct from and privileged over the history of their being taken up by the billions of people who have watched them since 1894.

(Allen, 1990: 348)

There is a history of female cinematic spectatorship which has yet to be written. The investigation of the historical reception of film raises important questions about the relationship between the cinematic institution and the female spectator. What do spectators bring to films from their own specific historical and cultural locations which then determine their readings? How do the discourses of particular historical conjunctures limit the possible readings a spectator may make of a film?

As I outlined in the previous chapter, within much feminist film criticism this relationship between text and spectator has been conceptualised within semiotic/psychoanalytic textual analyses of films, removed from their historical locations, and with little attention to the social identities of particular audiences. Within cultural studies, this relationship has been studied within specific locations, and analysed in terms of particular audiences, but the focus has been mainly on popular fiction, television or video.[1] However, as I have argued, there remain few investigations of historical cinema spectators within feminist film criticism.[2] In this chapter, then, some of the methodological issues of undertaking such research will be discussed.

Challenging the supremacy both of the text, and of the individual spectator, as the singular location of meaning production, Janet Staiger has argued that:

49

What we are interested in, then, is not the so-called correct reading of a particular film but the range of possible readings and reading process*es* at historical moments and their relation or lack of relation to groups of historical spectators.

(Staiger, 1986: 20)

As Staiger goes on to highlight, however, the investigation of the historical spectator presents the film researcher with a whole series of complex methodological and theoretical questions: what status do audience's accounts of films have; how are these to be found; and which interpretive frameworks might be useful in analysing such accounts?[3]

Methodologically, important questions about what should count as 'data' and how this material should be treated by the researcher are raised by the historical study of cinema spectators. Finding the material in the first place is a problem, since availability is clearly difficult in the historical study of film reception. But in addition, questions of interpretation are complex, since the material cannot be seen to 'speak for itself' as if it was separate from discursive and institutional forces. What audiences tell researchers will always be shaped by discursive factors and will produce a very particular set of selective knowledges. This leads to theoretical questions about subjectivity and meaning: should it be assumed that the conscious retelling of the response to a film tells us how this film works? What about the processes of spectatorship which are less directly accessible? Staiger (1986) argues that such problems have meant that even in the cases where film studies work has engaged with historical concerns, it has tended to focus on the institutional factors which may have shaped spectators' readings of particular films and has tended to ignore 'actual' spectator responses.[4] According to Staiger, this evasion has been for good reason: the result of the practical, theoretical and methodological complexities that such studies pose.

As I suggest in Chapter 1, in addition to the problems Staiger raises, there are more specific reasons for the reluctance on the part of feminist film theorists to venture into the area of audience research.[5] A feminist analysis of 'real cinema spectators' such as I have undertaken for this book, then, is a potential minefield of methodological, theoretical and political problems to which I shall now turn in more detail.

In retelling the story of this research I am aware of the temptation to represent the research project as a seamless narrative in which the next step seems inevitable. The dead-ends, the U-turns, the frustrations and the despair tend to get written out as the logic of the research project is imposed retrospectively. Such stories have been seen as problematic for the ways in which they reproduce the dominant narrative of 'history' (and, indeed, of much Hollywood cinema), in which events follow each other in a cause-and-effect logic, and in which the end point is shown to be the enlightened place of conclusion from which to assess the mistakes of the past. For the writer, this narrative offers structure and form with which to organise what are often rather haphazard and arbitrary steps in the research process; for the reader, it offers the pleasures of discovery, of recognition and of resolution; for both, order is imposed upon what once seemed chaos, and process becomes product. Within the conventions of academic presentation, this process aims to justify the specific research project, show the limits of previous ones, and point to the way forward.

Working within, and yet against, these conventions, feminists have constantly had to strike a balance between challenging some academic conventions and adhering to others. In this chapter, I am both conforming to certain conventions of retrospective reconstruction, and yet undermining the smoothness of the finished product usually presented under such circumstances. Some of the narrative pleasures will therefore be offered to the reader: a chronological sequence, a move towards resolution and the retrospective interpretation of the meaning of baffling evidence by the authorial 'voice-over'. However, I hope to disrupt this streamlined linearity by focusing primarily on the *processes* of this research and the methodological issues they raise and by including some discussion of the less fruitful avenues I pursued as well as those which ultimately led in more productive directions.

INVESTIGATING THE AUDIENCE: 1. MASS OBSERVATION

It had come to my attention through various publications and talks that the Mass Observation Archive at Sussex University had historical material from the 1940s and 1950s and that some of it concerned the cinema.[6] I thus started out by looking for clues about the whereabouts of historical material on women as cinema audiences at this Archive. The cinema proved to be an important aspect of everyday life in Britain at this time; the Archive today has more files on the cinema than on any other single topic. The collection of papers on the cinema includes some fifty reports on cinema-going in Britain between 1939 and 1945. The topics range from general material, such as 'Report on audience preference in film themes', or 'The film and family life', to detailed observations on responses of audiences to particular films, or descriptions of people's behaviour in a cinema queue!

The beginnings of the sociology of film and mass communication studies can be found in reports like the 'Worktown project'[7] and those on cinema-going in wartime Britain,[8] in which observers speculate about the (possibly damaging) effects of films on their audiences and the relationship between fictional films and people's lives outside the cinema. For example, in 'The film and family life', it is claimed that studies in America have shown: 'that the youth of America founded its ideas of sex, crime, travel, etc., almost

51

entirely on what they saw at the movies' (England, 1944: 7); it is also claimed that 'the influence of Hollywood on clothes is now greater than that of Paris, and hairstyles of such stars as Veronica Lake are copied by millions'; and a final example: 'psychologists say that the whole set up of the cinema, the dark, the reasonably comfortable seats, etc., are all conducive to a mild sort of hypnotism' (*ibid.*: 7). More detailed analyses of audiences' responses to particular types of films, newsreels or Ministry of Information shorts were also carried out, and can now be easily accessed in *Mass Observation at the Movies* (Richards and Sheridan, 1987).

Thus, although much Mass Observation material might appeal to the film historian for its 'independence' from the film industry, nevertheless it was closely related to government departments. This doubtless influenced the kinds of questions asked and the kind of information produced. Similar considerations must influence the interpretation of the two reports on cinema-going in Britain during the 1940s: the Wartime Social Survey (Box and Moss, 1943) on *The Cinema Audience* and The Bernstein Questionnaire.[9] The former offers important statistical data on cinema attendance, broken down by age, gender and occupation. It demonstrates, for example, general patterns, such as that those in the sample who attended the cinema more than once a week, labelled 'cinema enthusiasts' by the study, were found to be 61 per cent women and 39 per cent men (*ibid.*: 11).

The Bernstein Questionnaire, carried out by Sidney Bernstein on patrons of London cinemas (the Granada group) with which he was associated, had been started in 1927 and issued again in 1937, and thus the results of the 1946–7 questionnaire are compared with previous data from the first two. This research was carried out primarily for the film industry to gauge audiences' taste. Questions about taste in genre, director, American or British film, and stars were asked. Interesting data on Hollywood stars emerged in the results of the questionnaire. Of the female stars at the top of the favourites list in 1937, for example, only seven remain in the top thirty in 1946–7: Ginger Rogers, Claudette Colbert, Loretta Young, Barbara Stanwyck, Rosalind Russell, Anna Neagle and Bette Davis. The top five female stars in 1946–7, according to this sample, were Margaret Lockwood, Ingrid Bergman, Bette Davis, Phyllis Calvert and Greer Garson (Bernstein, 1947). This was the first time that a British star had been the favourite, which is not surprising, as 1946 was the peak year for the British film industry.

My brief discussion here of the Mass Observation Archive Reports is intended to give some idea of the kind of material available there. However, interesting as this material may be, it was not the kind of qualitative detail I sought in order to begin to develop arguments about how female spectators made sense of the cinema during this period. Together with box-office statistics of cinema attendance, these reports can give us an indication of which films, and perhaps which stars, were popular and when.[10] Film magazines such as *Cinematograph Weekly* or *Picturegoer* also ran popularity polls on stars, and these indicate in more detail which stars where favoured, when, and for how long. This information, whilst it may give a broad indication of likes or dislikes, offers little insight into the more qualitative dimensions of those preferences.

In addition, there are the methodological problems of the source of much of this information which will necessarily be partial and shaped by the interests of the institution in which it was produced. As Janet Staiger argues:

> Audience response research is invariably linked into commercial and academic institutions, already mediated by economic and theoretical projects at odds with any political goals of de-centering dominant practices or discourses. Marketing analyses, audience opinion polls, film reviews, interviews and letters to editors of periodicals are bound up with an apparatus of perpetuating the pleasure of the cinematic institution. Even if we acknowledge mediation and distortion these stumbling blocks can never be fully overcome.
>
> (Staiger, 1986: 21)

Another troubling question for me when looking at this material was the connection, or rather lack of one, to the existing debates in the field I sought to address. The questions put on the agenda by feminist theory seemed to bear no relation whatsoever to the questions of general cinema-going habits of women at different times. For example, two striking issues emerged from the historical material: first, the great significance of the cinema in women's lives in Britain in the 1940s, especially during the Second World War (see Chapter 4), and second, the rivalry between British and American cinema. Most feminist literature on Hollywood cinema and female spectatorship, however, pays little attention to the battle over national identities in relation to the cinema.[11] In *retrospect* these seem interesting and theorisable questions; however, early in my research, they led to confusion and disorientation, not least because they seemed disconnected from the theroretical concerns of feminist film criticism.

Fortunately, the summer at the Mass Observation Archive proved more fruitful than these early explorations might have suggested. The Archive held two sources which offered more qualitative material: the war diaries and the letters to *Picturegoer*. Mass Observation requested volunteers to write full personal diaries when the Second World War broke out in 1939. Approximately 500 people kept diaries and sent them to the Mass Observation in monthly instalments during the war. The cinema was one of many recurring topics that can be found in the diaries, which are stored in the Archive on microfiche. For the purposes of this research, the problem with this material is that the references to the cinema are very dispersed. Thus hours were spent reading the diaries to emerge at the end of the day with four or five rather disparate quotations from which I could conclude few general patterns or themes.

A more generative source was the *Picturegoer* letters (Topic collection 17, Boxes 5 and 6). The Archive holds several boxes of letters sent to the British cinema weekly publication *Picturegoer*. The magazine had a letters page entitled 'Dear Thinker'! All the letters (1,536) which were written to *Picturegoer* between May and November in 1940 are held by the Archive. Looking through these letters, I seemed at last to have some kind of lead. Here were letters written at the time from which one could analyse how female spectators had understood Hollywood cinema in the 1940s.

It was through the analysis of these letters that a more focused topic for this research emerged. The overwhelming interest in cinema in the 1940s was in the stars. Indeed, over 40 per cent of the letters concerned film stars, as Table 3.1 shows.

Table 3.1 Topics of readers' letters sent to *Picturegoer* in 1940

Category	Number of letters	Per cent of letters
Films	217	14
Stars	668	44
Newsreels	6	–
Industry	102	7
Subject matter	167	11
Propaganda	57	4
Picturegoer	96	6
Miscellaneous	223	14

Source: Mass Observation, Box 5/A, Folder 1.

Of the letters about film stars sent to *Picturegoer* at this time, 59 per cent were from women. It was this overwhelming interest in the stars which convinced me that the focus for this research should be female spectators and Hollywood stars. As I discussed previously (see Chapter 1), the absence of current feminist work on stars of that period was in striking contrast to the female spectators' interest in them.[12] The focus on female stars and female spectators was partly because this seemed to be the extent of the interest expressed in the letters, and because it remained an unexplored issue in the existing literature.[13]

WILL THE REAL AUDIENCE PLEASE STAND UP!

The letters concerning stars mainly addressed two issues: praise for, or criticism of, performance, acting ability, and so on, of existing stars, or pleas for acknowledgement of the talent of unknown actors. Both these subjects were encouraged by articles in the magazine; for example, readers were asked to write in with their suggestions of ten stars who should be given the sack, or to argue for the merits of unknown actors. The comparison of British and American stars was a constant theme encouraged by *Picturegoer*, demonstrating well the connection between editorial policy and audience opinions published in the magazines.

This connection highlights some of the important methodological limitations of letters pages as a source of historical evidence for the analysis of cinema audiences. First, it is clear that many of the letters are written in response to articles and features in the magazine, suggesting that the agenda for legitimate topics is largely framed by the producers of the magazine. Thus whilst letters pages in magazines such as *Picturegoer* may at first seem to provide suitable material for the study of consumption, further consideration of the framing of the content of such letters demonstrates the inextricability of production from consumption in this case. Such letters, then, provide material of audiences' responses to the discourses of stardom produced by the industry at the time. A second problem with this source is that the opinions of more marginal groups may not be expressed within the established pages of such mainstream publications. Letters printed can thus not be read as representative of all spectators (Staiger, 1986: 20–2). Thus the selection by producers clearly determines what is printed, which is therefore only a partial representation of audiences' feelings and opinions more generally.

In the case of the Mass Observation material, the situation is rather different. Holding all the letters from one particular period, some of which had been published and some had not, the editor's selection would not have influenced the material available. Moreover, in a report of the comparison of these letters with a hundred letters printed in *Picturegoer* it has been claimed that: 'the letters printed are a fair indication of the letters received. For instance, 47 per cent of the letters received are about stars, as are 43 per cent of the letters printed' (Mass Observation, Folder 1, LE 13.1.41).

Furthermore, the Mass Observation letters confirm that audience/ readers do actually write to magazines. Certainly there has been understandable scepticism about using letters pages as evidence of audience/ reader opinion, since those printed may well be concocted by office staff at the magazine.[14] Contradicting this suspicion, the letters held by Mass Observation were written or typed by many different readers, and thus seemed to be 'genuine', demonstrating that readers did, in fact, write to *Picturegoer* at this time.

However, although this finding sheds some light on the question of the validity of readers' letters, it does not detract from some of the other limitations of using them as a source for the study of the historical reception of film. These letters cannot be analysed outside a consideration of how the discourses of the cinema and of stardom are organised within the specific magazines. In addition, the generic conventions of letter-writing for publication would need to be taken into account. Particular types of letters, such as complaints, criticism, appreciation, humorous anecdotes, and so on, are recognisable forms for readers and editors, and knowledge of such forms will shape the kinds of letters written and selected for publication. Indeed, I found that the formulae for letters pages in the 1940s differed little from those published in the Birmingham local paper in the 1980s.

To argue that this material should therefore be discounted by film historians, however, would be mistaken. Janet Staiger's claim that 'Even if we acknowledge mediation and distortion these stumbling blocks can never be fully overcome' (Staiger, 1986: 21) implies the possibility of an unproblematic source of audience response beyond such stumbling blocks. 'Mediation' and 'distortion' suggest that there is pure cinematic experience beyond the limitations of representation. I would argue that all audience researchers must deal inevitably with the question of representation not as a barrier to meaning, but rather as the form of that meaning. Given that language itself is a system of representation, any expression of taste, preference and pleasure is necessarily organised according to certain conventions and patterns. Perhaps some material is less defined by the institutional boundaries of the film industry, but all audience 'data' has its textual formations, produced within particular historical and cultural discourses.

The problem with the Mass Observation *Picturegoer* letters for my purposes, then, was not their '*inauthenticity*', but rather that they all came from one year and thus offered few points of comparison. Since my general aim was to analyse historical change and continuity, these particular letters were unlikely to offer any conclusions. However, I left Mass Observation with a more focused topic for my research project, and with the intention of finding some comparative material of a similar kind elsewhere.

INVESTIGATING THE AUDIENCE: 2. THE BRITISH FILM INSTITUTE

The library and archive at the British Film Institute in London hold a number of potential sources for research into the history of female spectatorship. Initially, I expected to base my research on the material here. Primarily I was looking for material that female spectators had written at the time about Hollywood stars. Following my leads from the Mass Observation Archive, I began by analysing all the cinema magazines available at the time in the hope of finding letters pages for comparative purposes. The first task was to find out what magazines existed in the 1940s and 1950s and whether they had letters pages or not. The library holds many, but not all, of the cinema magazines from that period.

After analysing all the magazines held by the library, it became clear that *Picturegoer and Film Weekly*, with its full page 'Dear Thinker' with fully signed letters, proved to be the only cinema magazine at the time that promised to offer the material I could use.[15] All the issues of *Picturegoer* from 1940, 1945, 1950 and 1955 were then analysed in terms of letters written by female spectators about female stars. Since this was a weekly magazine, I decided to sample those particular years, rather than attempt a comprehensive analysis of the letters from each issue. Articles on female stars were also analysed, since these often became the subject of the letters the following week.

This study showed the recurrence of particular discourses of stardom: national identity, glamour and sexuality, and acting and performance.[16] The first, national identity, to some extent overlapped with the second and third, since the appeal of American or British stars was contested through assessments of glamour versus acting ability. For example, British 'woman-liness' versus American 'sex appeal' is the subject of one letter (Iris Tasker, *Picturegoer*, 20 July 1940). British stars are favoured as 'charming', 'natu-ral' and 'graceful', in opposition to American stars who are criticised as 'artificial', 'glamorous' and 'cheap'. Similarly, British stars are perceived to have 'personality' as opposed to the American stars' 'looks'. This differ-ence is reinforced through the discourse of acting and performance, British stars being associated with 'acting' and its high cultural associations: 'many British actresses brought their charm to the screen via the theatre after training in repertory, or ballet' (*Picturegoer*, 9 December 1950). In con-trast, American stars are seen to lack acting talent and possess only glamour. The combination of these discourses can be seen in this example:

> Our girls don't need glamour, Mr. and Mrs. America, they've got something far more real and precious – charm and natural refreshing beauty. I've always looked upon British film stars with relief from the tinsel and painted 'angels' of Hollywood. English beauty and talent is here in plenty, it merely wants publicity, not a cloak of glamour. You see in Britain, we believe in delivering the goods, not dressed up substitutes.
>
> (Shelia Coxhill, *Picturegoer*, 17 March 1945)

National identity is thus a central discourse through which stars are evalu-ated by spectators: Britishness is articulated here through notions of respectable female sexuality. As Jane Gaines has argued, 'high femininity' equals 'low sexuality' within discourses of gender and respectability at this time (Gaines, 1986). Class differences are clearly implied within such distinctions: middle-class femininity being respectable in contrast with working-class 'high femininity' which is not. Thus national differences and class differences are mapped onto one another and the assertion of 'respectable' British femininity becomes an assertion of middle-class norms: 'true' *British* femininity is middle-class and is not 'painted' or glamorous, and by implication, not explicitly sexual.

The battle over American and British stars, encouraged by features in *Picturegoer*, was most striking in the 1940s. It reached a peak in 1945 when the two industries were in bitter competition. By the mid-1950s the battle was less pronounced, in the *Picturegoer* letters at least. This striking shift within this major film weekly suggests the importance of changing historical circumstances in the meanings female spectators may have made of the films they saw during this period. The pleasures Hollywood stars offered female spectators may have been very different depending on changing definitions of femininity in Britain at this time.

Analysing the letters brought me up sharply against some of the methodological issues of using letters pages as discussed above. These letters are interesting cultural texts in so far as they cut across the usual cultural divides of public and private, production and consumption; they are a conventionally 'private' form – the letter – and yet written for public consumption. In addition, they are written by cinema spectators, but within the institutional constraints of editors and often in response to agendas set by film magazines which are part of the film industry.

For my purposes, then, the problem was not that these letters were not 'genuine' enough, but rather that they did not provide enough material for my research project. This was particularly true of the 1950s letters, since the magazine form changed, and the 'Dear Thinker' page, so prominent in the 1940s issues, decreased in size considerably throughout the 1950s. Letters were also more heavily edited, often amounting to one or two lines, rather than a full-length letter. Thus the comparative aim of the project also became more problematic, since there was a marked lack of symmetry between the 1940s and the 1950s material.

INVESTIGATING THE AUDIENCE: 3. FAN CLUBS

I therefore decided to look for further sources to supplement the letters from *Picturegoer*. Reading these letters, I had thought repeatedly about fan mail written to stars during this period. This seemed an appropriate addition to the letters I had analysed, since both took letter form and were written at the same time. Nevertheless I anticipated considerable differences between the 'private' fan mail and the 'public' letters to editors.

Sitting on a shelf somewhere, I fantasised, were hundreds of old letters, like those I had found in the Mass Observation Archive, written to favourite stars and articulating the likes and dislikes of female spectators. I wrote to every possible source I could think of to find addresses of fan clubs here and in America. I was unsure where the old letters would be, given the Second World War, the break-up of the studio system, and other intervening factors. I managed to find the addresses of about ten Hollywood stars and I wrote asking if any fan mail remained, and whether I could have access to it.

Clearly fan mail would again be a very specific form of information about cinema audiences. Most obviously it is from fans rather than a cross-section of the audience, some of whom would be keener on Hollywood than others. Reading fan mail as evidence of a typical audience's feelings about the cinema, then, would be problematic. There would also be little information about dislikes, in contrast to letters pages which give a wide range of complaints as well as praise.

However, my anticipations of such difficulties were wasted, since I received no positive responses to my requests. Some letters were returned unopened, others never produced a reply. A postcard from Doris Day, however, saying sorry, no, she could not help, but good luck with the project meant my search had not been completely in vain. I decided to give up on the fan clubs. It seemed to me I had come to the end of the road in terms of finding historical material written in the 1940s and 1950s about female stars. It was time for a rethink and a change of course.

INVESTIGATING THE AUDIENCE: 4. A TRIP DOWN MEMORY LANE

It seemed to me that my final option was to follow the lead of others in the field and advertise for women to write to me about their memories of their favourite film stars. As long ago as 1950, Leo Handel used the method of advertising for audiences to recount their cinema-going experiences. More recently, Helen Taylor (1989) and Richard Dyer (1986) advertised for audiences to write to them with their memories of *Gone With The Wind* (1939, Victor Fleming) and of Judy Garland respectively. Initially, I had wanted to look at the discourses which existed at the time, rather than those reconstructed retrospectively, but it became increasingly clear that if I wanted fuller qualitative material I would have to be willing to consider memories of Hollywood stars as a possible source.

I sent a letter (see Appendix 1, p. 243) to the four leading women's magazines whose readerships were generally women of fifty and over. Hollywood stars were focused on for two reasons: first, it became increasingly evident that a choice needed to be made, since British and American stars seemed from the letters pages to be read in very different ways; second, much feminist theory in which I wished to intervene primarily concerned Hollywood, rather than British cinema.

'Keen cinema-goers' from the 1940s and 1950s were asked to write to me and tell me which Hollywood stars they had liked and disliked, and why. I mentioned a few names as memory-joggers, or as eye-catchers: Bette

Davis, Katharine Hepburn, Barbara Stanwyck, Marilyn Monroe and Jane Wyman. Readers were also invited to request a questionnaire. This option had been added with the intention of avoiding too much quantitative material, such as lists of favourites, at the expense of more detailed preferences and pleasures.

I sent the letter to *Woman*, *Woman's Own*, *Woman's Weekly* and *Woman's Realm*. These were the most popular magazines in terms of having high sales, and also caught a readership of the age group who were likely to remember the cinema in the 1940s and 1950s. Wanting to analyse cinema-goers of forty and fifty years ago, I needed to contact women of at least fifty or sixty years old. Two magazines, *Woman's Realm* and *Woman's Weekly*, published my letter and had an overwhelming response. Altogether I received over 350 letters, and they continued to arrive from Canada, Australia, and New Zealand, where the magazines come out some months behind Britain, two years later. The letters varied enormously: some were ten pages long offering remarkably rich details, others were simply requests for a questionnaire.

The questionnaire (see Appendix 2, pp. 244–51) was then compiled according to the themes emerging from the letters. Thus the material from respondents generated the structure and content of the questionnaire. It was the specific interests and concerns of these female spectators that shaped the future direction of my research at this stage: rather than just asking about stars, which had been my original intention, I decided to situate the stars questions within a broader remit. The questions were grouped into four sections: 'Your picture-going background', 'Stars', 'Fan clubs and film magazines', and 'Details about you'. The first section asked for background information about cinema-going in this period. The second section asked about taste in stars, focusing on Hollywood, but offering space for information about British stars as well. This section contains the key question in the research, question 19, which asks respondents to write about their favourite star from the 1940s and then from the 1950s in detail. In the introductory paragraph to the questionnaire, there is advanced warning of the centrality of this question to my research, to prepare respondents for this and encourage them to save time, energy and information for this question. The third section asked questions about 'film star culture': the fan clubs and magazines which connected spectators and stars. The final section asked for information about the age, class, and ethnicity of the women themselves.

This structure was designed to facilitate the processes of recollection. Rather than simply being asked detailed questions about stars cold, respondents were first asked to answer questions about their general cinema-going habits at that time. The more practical details of cinema-going – how often, with whom, how this changed, reasons for visit, and so on – were thus designed to encourage the respondents to submerge themselves in their memories of this period. It also resulted from the way in which women had written about Hollywood stars in their letters as embedded in stories about cinema-going practices more generally.

The form of the questionnaire was a mixture of structured and more open-ended questions. This was finally decided upon by referring to existing work using questionnaires, such as those of Radway (1986) and Taylor (1989), and advice from experts in the field.[17] Although no official pilot study was carried out, the questionnaire was tried out informally upon a number of respondents, and critical feedback was obtained from those with experience of questionnaire design and construction. The structured, multiple-choice questions were designed to offer a contrast to the open-ended questions, and to offer respondents the pleasure of quick, easy selection of categories in which they recognised themselves. The more open-ended questions were to encourage them to provide the qualitative material I was interested in for more in-depth analysis.

The questionnaire had a specific function as a supplement to the letters; the form and structure of the questionnaire privileged question 19, which encouraged respondents to give full answers in their own words. Many respondents who requested a questionnaire continued their contributions from the letters in fuller and more focused accounts. Question 19, in particular, was frequently answered in a similar style to the letters written previously. Thus the more personal style of the letter form was not lost by the imposition of what, in contrast, could have seemed like a rather anonymous, quantitative form.

Of the women who requested a questionnaire only twenty decided not to return it. This high return rate is clearly due to the fact that these questionnaires were requested by a group of cinema enthusiasts, and not a group of randomly chosen respondents. Many sent me diaries, scrapbooks, old photos and leaflets, as well as their completed questionnaires. On the whole, the questionnaires were completed very fully, and the description of favourite stars often went on to two or three extra pages, if not more.

Since most respondents were readers of the same two leading women's magazines they comprised, not unexpectedly, a relatively homogeneous group. The questionnaire asked about their education, qualifications, housing and employment with the aim of analysing their class positions. Defining women's class position has frequently presented difficulties for researchers: women's paid employment patterns are often more variable than men's (partly because of childcare) and thus women have tended to be classified according to their husbands' occupations. In this case respondents typically shifted across the usual class categories of 'middle class' and 'working class'. Thus, what unites the majority of these respondents is precisely such variability within class positions; whilst most of them left school at 14 with few or no qualifications, working in clerical or 'unskilled' jobs and did not initially own property, many later moved towards more

61

middle-class positions through marriage or a return to education. Nevertheless the variability took place within the class categories of C1, C2 and D as defined by the readership information of these magazines (see Chapter 4 and Appendix 3).

The respondents to my advertisement were all white women. This is not surprising, given the magazines that agreed to print my request; both *Woman's Weekly* and *Woman's Realm* appeal predominantly to a white readership. Thus the study remains a study of white female spectatorship in relation to Hollywood stars. It is a study of white fantasy and the relationships between white female spectators and their ideals on the Hollywood screen. A further study would be necessary to look at black women's relationship to Hollywood stars and such a study would doubtless reveal a specific set of issues for black female audiences (see Chapter 4).

The outcome of this fourth investigation, then, was a proliferation of material from a very specific group of female spectators. The shift from a scarcity of historical material to an abundance of memories of Hollywood and 350 letters and 238 questionnaires (12 pages long) to analyse. The sheer volume was daunting, if exciting, and the methodological implications were increasing in their complexity.

Decisions about the focus of the research had to be taken. My original idea of supplementing the *Picturegoer* letters written in the 1940s and 1950s seemed increasingly unworkable. There was the problem of the gap of fifty years between the writing of one set of material, the letters to *Picturegoer*, and the other, letters and questionnaires written recently remembering the meaning of stars in the 1940s and 1950s. One would have been a set of letters informed by the institutional discourses and editorial policies during that period, the other would have been memories prompted by a researcher in the 1980s, which would have been shaped by the events of the intervening years.

Also abandoned was the idea of going back to the Hollywood stars, both their films and the publicity which constructed their star images, in order to attempt a combination of analyses based upon production, text and reception. However theoretically desirable, it promised to prove practically impossible, given the quantity and quality of material I had received. The letters and questionnaires proved such a rich source of material that it became increasingly clear that this should be the focus of the research project. Thus, rather than dealing with material written in the 1940s and 1950s, I decided to focus specifically on these female spectators' memories of Hollywood stars in Britain in the 1940s and 1950s.

FORMATIONS OF POPULAR MEMORY AND CINEMA HISTORY

'history' is a record of subjective readings of the past; it exists only in the perspective of the lens through which it is viewed. . . . History is not simply a study of the *past* by official historians. We are all historians of the *present*; 'popular memory' is produced socially and collectively as a précis of the past and everyone is a kind of historian.

(Taylor, 1989: 203)

Memory alone cannot resurrect past time, because it is memory itself that shapes it, long after historical time has passed.

(Steedman, 1986: 29)

The question of the relationship between memory and history is a slippery one. Yet it is a crucial one for those interested in the historical reception of film, if we are seriously concerned with the history of cinema audiences and not just the history of films (Allen, 1990). The history of audiences necessitates some consideration of memory if it is not to remain at the purely quantitative level; in other words if film history is to engage with ethnographic methods of audience analysis, as well as detailing cinema attendance statistically, then memory has to be a central consideration. A critical analysis of the forms and mechanisms of memory is pertinent to all ethnographic studies of media audiences, since the process of retelling is necessarily at stake in some form or another: audiences always represent their readings to researchers retrospectively. However, in this research, the length of the gap between the events and their recollection (forty or fifty years) highlights the question of the processes of memory especially sharply.

Spectators' memories of Hollywood stars, then, drawn on here to con-struct an historical account of spectatorship, need to be considered within a critical framework highlighting these processes of memory itself. Memory is not a straightforward representation of past events to which we have direct access and which we can in turn retell to others. Instead, I would argue that it involves a set of complex cultural processes: these operate at a psychic and a social level, producing identities through the negotiation of 'public' discourses and 'private' narratives. These histories of spectatorship are retrospective reconstructions of a past in the light of the present and will have been shaped by the popular versions of the 1940s and 1950s which have become cultural currency during the intervening years.

Cultural studies work on popular memory has highlighted well some of the methodological issues of using memory for cultural and historical analysis.[18] Amongst these is the question of how personal investments shape the kinds of memories we produce and how we prioritise some of them above others: in other words the processes of selection and construction of memory. The concept of the 'treasured memory', for example, has been used to refer to memories people have in which they have a particular personal investment. Many respondents in my research wrote of such 'treasured memories' and of their continued pleasures in recollections of past times: 'I have memories I shall always treasure. Other things in life take over, visiting the cinema is nil these days, but I shall always remember my favourite films and those wonderful stars of yesteryear' (Mrs B. Morgan). Using a personal mode of address which introduces a feeling of intimacy and familiarity, another respondent writes: 'Oh Jackie, what lovely memories are being recalled – I do hope you are going to ask for lots more information as a trip down Memory Lane of this nature is most enjoyable' (Barbara Forshaw). Such memories have been likened to a personal possession never to be lost. Indeed, it has been argued that 'treasured' memories are particularly significant in conserving a past self and thereby guarding against the experience of loss (Popular Memory Group, n.d.: 26). 'Treasured memories' may thus signify past selves or imagined selves of importance retrospectively.

The notion of the treasured memory suggests a place which can be regularly revisited. One woman writes of the unexpected pleasures such a place has provided:

> My grandfather's boss was kind enough, every Christmas of my childhood, to give me a present of a film annual. I enjoyed them then, but never dreamt what a treasure trove they'd prove to be. Now in my 50s, I pore over them from time to time and it's like opening Pandora's Box (*sic*). Stars of yesteryear, long forgotten. Films I saw, but had forgotten all about. Hollywood at its height, the glitz and glamour. I can remember setting out a good hour before the film started to secure a front position in the queue.
>
> (Barbara McWhirter)

There are numerous reasons for our investments in treasured memories. It has been suggested that one such investment might be in memories as particular 'transformative moments' (Popular Memory Group, n.d.: 165). Such moments are especially pertinent to the spectator/star relationship because Hollywood stars embody cultural ideals of femininity and represent the possibility of transformation of the self to spectators. Indeed, as we shall see, many memories of Hollywood stars concern their role in the transformation of spectators' own identities (see Chapters 5 and 6). In addition, many respondents' memories are of a transitional period: their 'teenage' years, in which change and self-transformation were central to their desires and aspirations (see Chapter 5).

It has been argued that one of the pleasures of such memories might derive from the ways in which memories work as 'personal utopias' which offer a kind of escape from the constraints of daily life. This conceptualisation is particularly pertinent in the context of spectators' memories of Hollywood stars who could be seen as offering utopian fantasies to cinema audiences at that time (see Chapters 4 and 5). Thus the process and the subject of the memory both involve utopias of some form.

The kinds of personal utopias produced will partly depend upon present feelings about past events. Memories depend upon past expectations and the extent to which these were met or not, since unmet needs and desires may influence the continuing significance of particular memories; in other words, some memories continue to be of central importance because of past frustrations, disappointments and unfulfilled fantasies. Thus it has been suggested that memories might usefully be considered as 'stories of unfinished business' (Popular Memory Group, n.d.: 30). Women's expectations and subsequent experiences of romance, motherhood or paid work, for example, may shape their reconstructions of their relationship to Hollywood ideals of femininity in the 1940s and 1950s.

Many women looking back at the cinema of the 1940s and 1950s may have developed a critical awareness of their love of Hollywood and its stars at that time. One woman writes:

> In retrospect it's easy to see Hollywood stars for what they really were . . . pretty packaged commodities . . . the property of a particular studio. At the time I did most of my film going, while I was always aware that stars were really too good to be true, I fell as completely under the spell of the Hollywood 'Dream Factory' as any other girl of my age.
>
> (Kathleen Lucas)

Reflecting upon the role of the industry in constructing the glamour of the female stars and upon her changing feelings about this in retrospect, she continues: 'I came in contact with the glamour and expertise of film making at a particularly impressionable age. Looking back, I can see much of what I took as authenticity was really technical skill. . . . Later on I realised just how much money and expertise went into creating the "natural" beauties the female stars appeared to be' (Kathleen Lucas). Thus, memory works here to define present self in contrast to past self, and whilst there may be a suggestion of retrospective wisdom, there may also be a sense of loss for the effects of the powerful magic of Hollywood.

Such feelings may be especially pertinent to an understanding of women's memories of the 1940s and 1950s, given the 'impossibility of femininity' discussed in Chapter 6. Feminine ideals are, by definition, never realisable, since they fundamentally contradict each other (such as the constructions of motherhood and of sexual desirability). Memories of Hollywood stars, then, may have a particular significance for female spectators in terms of their representation of a fantasy self never realised. In addition, given the centrality of commodities to the 'successful' construction of feminine identities, the material constraints of certain periods in women's lives, such as the austerity of the 1940s and early 1950s, and the continuing economic constraints on women outside the growing 'affluence' of the middle classes, may have shaped the kinds of investments made in particular memories.

For women in the 1980s, nostalgia is clearly one of the pleasures of remembering 1940s and 1950s Hollywood cinema and its stars. Remembrance is simultaneously an acknowledgement of the loss of those times, and a means of guarding against their complete loss. The nostalgia evoked may be for former feminine identities, for the period itself and for the cinema and stars of that time. Thus the loss of youth and of innocence articulates with a loss of a particular kind of cinematic pleasure and star status. The perception that the cinema and the stars 'are not what they used to be', 'not like the old days' is an important motivator for respondents to express their opinions about historical change in the cinema.

It has been argued that nostalgia may have particular appeal for women. Psychoanalytic theory offers an explanation of why nostalgic desire should have such a gendered appeal. According to this model our adult feelings about loss, about the past and about nostalgia are based on our early childhood understandings of our place in the world and its sexual/symbolic hierarchies. The psychoanalytic account returns us to the different meanings of sexual difference for boy and girl children represented in the Oedipal and castration scenarios: whereas the boy fears losing what he has, as he believes his mother to have done, the girl regrets what she believes she has lost. Thus femininity and nostalgia are linked through an early desire to retrieve what is believed to have been lost (see Radstone, 1993 and forthcoming).

Such an account importantly foregrounds the links between femininity and nostalgia. I do not want to take issue with some of the basic tenets of psychoanalytic theory here, since that would constitute too extended a digression (see Chapter 2). Rather, I would like to add to these psychoanalytic investigations my own arguments about the appeal of nostalgia for women with particular reference to the relationship between female spectators and Hollywood stars as feminine ideals during this period.

My argument hinges on the extent to which femininity is defined in patriarchal culture as an unattainable visual image of desirability (see Chapter 1). To present oneself to the world for approval in terms of physical attractiveness is the ultimate demand made of femininity. Few women ever overcome the sense of mismatch between their self-image and feminine ideals in terms of physical appearance, and those that do live uneasily with the inevitability of its disappearance with ageing. The attainment of feminine ideals is thus typically ephemeral. Feminine ideals are youthful ones, and thus successful femininity contains loss even in the rare sense of its attainment.

Thus the sense of loss for women evoked by nostalgic desire, I would suggest, is bound up in precisely this unattainability of the ideal feminine image. Indeed, the centrality of the visual image to feminine ideals produces lasting and powerful memories of such ideals which endure the passing of time. The feelings of loss, often experienced in the gap between the self and the ideal at the time, is deepened and extended as feminine ideals become ever-increasingly a lost possibility. Agreeing with the psychoanalytic accounts, then, I would argue that women's nostalgic desire is indeed bound up with their particular sense of loss, but a sense of loss which is firmly rooted in the unattainability of feminine ideal images. Thus it is the particular designation of femininity as image which gives nostalgia such potency for women.

This is not to suggest that masculinity is not also an identity which is culturally constructed through a series of ideals. Men may also feel a nostalgia for a time when attainment of desired identities still seemed a future possibility. However, masculine ideals are more diverse, less based upon image and physical appearance than on status, power and activity, and offer the possibility of improving with age in some cases. Thus, I would argue that typically nostalgia for lost ideals is very different for men and for women.

As I have discussed elsewhere (see Chapter 2), Lacanian psychoanalysis would suggest that all our subjectivities are constituted in relation to the misrecognition of the self in an ideal which is ultimately illusory. However, this pre-symbolic process of 'the mirror stage' needs to be considered in the symbolic context of the centrality of the visual image in representations of femininity in this culture. The pull of such mis/recognitions may be based in very early childhood development, but its specific meaning to femininity can only be fully understood when situated within a critical analysis of representation of 'woman as image' within patriarchal culture.

The centrality of being an image to the definition of successful femininity in this culture may account for one of the forms of memory frequently used by women in this research: what I shall call iconic memory. Icon, originally used to refer to religious imagery, is apt here to describe the female stars, remembered as screen goddesses and as the objects of desire and even worship. Women's memories of 1940s and 1950s Hollywood often take the form of a particular 'frozen moment', taken out of its temporal context and captured as 'pure image': be it Bette Davis's flashing and rebellious eyes, Doris Day's fun outfits or Rita Hayworth's flowing hair. This is not only true of memories of the stars, but also of the spectators' memories of themselves. One meaning of icon is 'likeness' and this is pertinent to the use of iconic memory in this context in which female spectators remember themselves in such 'frozen moments'. One woman remembers sitting in front of the mirror brushing her hair trying to look like Bette Davis in *Dark Victory* (1939, Edmund Goulding) (see Chapter 5); thus her own reflection in the mirror has replaced the image of the star on the screen and becomes the subject of this iconic memory.

The second form of memory which occurred most frequently in this research is narrative memory. Women's memories of the cinema in this period offer the opportunity for the presentation of past and present subjectivities through processes of self-narrativisation. In contrast to iconic memories, narrative memories present temporally located sequential stories of cinema-going in the 1940s and 1950s. Women's memories of Hollywood stars are specific forms of self-narrativisation in relation to cultural ideals. Female spectators thus construct themselves as heroines of their own stories which in turn deal with their own heroines at that time. Memories of Hollywood stars are thus represented through the codes and conventions of narrative form structurally connecting self and ideal.

It is not simply the case that these female spectators remembered the narratives in which their favourite screen idols starred, but also that their relationships to the stars are often recreated through narrative form of memory. One example of the use of the narrative form most convention-ally associated with femininity is that of romance. This is used by some respondents in their retelling of the connections between self and ideal within the conventions of romantic narrative (see Chapter 5).

The ways in which I requested information may have encouraged women to use narratives to construct their memories. For example, question 13, 'describe your favourite cinema experience of the 1940s/1950s', asked respondents to tell stories. In addition, letter-writing employs certain narrative forms in the retelling of past events. Respondents wrote me letters in which they narrativised themselves in relation to their past ideals. This history of spectatorship is thus constructed through forms of private story-telling given public recognition in the research process.

Some memories combine iconic and narrative forms. Particular iconic memories may be of a narrative image, a scene from a film such as Jennifer Jones's 'last crawl towards Gregory Peck over the rocks' (Yvonne Oliver) in *Duel in the Sun* (1946, King Vidor) (see Chapter 5). Alternatively, women's iconic memories of themselves in the cinema of this period may be narrativised, such as descending the cinema staircase like a Hollywood heroine (see Chapter 4). The narrative memories of female spectators, however, are typically also iconic memories. Thus the 'hero narratives' of these female spectators involved forms of display as well as action. The gendered significance of the forms of narrative memory found in this research is discussed in Chapter 7.

Each of the processes of memory formation and selection discussed so far replicates, or is replicated by, distinguishing features of Hollywood cinema. Popular memories of Hollywood cinema in these accounts thus interestingly take cinematic forms. Memories are typically constructed through key icons, significant and transformative moments, narrative structures, heroic subject positions and utopian fantasies. Thus in analysing female spectators' accounts of popular cinema it is especially important to take account of these conventions of memory formation.

PRODUCING THE PAST

As is true of all the sources discussed in this chapter, the rules of the enquiry frame the kind of information elicited. The form of the request for spectators' recollections of Hollywood stars will have shaped the memories sent to me. The kind of advertisement for responses clearly had a determining effect on the material I received. Answers to an advertisement asking for recollections of favourite stars inevitably produce a particular set of representations resulting from a specific cultural context. Advertising for 'keen cinema-goers of the 1940s and 1950s', for example, addressed potential respondents as a distinct group; in recognising themselves in this category, respondents were constructed as a particular kind of authority: the 'amateur expert'. The private pleasures of collecting cinema memorabilia and of having film-star expertise is thus given a kind of public importance in such research. In turn, my recognition of their 'expertise' could have been perceived to be flattering, and indeed to have set up an expectation that their 'keenness' as cinema-goers in this period had to be demonstrated either through the detail of their accounts, or through an expression of the significance of cinema in their lives.

The request for information about a period at such historical distance also shaped the material I received: respondents may have felt recognised as a valuable source of historical information, and thus endeavoured to give as much detail as they could remember. Indeed, the recollection of detail may have been one of the pleasures for respondents in particpating in the research: 'I have enjoyed doing this questionnaire. It was so detailed, I really had to think back. Thank you for that experience' (Kathleen Sines). The detail of many of the memories is commented upon in the chapters which follow: the ability to recollect such detail might be considered evidence of devotion to favourite stars.

Furthermore, my advertisement suggested an academic recognition, or indeed, validation, of women's pleasure in Hollywood cinema during this period, thus combining two things rarely taken seriously or given much status: popular culture and its female spectators. In other research, women had expressed shame in their pleasure because they were aware of its low status (Taylor, 1989: 204). Thus my request for information served as a validation of the importance of their memories, and indeed of the significance of Hollywood cinema in their lives in the 1940s and 1950s.

The kinds of selections respondents made when remembering what

Hollywood stars meant in their lives would also have been framed by the subsequent histories of the stars in question: which stars were remembered and how they were remembered must have been influenced by the cultural constructions of those stars since that time. For example, audiences may have remembered stars differently depending on whether the stars were still alive, and if not, how they had died (such as Marilyn Monroe) and indeed when they had died (Bette Davis died during the time the questionnaire was with respondents); whether they still had a fan club (such as Deanna Durbin); whether the star had continued to have a successful career (such as Katharine Hepburn and Bette Davis); whether their films had been shown frequently on television and indeed whether the stars had gone on to have a television career (such as Barbara Stanwyck).

In addition to these factors, memories are recollections of the past through the changing historical discourses. Assessments of stars will inevitably have been affected by changing notions of acceptable femininity and female sexuality. The different constructions of femininity within Hollywood, such as the power and rebelliousness of Bette Davis or the sexual attractiveness of Marilyn Monroe, or the clean-livingness of Deanna Durbin, may have had particular appeal in retrospect, and they may have come to mean something over the years which they did not in the 1940s and 1950s. For example, what effect did the 'permissive' 1960s have on discourses of stardom and glamour?[19] To what extent might stars have been re-evaluated through a post-1960s understanding of female sexuality? How might women's increased participation in the public sphere have transformed the discourses through which Hollywood's 'independent women' stars have been read? To what extent might the increased visibility of lesbians and gay men in society have encouraged a re-evaluation of early 'attachments' to stars of the same sex? (See Chapter 6.)

What gets remembered and what gets forgotten may depend not only on the star's career and changing discourses since the time period specified, but also upon the identity of the cinema spectator. The kinds of representations offered will have been informed by issues such as the respondents' own personal histories. The ways in which their lives had changed, and the feelings they had about their past, present and future selves, will have been amongst the factors determining the memories produced for the purposes of this research.

What I have been foregrounding in these last two sections of this chapter is the specificity of the production of the memories of Hollywood stars which form the basis of this research and the conventions through which knowledge about the past is formed. Rather than seeing these conditions and conventions as *barriers* to 'the real past', as if it existed separately from our retelling of it, I have instead suggested highlighting them as an integral part of the research. What is important here is to recognise the factors shaping these women's memories of Hollywood stars and to analyse the conventions through which such material is represented. Popular memories of the cinema, I have argued, replicate particular narrative and visual conventions of popular culture generally.

FROM THE TEXTUAL SPECTATOR TO THE SPECTATOR AS TEXT

The question of the textual conventions of popular forms is one that bridges debates about popular memory and those about ethnography, since both involve the problem of the interpretation of personal accounts. This is, however, a general issue in the analysis of media reception, be it of interviews, letters, or questionnaires. Within cultural studies audience research, attention has been paid to such conventions, in contrast to accounts which simply let the audience 'speak for itself'.

As Ien Ang has argued, when analysing the responses she received to the question 'why do you like watching *Dallas*?'·

> [I]t would be wrong . . . to regard the letters as a direct unproblematic reflection of the reasons why the writers love or hate *Dallas*. What people say or write about their experiences, preferences, habits, etc., cannot be taken entirely at face value . . . we cannot let the letters speak for themselves, but they should be read 'symptomatically': we must search for what is behind the explicitly written, for the presuppositions and accepted attitudes concealed within them. In other words the letters must be read as texts, as discourses.
>
> (Ang, 1985: 11)

Ang's approach here is methodologically exemplary of the shift from the textually produced spectator of film studies to the spectator as text within cultural studies.

For feminists, this presents particular issues about the politics of interpretation and research. In particular, the power of the feminist researcher to interpret other women's feelings and thoughts from a position of expertise in the academy is highlighted. There are certainly fewer moral dilemmas for feminists who continue to analyse film texts to which they are never held accountable in terms of the politics of research methods. As I suggested in Chapter 1, this dilemma may be a reason for the reluctance of feminist film critics to engage with audiences, as well as their anxieties about committing the cardinal sin of 'empiricism'. Those who have criticised the method that treats audiences' accounts as texts may argue that it is patronising to the women concerned. It may seem more 'democratic' simply to let women speak for themselves, since, many have argued, women are rarely listened to in this culture. Indeed, much early feminist oral history and documentary film aimed to 'give women a voice' and to make visible their experiences.

However, I would argue that some kind of interpretive framework is inevitable in academic research, and that avoiding analysis of women audiences because of embarrassment or anxiety about imposing such a framework merely perpetuates their absence from feminist film theory. The role of the researcher, I would argue, is to interpret the material that audiences produce within a critical framework which is appropriate to the material, and which is made explicit and can be contested. I shall argue for the importance of textual analysis of the stories that audiences tell researchers about what the media means to them, but in a framework which is demonstrably derived from the material itself. Thus a dialectical relationship emerges between the material studied and the theory which is used to analyse it. Female spectators' accounts of the cinema are used to criticise or confirm existing film theory, and indeed produce new or refined categories which could usefully add to our understanding of how audiences watch films.

This shift towards a textual treatment of spectators' readings of the media brings with it a host of methodological issues of central concern to ethnographers of media audiences (Morley, 1989). In reacting against one kind of textual determinism in film studies, in which the media texts produce their spectators (see Chapter 2), this approach, exemplified by Ang, might be accused of another kind of determinism, in which audience data is treated merely as a text. Is there, as Jane Feuer (1986) suggests, an inherent contradiction here?

> [T]he critic reads another text, that is to say, the text of the audience discourse. For the empirical researcher, granting a privileged status to the audience response does not create a problem. But it does for those reception theorists who acknowledge the textual status of the audience response.
>
> (Quoted in Morley, 1989: 24)

The problem of the interpretation of the text is thus displaced onto the audience, and, according to Feuer, the attribution of meaning is endlessly deferred (Morley, 1989: 23).

In addition to the problem of privileging the status of the audience as the focus for media research, and yet simultaneously relativising it by treating it as text, the question of the unconscious presents another methodological dilemma. As Feuer goes on to argue:

> They then have to read the unconscious of the audience without the benefit of the therapeutic situation, or they can relinquish the psychoanalytic conception of the subject – in which case there is a tendency to privilege the conscious or easily articulated response.
>
> (Quoted in Morley, 1989: 24)

The original challenge to the psychoanalytic textual models of analysis from these ethnographic audience studies has thus proved somewhat fruit-less, since, according to Feuer, these studies have no greater insight into the spectator's unconscious responses to a text than the speculations of the film theorist based on textual analysis (Morley, 1989: 24).

There are important reasons why studies of film spectatorship and those of television audiences have been held apart for so long (see Chapter 2). Not only are the models of 'female spectatorship' quite different, the one assumed to be a texual/theoretical construct, the other a woman in the audience, but certain basic theoretical positions are also incompatible. Film theory, associated with poststructuralism, generally assumes identity to be unstable, in flux and fragile. Indeed, the methodological emphasis on textual analysis within film studies has its foundations in the belief that feminine and masculine 'identities' are produced by textual practices, and not vice versa. This derives from the poststructuralist view that lan-guage speaks us, and not the other way around. Hence, theories of spectatorship in film studies frequently demonstrate little interest in the spectator before she enters the cinema, focusing instead on the pro-duction of *spectator positions* by film texts.

In contrast, as I have discussed, cultural studies work on television audiences has typically investigated *audiences' readings* of texts, situating them within the social context of the viewing practices of particular groups. Typically, such research does not see the film text as exclusively constitut-ing the viewers' identities. Instead it highlights many social determinations, such as class, gender, ethnicity or nationality, which shape the particular viewer's reading of specific media texts. The social relations of the viewing context have also been seen to influence the meaning of such media texts for audiences. So, for example, it has been argued that power relations within the domestic sphere affect how women and men watch programmes differently. Thus, social identities, already formed prior to the viewing of a programme, have been considered crucial to understanding media consumption.

In this research I follow cultural studies approaches in using the term 'female spectator' to refer to the woman in the cinema audience and in investigating how historical and national location affects the meanings of Hollywood stars for female spectators. Thus, the social identities formed outside the cinema are assumed to shape the kinds of readings made by female spectators of Hollywood stars in 1940s and 1950s Britain. Unlike some of the poststructuralist positions, then, I argue that historical and national locations are of significance for understanding female spectator-ship. However, I also show how the processes of cinematic spectatorship produce and re/form feminine identities. Thus, in a mode complementary to much poststructuralist theory, I analyse feminine identities 'in process', continually being transformed. Thus the relationship between image and identity is seen to be one of negotiation and process, during which there

73

are apparent moments of fixity within a larger picture of transformation.

Feuer's criticisms are useful in clarifying the issues and highlighting the theoretical and methodological problems in this area of research. However, she presents us here with a set of rather rigid oppositions – textual versus empirical, conscious versus unconscious – and fails to take account of the full complexity of more detailed questions of interpretation. What exactly is meant by empiricism, for example, which is easily dismissed by its mere mention within these debates?

Empiricism is a term with a complicated history. It generally refers to a reliance on the observation of experience and experiment as the basis for the production of knowledge. The assumption behind empirical studies, then, is that there is an external material reality whose truths can be observed and documented by the researcher. Historically, empiricism has been seen to be sceptical of the application of abstract concepts and ideas. Critics of empiricism have tended to challenge its atheoreticism and its so-called naive reliance on the unmediated observable truths of experience. Poststructuralist and psychoanalytic critics, in particular, have emphasised the ways in which meaning is mediated through symbolic signification and unconscious processes. Thus, 'experience' is seen to be a process which is constructed within specific cultural discourses, rather than as a self-evident phenomenon which can be straightforwardly observed. Whilst many of these criticisms of empiricism are well-placed, there are nevertheless problems with the ways in which the term 'empiricism' is employed within film studies. It is frequently used very loosely to dismiss categories of research, such as audience studies, without attention to either the exact meaning of empiricism as a term, or sufficient consideration of the differences between the studies in relation to that particular limitation. Thus all audience studies are often rejected as 'empirical' whether or not their method is that of empiricism. The source of the study – the audience – is thus seen to define the research as empirical whether or not the researcher is working within such an epistemology.

How, then, might audiences' accounts be considered as texts, and yet maintain a different status from the texts of film theory? How might we move beyond the simplistic ascription of audiences' responses as the 'authentic truth' about media meaning, whilst avoiding treating them as simply another kind of narrative fiction? How might some aspects of the psychoanalytic conception of the subject be retained, if modified, within studies of 'real audiences'? The material I received from my respondents which is analysed in the following chapters presented me with just such dilemmas. In addition to the usual methodological considerations of audience studies, I had to take account of the issues concerning history and memory discussed in the previous section of this chapter. In aiming to produce a historical study of women's memories of Hollywood stars in the 1940s and 1950s, I wanted to address some of the questions generated by the psychoanalytic feminist film theory, such as those about image and identity, using methods drawn from the very different traditions in cultural studies audience research. Feuer is not alone in highlighting the incompatibility of these two approaches. Indeed, my main purpose in Chapter 2 was to trace their very different histories.

However, what interested me when I began this research was the extent to which the psychoanalytic and the historical investigation of female spectatorship were *necessarily* incompatible. My aim was to critique the universalism of the psychoanalytic accounts of spectatorship within feminist film theory and produce an account of the historically located female spectator through an analysis of audiences' memories. This presented me with a number of tricky methodological and interpretive problems.

POSITIONING THE PROJECT: METHODOLOGICAL DECISIONS

First, there is the question of the focus on audiences in this research at the expense of analysing film stars and their films. This does not signify a conviction that the true meaning of the cinema lies with its audiences; rather, this focus should be understood in the light of the virtual absence of such work within the field. In film theory, any engagement with audiences has been dismissed as crudely or naively empiricist, and in film history there have been few ethnographic analyses of audiences, but rather studies of the institutional reception of films, or quantitative studies of cinema audiences in the past. As can be seen from the story of this research project, my focus was also partly determined by the size of the response I received which provided such a rich source of material and made me reluctant to move on to new sources, or to a more comparative model.

David Morley has defended his ethnographic method of interviewing television audiences as:

> a fundamentally more appropriate way to attempt to understand what audiences do when they watch television than for the analyst to sit at home and imagine the possible implications of how other people might watch television, in the manner that Feuer suggests.
>
> (Morley, 1989: 24)

What is implied by the term 'more appropriate' is crucial here. The suggestion is not that audiences are the only source of meaning, but that if we are concerned with questions of reception and cultural consumption, then the study of audiences will provide material not otherwise available to media researchers. Morley illustrates the dangers of Feuer's speculative method with the example of the discrepancies between Modleski's arguments about why women might like soap operas (Modleski, 1982) and the conclusions of an ethnographic study of a particular group of women soap opera viewers (Seiter *et al.*, 1989).

Similarly, I would argue that if we are interested in female spectatorship, an issue which has dominated feminist film theory for the past twenty years, then it is important to find out what female spectators say about Hollywood. In other words, I am arguing for the importance of putting spectators back into theories of female spectatorship (see Chapter 2). The kind of research methods and sources used need to be 'appropriate' to the subject of study. Thus I am arguing for the relativity of research methodologies, depending on the context and topic of research, rather than an absolutist model with its abstract prescriptions.

Second, there is the question of the status of this material. As I have argued, audiences' responses are not self-evident truths about what the media means; this would completely ignore the ways in which subjectivities are constituted through ideological discourses. The Althusserian and Lacanian work in the 1970s may have ascribed too much power to the dominant ideology and the symbolic order respectively (see Chapter 2), negating any notion of the historical agency of subjects; but to ignore issues of power relations is equally misguided. Thus these memories of Hollywood stars do need to be treated as texts in so far as they are forms of representation produced within certain cultural conventions. I would argue that the analysis of any form of representation requires a consideration of these conventions. Indeed, these conventions should not be seen as a barrier to the real meaning underneath, but rather as forming *part of the meaning itself*. In this research, for example, the processes of self-narrativisation discussed above would be one such convention which needs to be seen as part of the mechanisms of memory formation (see above). I have argued for the importance of seeing my material as narrativised accounts of the past which produced particular 'treasured memories' in which the respondents may have had certain personal investments.

However, to take such an approach is not to argue that what my respondents wrote to me is fictional, and thus of only relative significance to other fictions. Taking account of the narrative formations of audiences' memories is not to rob them of their specificity, or to treat them as fictional narratives like the films they were watching. This would be to confuse the categories of narrative and of fiction.[20] To argue that audiences produce narrative accounts of their responses to Hollywood is not to say that they may as well have made them up! Indeed, the importance of taking account of the cultural conventions of audiences' stories is precisely intended here to deal with them *in their specificity*. Audiences' memories of Hollywood stars, then, are obviously texts, but they are specific kinds of texts produced within a specific set of conditions. The readings of Hollywood that they produce need therefore to be situated within the context of their production.

What I have highlighted so far is the importance of audiences as a source for the study of the reception of film, without rendering them supreme, or transparent conveyors of historical truths. However, I *am* arguing for a method of analysis that takes what audiences say seriously. The three subsequent chapters which analyse women's memories of Hollywood cinema are organised around discourses generated by the material itself: escapism, identification and consumerism. Thus spectators' memories form the basis for the study, but they are situated within a critical discussion of the context of their production.

A third question which needs to be discussed in terms of the interpretation of audiences' memories is that of the incompatibility of ethnographic method with a belief in the unconscious, raised by Feuer above. These two approaches, it is argued, are incompatible because ethnography deals with 'conscious and easily articulated response' and ignores the unconscious, whereas psychoanalytic readings would mistrust audiences' accounts, emphasising instead the importance of unconscious processes to the meanings of visual images. Feuer is right to suggest that there are several methodological problems here, but her model offers only two possibilities: either there is the empirical description of what audiences choose to tell researchers of their conscious responses to the questions asked, which remains at the conscious level; or the researcher puts herself in the position of analyst and produces a reading of the unconscious of the audience.[21]

There are important feminist objections to an approach which seeks to psychoanalyse the audience. There are particular implications here for the politics of the power relations between the researcher and those being researched discussed earlier. To analyse their responses in terms of their unconscious psychic structures which the researcher, but not the researched, can identify is to impose the greatest degree of power difference between the two parties. The assumption behind such a method of interpretation is that audiences have offered information, but that the researcher can read between the lines for the latent meanings which reveal unconscious responses that are more significant than those apparently offered by the respondents. In some ways the question of the use of psychoanalytic theory here only intensifies the general problems of the power of the researcher to interpret audiences' responses. After all, critical analysis of the narrative structures of, or personal investments in, memory also involves highlighting hidden mechanisms. However, the question of the unconscious puts these issues into particularly sharp relief: it could be argued that psychoanalysing audiences' responses invests the researcher with maximum power and the audience with least agency.

However, another problem with this rigid division between ethnographic empiricism and theories of the unconscious is that it ignores much of the feminist work which has sought to combine elements of these two approaches such as Walkerdine (1986) and Radway (1984), discussed in

Chapter 2. Furthermore, it somewhat evades the methodological issues involved in the psychoanalytically informed textual analysis of film (rarely discussed in film studies) which similarly speculates about the unconscious of the audience 'without the benefit of the therapeutic situation'.

In this research the boundary between empirical audience research and psychoanalytic textual analysis cannot be drawn as straightforwardly as Feuer suggests. Instead my material demanded a consideration of cultural processes such as those of memory, identity formations, fantasy and day-dreaming which involve unconscious processes, but also need to be analysed in terms of the conscious everyday meanings they have for cinema spectators. I would argue that there are many modes of perception significant to the analysis of spectator/star relations in the 1940s and 1950s. A consideration of psychoanalytic theory and ethnographies of media audiences, therefore, needs to take account of the potential complexity of the relationship; it may be that methods of interpretation, theoretical perspectives, object of study and research questions cannot be collapsed into the straightforward choices Feuer advocates.

However, I would not want to deny the difficulties of combining a psychoanalytic with an historical approach. Indeed, the differential engagement with psychoanalytic theory in the ethnographic chapters that follow is indicative of this problem: whilst Chapter 5 engages directly, albeit critically, with psychoanalytic theory, Chapters 4 and 6 remain more historically based. The final chapter, Chapter 7, combines a consideration of the psychic with the historical moves beyond the details of the ethnographic material to a more generalised level of abstraction (although I have related the arguments back, as closely as possible, to the ethnographic accounts).

The ethnographic chapter in which psychoanalysis appears most prominently, albeit under a critical lens, is Chapter 5. This is the only one of the three in which there is an overlap between the audiences' category describing their relationship to Hollywood stars and a psychoanalytic category: namely, identification. In this chapter, after criticising the limits of the term within psychoanalytic theory through an analysis of the categories of identification generated by female spectators, I nevertheless return to alternative psychoanalytic accounts of the formation of gender identities, which I argue work more satisfactorily in relation to my material.

In contrast, in Chapters 4 and 6, psychoanalytic theory proved less useful than an historical framework. In Chapter 4, for example, I investigate the meaning of the commonsense term of 'escapism' used widely to explain the pleasure (especially for women) of popular culture. In their memories of Hollywood stars, respondents frequently employed the term to describe their reasons for going to the cinema. The material concerning escapism mainly related to wartime Britain and to the 1940s, hence the historical focus of the chapter. Reasons for cinema-going in this period were primarily presented through stories relating to the war, rationing and austerity in Britain at this time. Analysis of this material warranted a particularly detailed historical account, providing analyses of these circumstances which had clearly shaped women's cinema-going experience so forcefully.

Similarly, in Chapter 6, memories of cinematic spectatorship are analysed in terms of the changes in consumer culture in 1950s Britain. Again the importance of commodity consumption to female spectatorship emerges from the recollections of Hollywood stars by audiences. The material required a certain amount of discussion of the significance of changes in women's relationship to consumer markets and how this affected their readings of Hollywood stars. It is no coincidence that the psychoanalytic and the historical have remained somewhat separate, despite my efforts to bring them together. What is important here, however, is to highlight the importance of using theoretical frameworks appropriate to the material produced by the cinema audience.

In this research, then, I have taken different approaches in using spectators' accounts, depending on the issue at stake. Thus, at some points they have been used more illustratively: to analyse cinema-going practices in wartime Britain, for example. At others, they have been used to reflect upon existing theoretical debates: to assess theories of identification, for example. Finally, at other points, they have been treated as texts, and their narrative codes and conventions have been highlighted: to investigate the spectator's representation of devotion to a Hollywood star. Thus the material collected for this research has not been analysed within one single methodological or theoretical framework, but rather has been approached in a variety of ways to explore the multiple dimensions of female spectatorship at many different levels.

My own perspective then could be summed up as follows: although I have continued to address issues generated by psychoanalytic film theory, I have done so from a critical perspective which has also sought to question its universalist claims about female spectatorship and Hollywood cinema. What the project aims to offer is an investigation of the ways in which psychic investments are grounded within specific sets of historical and cultural relations which in turn shape the formation of identities on conscious and unconscious levels. How, for example, are spectators' fantasies and desires formed differently within specific contexts? In short, my investigation analyses the relationship between psychic and social formations, challenging the ways in which the latter have so often been ignored at the expense of the former within feminist film criticism.

4

HOLLYWOOD CINEMA – THE GREAT ESCAPE

This is the first of three chapters which analyse the letters and question-naires I received concerning Hollywood cinema and stars in Britain during the 1940s and 1950s. Each chapter deals with one of the three central discourses of spectatorship to emerge from the material I received from my respondents: escapism, identification and consumption respectively. Thus the first investigates the question of escapism and looks at the reasons why women went to the cinema; the second analyses the processes of spectator-ship in terms of a range of spectator/star identifications; finally, a key consequence of film viewing, namely commodity consumption, is analysed further in the last of these chapters. The differing historical foci of each of these chapters results from the varying emphases found in the material: significantly, the discourse of escapism is most closely articulated with wartime Britain and the discourse of consumption most closely with post-war Britain. However, this applies only at the most general level and there are numerous examples of overlap and of the blurring of these periodic boundaries.

Before moving on to analyse spectators' memories of Hollywood cinema, it is important to set out some of the features of cinema-going in Britain during this period. This will serve first to specify more clearly the cinema-going practices of audiences in Britain during this period; second, to analyse more closely the audience composition at this time; and finally, to include some discussion of my respondents in relation to audiences more generally. Thus the following section acts as an introduction to all three subsequent chapters by offering an analysis of cinema-going practices and their significance in terms of specific groups of spectators in Britain during the 1940s and 1950s. However, the introductory section is also especially relevant to an analysis of escapism in so far as it gives some general indications of Hollywood's mass appeal in Britain at this time. The stat-istics offer some of the quantitative details necessary to convey the centra-lity of Hollywood cinema in women's lives in Britain during the 1940s and 1950s.

HOLLYWOOD CINEMA IN 1940s AND 1950s BRITAIN

The significance of the cinema

Going to the pictures was not just an entertainment, but a way of life.

(Sonja Robinson)

The cinema meant so much to us in those days. We would rather have gone without food, and often did, than miss our weekly visits.

(Pat Robinson)

I loved all the stars of Hollywood in the 1940s and 1950s. I was a teenager in the '40s and the cinema was my world.

(Anon)

The significance of the cinema in women's lives in the 1940s and 1950s cannot be overestimated. The considerable response I received from my advertisement (350 letters) and the high return rate of the follow-up questionnaires (238 out of 258) attest to the value women continue to place on the subject of Hollywood and its stars in their lives forty and fifty years later. The pleasures of recollection, remembering and reminiscing were constantly referred to in the replies I received: I was frequently thanked for offering the opportunity for 'a trip down memory lane' (see Chapter 3). Hollywood stars during this period, it would seem, provide an abundance of 'treasured memories' which demonstrate their lasting significance for female spectators at this time. My advertisement signified to respondents a recognition of important experiences many feared were no longer relevant, and catalysed a powerful expression of renewed enthusiasm and passion for Hollywood cinema:

> I saw *Calamity Jane* 88 times . . . My favourite star of all time, even now, is Doris Day. To me she was my idol, I loved every film she ever did, and watched most of them several times. . . . I belonged to her fan club, collected all her photos and kept a scrap book, which sad to say was stolen in the 1970s. *Calamity Jane* was my all time favourite.
>
> (Veronica Millen)

Spectators' enthusiasm for particular stars and particular films is striking. A high percentage of respondents remembered going to the cinema two or three times a week during this period. Although the women responding to an advertisement for 'keen cinema-goers' are likely to have gone more frequently than many audiences at that time, cinema attendance *was* very high during this period, especially during the 1940s. Statistics of cinema attendance during the 1940s and 1950s are sporadic and partial. There are, in fact, very few sources for such information.[1] However, piecing together what is available indicates high attendance rates, high frequency of attendance and huge profits made by motion picture industries, suggesting some-

81

Figure 4.1 'I saw *Calamity Jane* 88 times . . . My favourite star of all time, even now, is Doris Day.'

thing of the role cinema played in people's lives at this time.

A table of the gross box-office receipts, for example, between 1935 and 1980 offers some indication of the enormous popularity of the cinema in the 1940s and 1950s (see Table 4.1).

As Table 4.1 makes clear, the gross box-office receipts totalled £114.2 million in 1945, which is nearly three times the equivalent figure in 1940, and about nine times the figure for 1980 based on the 1980 prices scale. In 1946, when cinema attendance in Britain was at its peak, cinema admissions takings totalled £121,000,000 (1946 prices) which was 'roughly one-fifth of the nation's annual clothing bill, one-seventh of its yearly outlay on rent and light, or one-thirteenth of its expenditure on food' (Swann, 1987: 36). Even in 1955, when cinema-going had become less popular, the net takings were £105.8 million (£632.7 million by 1980s prices).

Cinema-going was the main form of leisure activity in Britain in the 1940s and 1950s. In the early 1950s, twice as much money was spent on going to the cinema as on 'going to theatres, concert halls, music halls, skating rinks, sporting events and all other places of popular entertainment' (Swann, 1987: 150). Indeed, figures for 1950 highlight the popularity of the cinema over other leisure activities: in 1950 the number of cinema admissions totalled 1,611 million, compared with theatres and music halls, or football matches, each totalling 84 million (Corrigan, 1983: 24). The number of cinemas in Britain in 1940 was 4,671 and this rose to a peak of 4,703 in 1945.

Cinema admissions peaked at 1,635 million in 1946 in Britain, and did not drop below 1,000 million between 1940 and 1955. According to Corrigan, cinema attendance in England, Scotland and Wales was higher than in any other country: it 'averaged twenty-eight admissions per head in 1950, compared with twenty-three in the United States' (Corrigan, 1983: 25). As well as the extremely high numbers of people going to the cinema each week in Britain during this period, the frequency of attendance is also striking (see Table 4.2). The results of the Wartime Social Survey 1943, *The Cinema Audience* (Box and Moss, 1943), show a high percentage of audience members attended the cinema more than once a week, especially within the younger age ranges, and that a slightly higher percentage of women attended more frequently than men.

Although the statistics in Table 4.2 do not distinguish between Hollywood and British films, a large proportion of the films seen were American. In 1939, for example, 80 per cent of films shown in Britain were American (Lant, 1991), and in 1945 a total of seventy-six British films (over thirty-three-and-a-half minutes) were registered with the Department of Trade, compared with 374 'foreign' films (of over thirty-three-and-a-half minutes). Indeed, Hollywood found its most important export market in Britain. 'In 1946, for example, between them, the United

Table 4.1 Gross box-office receipts

Year	£ millions (at then current prices)	£ millions (at 1980 prices)[1]
1935	38.7	
1940	44.9	(485.4)
1945	114.2	(1027.8)
1950	105.2	(779.5)
1955	105.8	(632.7)
1960	63.6	(338.4)
1965	61.7	(278.9)
1970	59.0	(213.0)
1975	71.2	(139.6)
1980	135.7	(135.7)

Note: 1 This column, in which the purchasing power of the pound in 1980 has been reckoned as a constant 100p, shows the comparable figures for box-office receipts from 1940 onwards; VAT is included where relevant.
Source: The statistics are issued by the Department of Trade (Pirelli, 1983: 382).

Table 4.2 Frequency of cinema-going in the UK in 1943

Frequency	Sex	Age 14–17 (%)	18–40 (%)	41–5 (%)	46–65 (%)	Over 65 (%)
Once a week or more	M	76	38	24	15	5
	W	81	45	28	119	5
Less than once a week	M	21	43	48	40	26
	W	15	36	43	42	25
Not at all	M	2	19	27	43	69
	W	2	18	28	38	70
Sample	M	151	841	378	897	193
	W	153	1527	336	795	261

Source: Box and Moss (1943), Mass Observation File 1871.

States and Great Britain accounted for 120 million out of the 235 million worldwide cinema admissions each week, 30 million of these being in Britain' (Swann, 1987: 9).

Table 4.2 suggests that my respondents would have been amongst those attending the cinema most often, since the combination of being young and female puts them in the highest attendance category. Most respondents are women who are now over 50 years old and thus most of them would be included in the first two age brackets in this particular survey.

The feminisation of the spectator

There has been a great deal of work investigating the masculinisation of the cinema spectator within a psychoanalytic approach to the pleasures of Hollywood cinema (see Chapter 2). However, historically, it has been the female spectator who has been of most interest to the cinema and other related industries. Leo Handel (1950) argues that Hollywood studios believed women made up the highest proportion of cinema audiences and thus went to great lengths to produce films which appealed to women. Handel's summary of Hollywood's own market research reveals that gender-differentiated surveys were conducted to find out what female spectators wanted to see.

This 'feminisation' of the cinema spectator is also identified in Maria La Place's illuminating analysis of the 1930s and 1940s 'woman's film' as the embodiment of many of the criteria found to be particularly desirable by female spectators:

> a set of criteria were [sic] developed for attracting women to the movies; it was concluded that women favoured female stars over male, and preferred, in order of preference, serious dramas, love stories, and musicals. Furthermore, women were said to want 'good character development', and stories with 'human interest'. In one sense, the woman's film can be viewed as the attempt to cover as much of this territory as possible.
>
> (La Place, 1987: 138)

A further reason Hollywood marketing strategies paid particular attention to female spectators related to consumerism. The coincidence of the development of Hollywood cinema with the rise of consumerism more generally, in which women played a key role as consumers, has led to a consideration of the specific relationship between female spectators and Hollywood cinema. Although the theme of Hollywood cinema and consumerism is more relevant to the 1950s, when markets expanded in Britain and commodities became more widely available (see Chapter 6), it has been argued that the cinema industry (linked as it was with other consumer industries) has always addressed its female spectators as consumers more generally. Some critics have made the argument that because of the central role of the spectator as a consumer, and because it was women who were primarily addressed as consumers, a case can be made that the cinema spectator was increasingly envisaged as female:

> In the 1920s, theatre managers' trade journals described the motion picture theater not only as a temple of a secular religion, but as an environment designed to stimulate the adoration of the female spectator in particular. A 1927 article in *Theater Management*, for example, stressed the importance of women as the primary com-

ponent and motivators of film attendance and argued that both the appeal of the film and the theater must be geared to pleasing women's sensibilities.

(Allen, 1980: 486)

This is not to deny the fact that men attended the cinema regularly too. Indeed, many women remember the cinema as the main place for the pursuit of heterosexual romances and 'courtships', and thus men's presence was a necessary component of much cinema-going during this period. Ironically, this public place offered the only opportunity for the necessary privacy for many heterosexual couples before marriage:

> It seems that most of our courting was done in the pictures. It was the nearest thing to privacy any of us had in those days.
>
> (Jean Sheppard)

However, men's attendance does not necessarily undermine the fact that it was women who were seen as the key *motivators* of cinema-going, and thus a crucial audience to target in Hollywood's marketing strategies.

In addition to the popularity of Hollywood films in Britain, there were many other cultural forms, associated with Hollywood, which attest to its significance in women's lives at this time. For example, in the late 1940s there were at least twenty-seven magazines about the cinema on sale to the general public. There were also several film journals aimed at more specialised audiences. Women were seen as a particularly receptive market for stories on Hollywood cinema in magazines generally (Swann, 1987: 41). Fan newsletters were also prolific at this time and had high circulation figures among female spectators: 'It was possible for a fan newsletter such as the *International Jean Kent Fan Club* to have a circulation rivalling that of the *Spectator*' (*ibid.*: 42). As well as specialist publications, the purchasing of daily newspapers was also related to the cinema: 'in a postwar survey, a majority of newspaper readers said that local film listings were the second most important reason for buying a newspaper, whilst fully a fifth of the respondents in this survey said cinema listings were their most important reason for buying a newspaper' (*ibid.*: 42).

Class differences

Another important factor in determining the composition of cinema audiences was class difference. According to *The Cinema Audience* (Box and Moss, 1943: 8), the highest proportion of cinema-goers who visited the cinema more than once a week in 1943 were those who worked in light munitions and other manufacturing and in clerical work. Only a small proportion of people in these groups did not go to the cinema. Agricultural workers and the retired and 'unoccupied' had the lowest cinema attendance. Those belonging to the managerial and professional classes represented a high proportion of the group who went less than once a week. Under the rather problematically general category 'housewives', a rather lower-than-average proportion went to the cinema once a week or more often. But the researchers point out that, compared with other groups, there is a high proportion of older people in this group and that younger women would more often be wage earners.

One source of research on class difference and cinema audience composition and frequency of attendance is the findings of Mark Abrams' Research Services Company. This research was produced for the Rank Organization with a view to using films to market other consumer goods. Drawing heavily on the results of the Hulton Surveys, Abrams highlighted the extent to which the cinema audience was drawn from working-class people and from younger sections of the population. In an article written for the *Hollywood Reporter*, Abrams claimed that: '[t]he Working Classes flock to the movies with such avidity that they account for more than 70% of the audience' (quoted in Swann, 1987: 46). As Paul Swann goes on to comment, there are many competing claims about the demographies of British cinema audiences in the postwar period, but all suggest this kind of class difference in its composition.

Class position, as I have already stated, is notoriously difficult to ascertain for women, since a woman's class position is frequently defined through her husband's paid employment, and the category 'housewife' that many women use to describe themselves is one which does not explicitly indicate class position. The readers' profiles of the two magazines in which I advertised, *Woman's Realm* and *Woman's Weekly*, show that over 50 per cent of their readership come from classes C1 and C2: clerical and skilled workers (see Appendix 3, pp. 252–4). Based upon information about respondents' backgrounds, such as ownership of accommodation, educational qualifications and employment of the respondents and their spouses, my respondents typically come from similar class backgrounds. This is also consistent with the statistics available on the composition of the cinema audience during this period. However, although most of my respondents tended to come from similar class backgrounds in the 1940s and 1950s, many of them have since shifted class positions through marriage or changes in education, training and employment (see pp. 61–2).

Ethnicity

To my knowledge there are no comparable surveys about the different ethnicities of cinema audiences at this time. The Hollywood audience in Britain during the 1940s and 1950s has been perceived as predominantly white, despite the fact that its ethnic composition changed considerably, particularly during the 1950s when Britain's black population grew with the need for labour from Britain's colonies (The Runnymede Trust and the Radical Statistics Group, 1980). The so-called age of affluence in 1950s Britain was heavily dependent upon the importation of black workers from Britain's colonies (Fryer, 1984). The cinema was also a central source for the dissemination of government 'lines' to white audiences about the new workers from the colonies. Afro-Caribbean and Asian workers were sought out by British companies and encouraged to come to Britain with the promise of employment and prosperity. In fact, they were mainly employed at low wages to do the work which many white workers were unwilling to do. The ethnic composition of Britain thus changed greatly during this period of economic expansion (Fryer, 1984: 373–81). However, details about changes in the ethnic composition of British cinema audiences remain unresearched.

Furthermore, there has been very little research into the question of black audiences and their relationship to dominant white Hollywood. Until recently Elizabeth Ewen (1980) and Judith Mayne (1982) were two of the few to consider the issue of ethnicity and audiences. However, there is an increasing amount of textual criticism of Hollywood cinema in terms of its traditions of racist representations and, indeed, two recent collections on female spectatorship have included some new work on black female spectatorship. Jacqueline Bobo (1988) examines black women's readings of the film *The Color Purple* and Jacqui Roach and Petal Felix (1988) analyse questions of the black look in popular culture (see Chapter 2).

The respondents to my advertisement were all white women. This is not surprising because of the readership and orientation of the magazines which agreed to print my request. Both *Woman's Weekly* and *Woman's Realm* appeal predominantly to a white readership. Many of my respondents expressed surprise, irritation and confusion at being asked to describe their ethnicity (see Appendix 2 question 45). Some felt the question was irrelevant; others felt indignation at being asked; others still expressed anger at the categories I had chosen and crossed them out altogether. In particular, the respondents resented the category 'white European' and asserted instead their 'Englishness' or 'Britishness' which they assumed to be a white identity.

Given the predominant whiteness of Hollywood and its stars, the question of ethnicity and the appeal of Hollywood cinema at this time is a pressing one. Black female spectators have yet to be asked about their feelings about white Hollywood cinema. Certainly, in some black writing, Hollywood stars have signified desirable white femininity, producing fantasies of glamour, power and status for those women denied such 'privileges', as the opening to the novel *I Know Why The Caged Bird Sings* demonstrates:

The dress I wore was lavender taffeta, and each time I breathed it rustled, and now that I was sucking air to breathe out shame it sounded like crepe paper on the back of hearses.

As I'd watched Momma put ruffles on the hem and cute little tucks around the waist, I knew that once I put it on I'd look like a movie star. (It was silk and that made up for the awful color.) I was going to look like one of the sweet little white girls who were everybody's dream of what was right with the world. Hanging softly over the black Singer sewing machine, it looked like magic, and when people saw me wearing it they were going to run up to me and say, 'Marguerite (sometimes it was "dear Marguerite"), forgive us, please, we didn't know who you were,' and I would answer generously, 'No, you couldn't have known. Of course I forgive you.'

. . . . Wouldn't they be surprised when one day I woke out of my black ugly dream, and my real hair, which was long and blond, would take the place of the kinky mass that Momma wouldn't let me straighten? My light-blue eyes were going to hypnotize them. . . . Because really I was white and because a cruel fairy stop mother, who was jealous of my beauty, had turned me into a too-big Negro girl with nappy black hair, broad feet and a space between her teeth that would hold a number two pencil.

(Angelou, 1984: 3–5)

As Maya Angelou highlights, Hollywood stars produce cultural ideals of whiteness. The 'difference' between 'Marguerite' and the white movie star she fantasises resembling can be seen to intensify the appeal in a racist society where ideals of beauty and glamour have always been white. Indeed, in the 1950s this is especially the case, when Marilyn Monroe's blondeness, for example, was a key signifier of her glamour (Dyer, 1986).

The decline of the cinema in the 1950s

It is important to highlight the fact that cinema attendance was by no means consistent during the 1940s and 1950s. In fact, attendance fell considerably during the late 1940s and the 1950s as Table 4.3 indicates. Reasons for this are too numerous to discuss in detail here, but tend to be attributed to changes in the Hollywood industry, especially the break-up of the studio system, the diversification of leisure markets, particularly the emergence of television, and finally to the restructuring of housing in postwar Britain, moving people away from areas with accessible local cinemas. Hollywood feature films also began to be shown on television from 1953/4 onwards.

However, whilst it is important not to treat the 1940s and 1950s as a unified time period during which the popularity of the cinema was constant, it is also true that cinema-going was an immensely popular practice

Table 4.3 Cinema admissions and net box-office takings (UK)

Year	Admissions (millions)	Net takings (£ millions)
1945	1,585	73
1947	1,462	68
1949	1,430	67
1951	1,365	71
1953	1,285	72
1955	1,182	73
1957	915	65
1959	581	59

Source: Adapted from Board of Trade Statistics (Kelly, quoted in Jarvie, 1970: 116).

that produced an enormous revenue throughout both decades in Britain. During this period, cinema attendance averaged over 1,000 million per year and net takings were over £68 million. Similarly, despite this decline in cinema attendance,[2] a 1961 survey, *The Cinema Audience*, carried out by the Screen Advertising Association, found the frequency of cinema attendance still significantly high: 30 per cent of the sample attended twice a week and another 33 per cent once a week (Jarvie, 1970: 112).

THEORISING ESCAPISM

The cinema was a night out, an escape into a more glamorous world.

(Jean Johnson)

It is a truism to assert that escapism is one of the most important pleasures of Hollywood cinema. But what exactly is meant by 'escapism'? A term often meant pejoratively, 'escapism' has been applied to forms of popular culture in order to dismiss them as insignificant and unworthy of critical or academic attention. Indeed, this has been particularly true of forms of popular culture enjoyed by women – soap operas or romance fiction and films. In the light of such attacks, feminist critics have insisted on taking women's pleasures in popular culture seriously and understanding exactly what is at stake in their consumption of these particular popular forms.

In this study my request for accounts of such pleasures contradicted the assumption that women's pleasures in popular culture are unworthy of academic attention. The overwhelming and enthusiastic response I received may partly be accounted for by the feelings of validation and recognition prompted by such a request. However, some women wrote about their enthusiasm for Hollywood stars with a kind of embarrassment or self-consciousness about their pleasure, acknowledging its escapist roots

90

which they feared might be perceived as 'trivial' or 'silly'. Respondents frequently questioned the importance of their contributions with comments such as: 'I hope this is helpful, though I fail to see how my scribblings are of interest'; or 'yes, please do quote me if you really want to, but I doubt if my memories will be of much use'. Thus, whilst keen to share their memories, some women simultaneously guarded against disparagement by building in their own auto-critique of the 'escapist' nature of their love of Hollywood and its stars. One respondent offers a retrospective analysis of her own pleasures in Hollywood 'dreams':

> In retrospect it's easy to see Hollywood stars for what they really were. This was pretty packaged commodities . . . the property of a particular studio.
> At the time I did most of my film-going, while I was always aware that stars were really too good to be true, I fell as completely under the spell of the Hollywood 'Dream Factory' as any other girl of my age.
>
> (Kathleen Lucas)

The reappraisal of the pleasures offered by Hollywood stars continues:

> Looking back, I can see much of what I took as authenticity was really technical skill . . . Later on I realised just how much money and expertise went into creating the 'natural' beauties the female stars appeared to be.
>
> (Kathleen Lucas)

Other respondents articulated a strong nostalgia for Hollywood cinema of the 1940s and 1950s precisely because of the escapist pleasures they longed to recapture. When contrasting their memories of Hollywood with the cinema of today it is escapism which recurringly characterises the pleasures many respondents feel they have lost:

> I think in those eras, we were more inclined to put stars on a pedestal. They were so far removed from everyday life, they were magical. . . . These days stars are so ordinary – the magic has gone. Hollywood will never be the same again!
>
> (Kathleen Sines)

Whether reappraised with critical hindsight, or longed for nostalgically, 'escapism' was one of the most frequent reasons given by these female spectators for their cinema-going enthusiasm in the 1940s and 1950s. There are few studies, however, that analyse what is involved in this cultural process so loosely dubbed 'escapism'.[3] Most studies fail to move beyond the level of generalisation in their discussion of escapism. Those that do have not considered the gendered dimensions of escapist pleasures which are of particular relevance to this study. This chapter therefore offers both an analysis of the meanings of escapism in relation to the cinema and an investigation of the relationship between escapism and the cultural construction of femininity.

Richard Dyer's article 'Entertainment and utopia' (1985) is one of the very few attempts to deconstruct the notion of 'escapism' in relation to Hollywood cinema. He argues that two of the taken-for-granted descriptions of entertainment:

> as 'escape' and as 'wish-fulfilment', point to its central thrust, namely, utopianism. Entertainment offers the image of 'something better' to escape into, or something we want deeply that our day-to-day lives don't provide. Alternatives, hopes, wishes – these are the stuff of utopia, the sense that things could be better, that something other than what is can be imagined and maybe realised.
>
> (Dyer, 1985: 222)

Dyer's article develops an analysis of what he calls 'entertainment's utopian sensibility'. Contradicting the usual exclusively textual focus of many film studies, Dyer argues that these signs work through a cultural code which can be related to a particular set of historical circumstances:

> it is important to grasp that modes of experiential art and entertainment correspond to different culturally and historically determined sensibilities. This becomes clear when one examines how entertainment forms come to have the emotional signification they do: that is, by acquiring their signification in relation to a complex of meanings in the social-cultural situation in which they are produced.
>
> (Dyer, 1985: 223)

Importantly for my argument, then, Dyer highlights here the connections between pleasure and the historical and cultural locations which produce particular forms of utopian sensibility. Additionally, by focusing on utopian *sensibility*, Dyer highlights another rather neglected question within film studies – the emotional dimensions of the cinema. Despite the preoccupation with the question of (visual) pleasure in film studies generally, an understanding of the emotional significance of the cinema to its audience has remained absent.

In order to develop an understanding of utopian sensibility, Dyer constructs a series of categories through which entertainment forms can be understood: abundance, energy, intensity, transparency and community. He then relates these categories to the inadequacies of society from which people may be seeking temporary relief through the utopian sensibilities of entertainment forms. Thus, attempting to construct a framework for how entertainment works, Dyer suggests the model shown in Table 4.4.

However, although Dyer's model provides one of the few analyses of the pleasures of escapism offered by popular entertainment forms, a number

Table 4.4 Dyer's model of the appeal of entertainment forms

Social tension/Inadequacy/Absence	Utopian solution
Scarcity (actual poverty in the society; poverty observable in the surrounding societies, e.g. Third World; unequal distribution of wealth)	*Abundance* (enjoyment of sensuous material reality, conquest of scarcity for self and others)
Exhaustion (work as a grind, alienated labour, pressures of urban life)	*Energy* (capacity to act vigorously; human power, activity, potential)
Dreariness (monotony, predictability, instrumentality of the daily round)	*Intensity* (experiencing of emotion directly, fully, unambiguously, 'authentically', without holding back)
Manipulation (advertising, bourgeois democracy, sex roles)	*Transparency* (open, spontaneous, honest communications and relationships, sincerity)
Fragmentation (job mobility, rehousing and development, high-rise flats, legislation against collective action)	*Community* (togetherness, a sense of belonging, communal interests and activities)

Source: Dyer, 1985: 224–8.

of questions need further elaboration. First, the audience is, in a sense, the structuring absence in Dyer's argument. The missing link between the social tension outside the cinema and the utopian solution offered on the screen in Dyer's model is, in fact, the cinema spectator. With its emphasis on the significance of context to the pleasures of escapism, Dyer's analysis demonstrates the necessity of situating the pleasures of the text within specific locations. Thus, different audiences might bring different needs and desires to the cinema depending on their historical and cultural circumstances. Second, as Dyer himself acknowledges, these categories work at the general level and need to be explored in terms of social divisions such as gender, ethnicity and class. It therefore remains for this model to be reworked and adapted in relation to particular audiences in specific contexts. The rest of this chapter thus extends Dyer's argument through an analysis of the escapist pleasures of Hollywood cinema in wartime and postwar Britain remembered by the female spectators in this study.

THE CINEMA AS DREAM PALACE

Previously, the question of cinematic pleasure has been primarily analysed in terms of the visual and narrative conventions of Hollywood films. Memories of the pleasures of the cinema in wartime and postwar Britain, however, are not limited to the film text. In order to understand how the cinema offered female spectators the pleasures of escapism at this time it is necessary to analyse the whole cinema-going experience, rather than simply focusing on the details of the film text.[4] Indeed, as Rachel Low has argued, the cinema audience during this period largely consisted of habitual cinema-goers for whom the cinema was 'an institutionalised night out independent of the artistic value of the entertainment' (Low, quoted in Swann, 1987: 36). It was often this ritualised night out which was remembered as particularly enjoyable by female spectators in my study: 'I loved the whole atmosphere from queueing outside, right through to the national anthem – after which it was a rush to catch the last bus home' (Kathleen Lucas).

The focus on the whole event, it might be argued, could be partly explained by the retrospective nature of these accounts. For example, the details of particular films might have been forgotten, and these 'ritualised nights out' might be more easily remembered fifty years later. However, many of my respondents also remember surprisingly detailed aspects of costume, gesture and dialogue from particular films (see Chapter 6). Instead, I would argue that what emerges from these repeated accounts of the pleasures of cinema-going practices generally is the importance of moving beyond the pleasures of the text to include the pleasures of the ritualised event.

A second issue to emerge from respondents' memories of cinema-going in Britain at this time was the material pleasure of the cinema itself. My respondents repeatedly offered vivid memories of the cinema as a physical space in which to escape the discomforts of their everyday lives. Shortages of fuel, clothes, food and other basic needs were frequently mentioned as contrasts to the environment of the cinema:

> Cinemas were warm, comfortable, attractive places, relaxing after a day's work. Sometimes one went to keep warm if coal was short.
>
> (Anon)

> For a few hours it made you forget about the war in the 1940s and after the war the drabness of everything in post war Britain. . . . We went more often during the war because you could forget the war for a few hours and the air raids that were often going on at the same time, also it was a place to be warm in the winter months, as coal was in short supply.
>
> (Joan Draper)

Cinematic pleasure, then, is remembered as having an important material dimension. Cinemas offered women a physical escape from the hardships of their lives at this time.

But cinemas were not merely recalled as warm, cosy buildings where films were screened. They were also remembered for their plush interiors, which offered a unique opportunity to enjoy the feelings associated with certain 'luxuries' rare in 1940s Britain:

> Like so many others, my life in the 1940s was pretty drab. We lived in a London flat. No electricity, no bath, no luxuries like refrigerators, telephones or cars, and of course no t.v. All we had to brighten up our lives were the radio and the cinema. For 1/9d we could enter another world. Oh the luxury of it, the red carpet, the wonderful portraits adorning the walls. The chandeliers hanging in the foyer and the smell!
>
> (Patricia Robinson)

Here, attention is drawn to the physical luxuries of the cinema in contrast to the very specific hardships of the domestic environment.

Remembering the 1940s from the vantage point of the late 1980s these contrasts between the luxuries of the cinema and the hardships of the home may have seemed particularly stark. Having lived through more prosperous years since, when many of these 'luxuries' became 'necessities' for women in Britain, the retrospective assessment of this period no doubt makes it seem even bleaker. For many women in this study the availability of mass market consumer goods, especially domestic ones, from the 1950s onwards highlights the relative hardships of the war years.

Many women included details of the cinema buildings themselves in their favourite memories of cinema-going. Cinemas in wartime and post-war Britain were remembered as very particular kinds of material spaces for the consumption of Hollywood films. In fact, memories of the cinemas were often as detailed as those of the films. Thus the architecture, design and interior decor can be seen as an integral and important part of the escapist pleasures of cinema-going. A favourite cinema experience of this time, for example, was remembered as:

> visiting an exotic cinema out of my usual district with a friend. The cinema was decorated like a moorish palace with fountains, star spangled ceiling etc.
>
> (Anon)

Cinema designs at this time encouraged the feelings of entering another world;[5] in this example, the imitation of an architectural style from an 'exotic' culture is constructed as 'other' and thus provides an exciting context for the consumption of Hollywood film. One kind of otherness, provided by the style of the cinema interior, offered the context for the enjoyment of another kind of otherness, the representations of American culture in Hollywood films. Escapism, then, was experienced not only in terms of the fictional narrative viewed on the screen, but also through a feeling of 'other worldliness' produced by the design of the cinema interior.

According to Allen (1980) cinema interiors were designed and furnished in ways intended to appeal to female spectators:

> Art works in the lobbies, attractive fabrics and designs for interior decoration, and the subdued and flattering lighting were important appeals to women's tastes and to their desire for comfort and relaxation.
>
> (Allen, 1980: 486)

Responsible for the domestic space at home, and thus acutely aware of its limitations, women could thus be relied upon to respond to the promise of luxury offered by many cinemas. The fact that women were typically responsible for the domestic organisation of households at the time meant that their desire for escape from such hardships may have been especially intense.

One aspect of this appeal remembered by many of my respondents is the sensuousness of cinematic pleasures:

> Particularly in wartime, the cinema was an escape from shortages and restrictions. I revelled in the special effects – perfumed air spray, the exotic (to me) decor, the fancy lighting which was dimmed, then faded and finally turned off. The feel of the plush seats and the reaction of the audience.
>
> (Kathleen Lucas)

This quotation emphasises the luscious nature of the cinema-going experience, for four out of the five senses are mentioned: smell – the perfumed air spray; sight – the fancy lighting; touch – the feel of the plush seat; and sound – the reaction of the audience.

The pleasures of wartime cinema-going, then, did not involve only the sense of sight, as is so often assumed in analyses of visual pleasure which focus on the film text to the exclusion of other aspects of the cinema. The debates about pleasure within film studies have concentrated on the 'visual', rather than the 'other pleasures' of the cinema (Mulvey, 1989). These other 'pleasures' are analogous, to some extent, to Dyer's non-representational signs in films, such as lighting, colour and rhythm, which, he argues, have tended to be ignored in film analysis. Both have crucial roles in creating atmosphere and mood and thus contribute to the pleasures of the consumption of the film, but have remained relatively hidden within film studies analysis.

Whereas Dyer's categories of utopian sensibility work primarily at an emotional level, the factors I have identified so far work at a more sensuous, physical level, although these clearly have an emotional dimension. It is the sensuous pleasures of the luxury of the cinema that provide a contrast here with the material conditions of women's lives in wartime and postwar Britain. The cinema itself, then, not only functioned as the physical environment for screening Hollywood films, but through its architecture, style, decor and layout, it contributed to the pleasures of escapism remembered by these female spectators.

Moreover, these pleasures (scented smells, softness, visual attractiveness) associated with the cinema interiors were ones which have been culturally ascribed to femininity; perfumed air, the plush texture of the curtains and seats, the glistening chandeliers all contribute to what could be seen as a feminised environment for consumption. The emphasis on the sensuous pleasures of the interior, as a spectacle to be marvelled at, inviting touch and offering sweet smells, all connote femininity and echo the feminine qualities so admired in the female stars of Hollywood.

This analysis questions the distinction between 'popular' and 'bourgeois' aesthetics formulated by Pierre Bourdieu in his study of cultural taste and class differences (see Bourdieu, 1980, 1984). He argues that whereas popular aesthetics are characterised by an immediate emotional and sensual pleasure, bourgeois aesthetics are based upon formal and universalised criteria devoid of passion and pleasure. This distinction ignores the ways in which the pleasures of the cinema, for example, operate at a sensual and emotional level for female spectators. Clearly, these are also gendered pleasures at a number of levels. Indeed, it could be argued that the cinematic space in which Hollywood films were consumed was a feminised one.[6] It is precisely this feminisation of the context of cultural consumption which contributed to the pleasures of cinema-going at a time when such 'expressions' of femininity remained relatively unavailable to many women in everyday life in Britain.

The centrality of material pleasure to women's memories of cinema-going at this time is particularly important in understanding the appeal of *Hollywood* cinema and *Hollywood* stars. Associated as it was with luxury and glamour, in contrast to British drabness at this time, Hollywood was remembered as offering an escape to a materially better world. Thus the specific association of the luxury of Hollywood with the luxury of the cinema interiors at this time clearly contributed to the multi-layered meanings of escapism for female spectators.

One central difference which my respondents frequently remembered as significant between British and American cinema confirms this argument. Hollywood differed from British cinema in numerous ways, but one crucial difference perceived by audiences at the time was the 'glamour' of Hollywood and its *stars* in contrast to the seriousness of British cinema and its *actors*.[7] Thus the palatial surroundings of cinemas in the 1940s

Figure 4.2 'Coming down [the cinema staircase] one always felt like a Hollywood heroine descending into a ballroom.' (Publicity still of Joan Crawford.)

anticipated in a very particular way the pleasures which followed in the screening of Hollywood films.

Besides anticipating the glamour associated with Hollywood, British cinemas replicated the atmosphere many women associated with Hollywood films and indeed the kinds of roles female stars might play:

Our favourite cinema was the Ritz – with its deep pile carpet and double sweeping staircase. Coming down one always felt like a Hollywood heroine descending into a ballroom.

(Anon)

The glamorous interiors of British cinemas, then, provided the cultural space for the consumption of Hollywood's glamorous femininity. Their luxurious interiors enabled the audience to begin their 'escape' before the films had begun:

The moment I took my seat it was a different world, plush and exciting, the world outside was forgotten. I felt grown up and sophisticated.

(Betty Cruse)

The physical space of the cinema provided a transitional space between everyday life outside the cinema and the fantasy world of the Hollywood film about to be shown. Its design and decor facilitated the processes of escapism enjoyed by these female spectators. As such, cinemas were dream palaces not only in so far as they housed the screening of Hollywood fantasies, but also because of their own design and decor which provided a feminised and glamorised space suitable for the cultural consumption of Hollywood films.

The material pleasures of cinema-going discussed so far fall within Dyer's utopian category of abundance. Indeed the physical pleasures of the cinema environment, such as the thick pile carpets, the texture of the seating and the perfumed air, accord perfectly with Dyer's definition of abundance as 'enjoyment of sensuous material reality, conquest of scarcity'. However, my analysis here extends Dyer's model to include an account of the ways in which such escapist pleasures are historically and culturally located. Life outside the cinema is repeatedly used in these accounts as a point of contrast with the pleasures offered inside it. Thus the fulfilment of utopian fantasies of luxury and glamour can only be fully understood when situated in relation to the hardship of wartime and postwar Britain which intensified such pleasures for these female spectators. Moreover, memories of the pleasures of abundance offered by the cinema at this time demonstrate the centrality of the construction of femininity to such pleasures. This is true both in terms of the feminisation of the cinematic space and in terms of the connections between this space and the glamour of the female Hollywood stars remembered by these spectators.

A SENSE OF BELONGING

In addition to the importance of the physical space cinemas provided, the shared experience of escaping into that space was remembered as significant. Here again, the focus was not specifically on the films themselves, but rather on the many contributing elements of the cinema-going experience:

> The atmosphere in those days in the cinema was wonderful. Crowds of people queueing to go in, the music playing, the rustling of sweet papers, with usherettes darting up and down the aisles shining their torches.
>
> (June Kelly)

The feeling of a shared group identity was a central component of the 'atmosphere' referred to repeatedly in descriptions of the appeal of the cinema:

> The cinema was a night out, an escape into a more exciting more glamorous world. The watching of a film with a lot of other people heightened my enjoyment of it. . . . I particularly enjoyed the company of the audience around me, the comfortable surroundings, the ice creams and the getting away from everyday life for a few hours.
>
> (Jean Johnson)

This sense of belonging to an audience is an interesting extension of Dyer's category of community which he uses to describe one aspect of utopian sensibility in film texts: 'all together in one place, communal interests, collective activity' (Dyer, 1985: 228). One of the pleasures of escapism, then, was remembered as the collective sense of being part of another world:

> The cinema was a wonderful few hours of warmth, companionship and escape to a dream world, and we were part of it.
>
> (Joyce Lewis)

Indeed, sharing the appreciation of particular aspects of Hollywood was felt to connect members of the audience to each other: for example, the collective anticipation of the appearance of the favourite star was one of the unifying practices associated with being part of the cinema audience:

> What I particularly enjoyed about going to the pictures was the expectation of the shared intimacy, the waiting for the favourite star of the moment to appear.
>
> (Dawn Hellmann)

The connectedness to others through shared cultural consumption extends beyond the cinema itself and into everyday practices associated with cinema-going. Discussion of Hollywood and its stars at work and at home was one of the pleasures of the cinema frequently recalled:

> What I really enjoyed about going to the pictures was the atmosphere in the cinema – warm and friendly. It was something to look forward to and plan and then to talk about afterwards.
>
> (Mrs H. Cox)

This sense of community and of togetherness clearly broke down feelings of isolation and offered a sense of self with a collective meaning. The 'shared intimacy' and 'heightened enjoyment' of collective consumption could be read as further contributing to the feminisation of cultural consumption: femininity being culturally constructed as relational and masculinity as more individuated.

The notion of femininity as more relational than masculinity has been developed by some feminist theorists, such as Nancy Chodorow (1978), using object relations theory to analyse the social construction of gender inequality.[8] Chodorow argues that the mother/boy-child relationship can be characterised by separation: mothers relate to boys from the time they are born as separate and different from themselves, thus encouraging boys' individuation/separation from their mothers, and boys in turn negate their early sense of merging with their mothers on the basis of their difference from them. Mothers and girl children, on the other hand, do not relate through such a degree of individuation/separation: girls do not negate their early feelings of oneness with their mothers since they recognise themselves in their mothers; mothers regard their girl children as similar to themselves and identify with them, thus encouraging girls to develop a more relational sense of self.

Although there are limits to this model of gender differences between men and women, not least of which is the fixed version of masculinity and femininity which results, object relations theory nevertheless offers an interesting lens through which to analyse the pleasures of the utopian feelings of 'community' remembered by these female spectators. Indeed, it is the relational aspects of cinematic consumption that are emphasised in these aspects of collective consumption in cinemas in the 1940s. Thus escapism is not merely an individualised process, but rather involves a submergence of self into a more collective identity which could be seen to have a gendered specificity. In other words, the appeal of a utopian sense of community may be especially strong given the ways in which femininity is culturally constructed as generally more relational.

ESCAPING THE WAR

Unless you have experienced a totally blacked-out town, limited food and shops that were almost empty, you cannot comprehend the part films played in our lives.

(Gwyneth Wathen)

One of Dyer's central arguments in relation to utopian sensibility is that as well as investigating the pleasurable feelings the audience escapes *into*, it is also important to analyse what it is they are escaping *from*. The Second World War was, not surprisingly, a constant reference point in many accounts of cinema-going during the 1940s. Hollywood films were remembered as an important contrast to the hardships and strain of wartime Britain. This extreme and dramatic context in which fear, anxiety, loss and confusion became the emotions of everyday life produced a heightened desire to 'escape into another world'. Thus the specificity of the consumption of Hollywood in Britain during the war, and during the continuing austerity of the postwar years, necessitates careful consideration in understanding the pleasures of escapism during this period.

The sense of belonging discussed above, for example, took on a particular meaning during the 1940s in relation to the war: 'the war highlighted the sense of pleasure, the cinema was a warm, communal place to go in an air-raid' (Dawn Hellmann). In this context feelings of togetherness and community took on a special significance. The sense of community was enhanced because there was a common crisis from which to escape. One of the most popular memories of the Second World War has been an image of people 'pulling together' in a crisis. Togetherness, then, is a predictable recollection to be associated with this time. However, the cinema provided a feeling of togetherness with a difference: unlike the sense of community found in air-raid shelters and food queues, the feelings of community recalled in relation to cinema were linked to pleasurable forms of cultural consumption. Thus, although a feeling of community might have been stronger during the war than would generally be found in many parts of British society, this feeling had particularly pleasurable connotations in relation to Hollywood cinema.

Women's lives in Britain were constantly being fragmented and disrupted by death, destruction and dislocation:

> Women all over Britain were obliged to billet the odd assortment of war workers which included miners, mothers, professors, ex-convicts, students, salesmen and labourers. . . . They were paid a 'government guinea' a week (unless it was a private arrangement) to accommodate, feed and launder for the unnerving intrusion into their already disrupted lives. In September 1939 a third of all Britons changed address and in the course of the war sixty million changes of address in a population of thirty-five million were registered. Normal life ceased as schools, homes, places of work, pubs and cinemas closed or were filled with strangers.
>
> (Minns, 1980: 17)

Women were separated from relatives and friends by the war in several ways: most men were absent fighting the war, relatives and friends were under constant threat of being killed by the bombing, and children were evacuated to the country away from their mothers after severe bombing attacks. Throughout these stressful and traumatic times, the cinema was remembered as offering 'a prime source of escapism from the prevalent stresses and anxieties about my husband's serving abroad and all my young friends also serving' (Elizabeth Allan).

One of the key factors dominating life in Britain during the Second World War was the air-raids. For women in cities particularly, air-raids meant constantly living in fear of death, loss of family and friends and destruction of homes, workplaces and shops. Each new phase of bombing brought new grief and anxiety: 'the Blitz of September 1940 to June 1941, the 1942 Baedecker raids on historic towns, the renewed air attacks on London and other big cities in 1943 to 1944, and the V2 flying bombs and rockets of 1944 to 1945' (Braybon and Summerfield, 1987:160). Women in Britain were all subject to the horrors of the air-raids, and the cinema provided one of the only forms of relief:

> It was lovely to go to see the films – to see the lovely clothes and hear the music. It made the war seem further away, although we often had to go to the shelters during the raids, and come back and finish the film afterwards.
>
> (Kathleen March)

> It was a way of escaping from the blackout and going into a different world of the cinema, especially the musicals, as a young girl I enjoyed the music and clothes and make-believe.
>
> (Anon)

Although cinemas did close down in the first three months of the war, they were quickly re-opened, and they provided a much needed feeling of continuity during a time of unpredictability, loss and change. The relocation of people and of activities meant that few previously relied-upon daily routines and/or rituals could be counted upon. Despite the occasional disruption to cinema-going during air-raids, as mentioned above, most respondents remembered little change in their cinema-going habits as a result of the war. Cinema-going, then, proved to be an important and reassuring ritual during the war, offering a brief escape from the pressures on women of wartime life.

Changes were introduced very quickly into many areas of everyday consumption, and it was women who typically had to negotiate these new circumstances. Domestic consumption in particular underwent radical transformations due to shortages and the different requirements of a wartime economy. Contrary to popular memories of the state's intervention into unpaid domestic labour, Braybon and Summerfield argue:

> It is sometimes thought that the government stepped in like a beneficent uncle during the Second World War to take over many of the domestic jobs traditionally ascribed to women, in order to release them for war work. In fact government records and women's own

experiences suggest that state intervention into the domestic sphere
was limited.

(Braybon and Summerfield, 1987: 253)

In fact, rather than releasing women from their domestic burdens, they go
on to argue, government campaigns actually encouraged women to increase their domestic activities in order to meet the challenge of the
demands of the wartime situation:

> the government was actively encouraging women to enlarge their
> domestic role through the 'make do and mend' propaganda directed
> at the 'housewife'. Shortages were even more acute than in the First
> World War, and the state depended on women to make up the
> deficiencies in diet, clothing and comfort, an extra load for already
> burdened women to bear.

(Braybon and Summerfield, 1987: 235)

Shortages and rationing were time-consuming and frustrating for women
who had to put up with long queues at the shops and invent new recipes to
make limited food go further. Food rationing of basics like butter, cheese,
sugar, meat, tea and preserves was introduced during 1940–1. Making food
stretch to feed everyone was not easy for women on such limited
restrictions:

> In 1943 the basic weekly ration per person was 4 ounces of bacon,
> 1s 2d worth of meat (this was about the price of a leg of mutton),
> 3 ounces of cheese, 2 ounces of tea, 8 ounces of sugar, 4 ounces
> preserves, and a total of 8 ounces of fats (2 oz cooking fat, 2 oz butter
> and 4 oz margarine).

(Braybon and Summerfield, 1987: 247)

In contrast to such difficulties many women remembered the cinema as
providing a longed-for escape. Wartime restrictions, then, provided a very
particular context for the pleasures of 'abundance' discussed above:

> I wanted to forget, just for a short time, about being cold, lonely and
> yes, sometimes hungry . . . to think there was a world out there with
> no blackout, no rationing of food or essential clothing.

(Elizabeth Allan)

For a few glamorous hours, I could escape from the rationing, the
queues and all the frustrations of wartime Britain.

(Anon)

What I enjoyed about going to the pictures most was the glamour.
Escape from the worries of the war and its austerity. I enjoyed the
walk home afterwards, my head full of the film I had seen.

(Anon)

American culture in general, and Hollywood films in particular, were associated with glamour, extravagance and luxury, and watching American films in wartime Britain was associated with a temporary participation in a more affluent culture:

> The wonderful escape of wallowing in a lifestyle I would have liked for myself. . . . Cinema was one of the entertainment sources that kept me going throughout the war years – and took one's mind off the anxieties, fears and austerity of that time, particularly for a teenager/ early twenties girl who could not get the clothes she wanted and sometimes not even the make-up.
>
> (Mabel Stringfellow)

What is evident in these memories of Hollywood is the perceived difference between British and American culture in relation to material scarcity as opposed to material comfort and security, and the pleasures of the temporary escape into another world which offers these 'utopian feelings'. This may have had a specific significance for women on two counts; first, as I have suggested, it was women who primarily dealt with the shortages and rationing on a day-to-day basis. For women, the escape from austerity had particular significance, since it was their primary responsibility to provide for others. Even though so many women worked during and after the war, 'running the home' and catering for people's material well-being continued to be principally their responsibility. In other words, shortages and rationing affected everyone, but women had a particular responsibility for dealing with these problems and negotiating other people's relationships to them.

Second, since one crucial aspect of successful femininity has conventionally been defined through physical attractiveness, the contrast between American 'abundance' and British austerity would be remembered as especially appealing. American culture was remembered as offering 'abundant femininity', which was in turn associated with glamour and desirability, and which was unavailable to women in wartime Britain. What is important here is that the process of escapism involves the reproduction and consumption of highly gendered and historically specific forms of identity. Thus the utopian feelings experienced through Hollywood cinema in 1940s Britain need to be situated within this specific cultural context in order to understand fully their significance to female spectators.

THE CIRCULATION OF HOLLYWOOD STARS

Stars were – and are – what the American film was about, what the world went to see American films for, in preference to those from all other countries, including their own . . . the film star was the

American industry's contribution to film as a rapturous art.

(Kobal, quoted in Swann, 1987: 67)

Stars were as important for cinema spectators as the narrative of the film in which they appeared. They offered one of the key sources of pleasure to the cinema audience. Stars were the most common reason given for the choice of film made in the 1940s by cinema-goers in my research, although this is hardly surprising, given the wording of my advertisement which foregrounded Hollywood stars.

Hollywood's movie star system emerged as a 'business strategy designed to generate large audiences and differentiate entertainment programs and products, and has been used for over seventy years to provide increasing returns on production investments' (Kindem, 1982: 79). The rise of the star system in Hollywood, however, was not motivated solely by economic competition between movie companies, but also by 'the intense demand of movie audiences for specific performers' (*ibid.*: 80). The audience–star axis, then, has always been a crucial one to the success of Hollywood cinema.

Hollywood stars were controlled by studios during the 1930s and 1940s. An increasing concentration of the movie industry into the hands of the 'Big Five' (Warner Bros., Loews/M.G.M., Paramount, R.K.O. and Twentieth-Century-Fox) and the 'Little Three' (Universal, Columbia and United Artists) during this period meant that the American movie industry became an oligopoly: in other words, all the power in the industry was concentrated in the hands of these few companies. As this concentration of power in vertically integrated major studios increased, so the control over Hollywood stars tightened.[9] In contrast to the 1920s, stars had less independence, lower salaries and little artistic control over production decisions. Increasingly they were offered restricted contracts with one company for a fixed time period and were disciplined for breaking contracts and trying to work elsewhere. It was not until the gradual break-up of the studio system in the 1950s that stars regained some independence in Hollywood. This proved a mixed blessing, however: whilst the more popular stars turned this to their advantage, the less successful ones found little work in the film industry (Kindem, 1982: 88).

Hollywood stars were not simply sold to audiences through the films in which they appeared, but were surrounded by a huge publicity machine which offered audiences information about their lives and activities. Their careers were carefully planned and orchestrated to feed into popular demands and to create new ones. Audiences obtained information about stars from the huge publicity apparatus which was developed by the various studios to promote their stars and protect their investments in them. Stars made personal appearances arranged by studios to encourage their followers; they also circulated regular press releases to ensure fans kept up on

106

the details of the careers and lives of their favourite stars. In addition, fan clubs encouraged audience interests in particular stars. Cinema-goers wrote off for signed photos to the studio or the fan club and used them as 'pin-ups' in their own domestic environments. Some fan clubs had newsletters with wide circulation. The consumption of Hollywood stars, then, was by no means limited to the viewing of the films they appeared in; an extensive publicity apparatus existed which also constructed star images for audiences at this time.

There were, too, numerous publications about the cinema which were read regularly by cinema-goers during the 1940s. *Picturegoer*, the most prestigious film magazine in Britain, was started in 1911, although it took on its more familiar format from 1931 onwards. There were numerous other magazines about the cinema during this time, including: *Film Fantasy and Fact* (formerly *Film-Fan Fare*), *Film Post* (1947–51); *Film Forecast* (1948–51); and *Screen Stories* (1948–9) (Swann, 1987: 72). Certainly a very high percentage of the respondents to my research read *Picturegoer* regularly, and many of them mentioned reading at least two or three film publications at this time.

These magazines were devoted to representing the lives of stars, as well as to other features on topics such as new releases, fashion tips and results of audience polls. But women cinema-goers in my study read them to find out about the stars. They featured photographs of stars and a mixture of press releases and inside gossip. The material possessions, wealth and leisure time of individual stars were a source of constant fascination for readers: their cars, houses, swimming pools, holidays, clothes and extravagant American lifestyles were described in detail in film magazines at this time. Audiences in Britain during the 1940s were thus connected to consumption through regular information about the luxuries enjoyed by their idols.

The popularity of stars was continually evaluated by the Hollywood studios. This was hard to gauge and there continue to be competing estimations of the popularity of particular stars at any given time (Kindem 1982: 84–6). Fan clubs and fan magazines were used by studios to monitor the popularity of different stars. Fan mail was another indication of this, giving studios some idea of star popularity. Throughout the 1940s the film industry also used research carried out by George Gallup, who founded Audience Research, Inc. in 1938. This research, the 'Continuing Audit of Marquee Values', aimed not only to analyse the popularity of Hollywood stars, but also to ascertain their relevant importance in relation to other aspects of the cinema.

NATIONAL IDENTITY AND HOLLYWOOD STARS

The star system, it has been argued, is particularly characteristic of American cinema:

> This emphasis on screen talent, and the cinematic codes which evolved to render screen talent, such as the use of close-up, and 'glamour' lighting, made American film significantly different from that which evolved in much of the rest of the world. Although it should be acknowledged that subsequently many other countries, such as India, have adopted star systems based on the American model of spectacle, stardom has always been a characteristic closely tied to the American feature film.
>
> (Swann, 1987: 69)

For audiences in Britain, the Hollywood star system was in another league from the British film industry. Whilst stars did exist and were used to sell films in the British industry, they did not function on the same scale as Hollywood stars. British stars featured frequently in British film magazines and the British studio, Rank, put extensive resources into building a British star system. However, whilst British stars were extremely popular during the 1940s, and stars such as James Mason and Margaret Lockwood were often among the top-rankers in polls at the time, 'there was nothing really comparable to the big centralised industrial and marketing machinery of Hollywood' (Swann, 1987: 74). Furthermore, it is also important to note that, as Swann argues, 'British screen stars were never rooted in the ideology of consumerism in quite the way that American stars were as a matter of course' (*ibid.*: 69–70).

American stars acquired substantial and devoted followings in Britain during the 1940s and 1950s. Although it has proved impossible to find any figures for fan club membership for this period, the strength of the response to my advertisements and the passion with which women wrote about Hollywood stars both give some indication of the importance of American stars in British women's lives.

The appeal of Hollywood stars to British female spectators in particular needs to be understood in the context of the relationship between British and American cultures during this period.[10] In attempting to account for the specific appeal of Hollywood in postwar Britain, Paul Swann argues that the reasons cannot be entirely attributed to the economic imperialism of the Hollywood industry, since there were restrictions on the import of American films during this period when 'the British government pursued a vigorous campaign against the American feature film' (Swann, 1987: 31). Continuing a long-standing historical battle between the British and American film industries, the British government took steps to restrict the number of American films shown in Britain in an attempt to encourage the comeback of British film onto the entertainment market (Lant, 1991).

More important for understanding Hollywood's appeal, Swann argues, is the significance of American culture in Britain during this period. Daily life in Britain during the war and during the postwar period was dominated by hardship, rationing and loss of family and friends. Rationing did not stop when the war ended, in fact many items began to be rationed which had not previously been: for example, bread rationing was introduced in 1946. Generally there was a shortage of products available for purchase: food, fuel and clothes were all in short supply. Magazines advertised products that were not yet available on the British market.

In 1946 the 'Britain Can Make It' exhibition at the Victoria and Albert Museum was renamed by the popular press 'Britain Can't Have It', since so many of the new consumer products proudly exhibited were marked for export only (Swann, 1987: 35). One American magazine reported about life in Britain in 1948: 'Until recently, bananas, lemons, nylon stockings, potato chips, foreign travel for pleasure, a variety of sports equipment . . . were completely unavailable' (Dawson, 1948, quoted in Swann, 1987: 32). Indeed in 1947, only 3.3 per cent of people in Britain went on holiday abroad, and 43 per cent had no holiday at all (Swann, 1987: 45).

All in all, there were few escapes from the hardships of everyday life in Britain at this time. In this context Hollywood cinema had a particular significance in British culture:

> the cinema figured prominently in most people's lives as one of the few affordable luxuries which did not require a ration book. The authorities were very conscious of the manner in which films functioned as an important release from austerity, especially for the working class filmgoer. The British worker was on the front line in the export war and Hollywood regularly came up in discussions about schemes to maintain his, or more often her, morale and productivity.
>
> (Swann, 1987: 33)

Hollywood cinema offered audiences the possibility to be part of another world far away from the difficulties of everyday life in Britain. America was frequently represented as 'the land flowing with milk and honey' (Eileen Jenkins) in Hollywood films, and the pleasures of escaping from the drabness of life in Britain during the 1940s into the luxurious and glamorous worlds of Hollywood were considerable.

DESIRABLE DIFFERENCES

It has been argued that it was particularly women who became fans of Hollywood stars. Richard Dyer has claimed that:

> particularly intense star–audience relations occur amongst adoles-

cents and women. . . . These groups all share a peculiarly intense degree of role/identity conflict and pressure from the dominant articulacy of, respectively, adult, male, heterosexual culture.

(Dyer, quoted in Swann, 1987: 74)

The female spectators in this study would have been adolescents/young women during the 1940s and 1950s, since most of them are now in their fifties, sixties and seventies. According to Dyer's argument, these women would have been amongst the most devoted to Hollywood stars at this time. Many women mentioned age as a significant factor in their attachments to stars: 'as a young girl I enjoyed the music and clothes and make-believe' (Anon); 'we were young and impressionable then' (Anon); 'We were very young people then, shy country girls really, shocked, delighted and uplifted by some of the stars' (Elizabeth Allan).

Age difference between stars and audiences may have been significant for several reasons. There is an intensity of feeling often associated with adolescent attachment to desirable images of a more complete, confident and mature identity; adolescent adoration of adults takes many forms, such as teenage crushes, hero worship and fixation on cultural idols.[11] For young women whose identities are connected to having a desirable image for others in a patriarchal culture, female Hollywood stars played a very significant role. Feminine identity was, and still is, constructed in relation to idealised images of desirability and sexual attractiveness which few, if any, women ever feel they embody. For some young women, Hollywood stars seemed to embody a perfection of desirability which they themselves felt they could never hope to achieve:

I didn't want to see anybody being ordinary at the cinema. The cinema was the focal point of our lives at that time, and we all wanted the female stars to be something 'unattainable' and we put them on a pedestal.

(Mary Wilson)

Female stars in the 1940s were often read by young women in the audience in opposition to the older women in Britain at the time:

We talked about the stars [in terms of] . . . the kinds of clothes they wore, their hairstyles, their leading men, the way they danced, the different films they were in. . . . Most of the older women we knew were too busy coping with clothes, food and every other kind of shortage, to be leading a dancing singing glamorously clothed life – it was just a fantasy on our part.

(Mary Marshall)

However, it was not only adolescents who were caught up in the imaginary worlds of feminine ideals; Hollywood stars were remembered as offering female spectators, generally, images of femininity unattainable for most women in a time of austerity during the 1940s in Britain. Not surprisingly, given the centrality of physical, and particularly sexual, attractiveness to definitions of femininity, it was the clothes, make-up, hairstyles and general physical appearance which were the most common way British female audiences remembered Hollywood stars:

> The stars in Hollywood films were all very glamorous, their costumes were beautiful and it was like being in a different world, especially after the restrictions of the war. . . . I preferred stars with glamorous clothes and looks.
>
> (Phyllis Reynolds)

> Ginger Rogers wore such wonderful clothes, and for a couple of hours or so, we could forget the terrible things that were happening, and one could imagine wearing the beautiful frocks if only one could spare the clothing coupons.
>
> (Anon)

> I'm sure it was sheer escapism. We never had much money for clothes, hair or make-up, and also during my teens clothing was rationed and make-up was virtually unobtainable. The female stars I liked didn't have a black out or rationing and most of the films I saw were completely different from my own life.
>
> (Anon)

American femininity, then, was associated with particular consumer products unavailable in wartime Britain. It was the difference between women's own experience of wartime Britain and Hollywood stars that women wrote about again and again as pleasurable:

> Betty Grable was my favourite because of her clothes (ours were rationed), glamorous locations (shelters for us) and handsome escorts (ours were in the forces). We were living such a different life – this was the stuff dreams were made of.
>
> (Anon)

Hollywood stars were remembered in relation to the envied availability of key signifiers of glamour and desirability which were perceived as defining femininity. Thus it was the 'abundance' of signifiers of femininity represented by Hollywood stars that was seen as particularly pleasurable for the British women in the audience. Escaping the austerity of rations and shortages of the products that connoted femininity, such as clothes and make-up, women audiences remembered the pleasure of the temporary participation in the abundant American femininity of their favourite Hollywood stars.

The cultural construction of femininity in relation to Hollywood-idea-

Figure 4.3 'Betty Grable was my favourite because of her clothes (ours were rationed)'.

lised visual images is clearly not unique to wartime Britain. Indeed, it has been argued that fears about the negative effects of American influences on British culture can be traced back to the 1930s (Hebdige, 1988). However, during the 1940s and 1950s American glamour played a particularly significant role in the changing constructions of British femininity.

Hebdige argues that, by the 1950s, certain American products were seen to be desirable because of their streamlined and glamorous image which appealed to large sections of the British working classes. The appeal of certain imported American goods can thus be read as an expression of their discontent with 'traditional British values'. Cultural taste and national identity is seen here as an ideological battle ground in which 'American-ness' functioned to offer the possibility of opposition to dominant values.

This argument about cultural taste and the rejection of bourgeois values can be extended here to account for the appeal of Hollywood stars to British female spectators at this time. American femininity clearly signified excitement, glamour and sexuality in ways which rejected what were perceived as conventional definitions of British traditional femininity. It was not until well into the 1950s, however, that female spectators were able to purchase commodities enabling them to become more like their American ideals. I would argue that Hollywood stars had an especially intoxicating effect on British women in the 1940s, precisely because of the stark contrast between their lives and the images they saw on the screen. The lack of availability of even the basic commodities sold to women to encourage particular ideals of feminine attractiveness in Britain at this time intensified the appeal of the abundance signified by Hollywood stars.

Hollywood stars, then, played an important role in the reproduction of feminine ideals at this time. One distinction drawn between British and Hollywood stars was that the latter were associated primarily with 'glamour' and the former with 'acting'. As Paul Swann points out, glamour was perceived as something not belonging to British culture. He quotes a contemporary commentator on Hollywood cinema and its influences on British taste in 1946, who wrote that 'American clothes – "trick" clothes for men, snappy shoes for young women, and so on, have become intensely popular over here, "glamorised", of course, by the Hollywood movie'. Swann points out that 'it is significant that the notion of glamour was sufficiently alien to a British writer to warrant quotation marks' (Swann, 1987: 42).

The appeal of Hollywood stars was typically remembered in terms of their 'glamour'. A frequent feeling expressed was that glamour belonged to American femininity, and thus Hollywood stars were preferable to British ones:

> I preferred Hollywood stars in the forties. It had mostly to do with glamour. No matter what our girls did, they just couldn't hold a candle to the American girls. I remember I went to see a British musical called *London Town* the attempt at glamour was so awful it just made us giggle.
>
> (Patricia Robinson)

The contrast between British female spectators and the kinds of feminine ideals on the Hollywood screen would have been especially intense in terms of affordable consumer products. However, it was not simply the case that British women could not reproduce the glamorous images they saw on the screen through their own appearances, but rather that the purchasing of *any* clothes at all was a rare occurrence. Clothing was rationed in Britain from 1941. Everyone was issued with a basic allowance of clothing coupons. Clothing prices rose drastically during the war: 'by 1943 a pre-war 25s nightie cost about £13, a 14 guinea coat and skirt £42, and a guinea hat between £6 and £8' (Minns, 1980: 154). The average weekly wage rose from £2 13s 3d to £4 16s 1d. Some women from very wealthy classes continued to buy new clothes, but for most women, certainly for most of the women involved in my research, buying new clothes was very unusual:

> I preferred stars with glamorous clothes and looks as it came as a light relief after the war years when the buying of clothes was a rare occasion.

> (Phyllis Reynolds)

Booklets showing women how to 'make do and mend' were issued by the Ministry of Information. 'Austerity regulations dictated the number of pleats, seams, pockets and buttonholes. Embroidery and sequins were banned. Underclothes were limited to six shapes' (Minns, 1980: 154).

In 1942 the *Observer* wrote about the new first-aid classes for clothes, 'Women must expect to wear clothes now until the elbow wears out, but garments can be sent back to be refashioned as above – elbow sleeved dresses – or to have sleeves remade' (Minns, 1980: 154). Clothing exchanges were set up where worn children's clothing was exchanged, but it had to be renovated by the mother first (see Minns, 1980: 148). For many women these tasks put added pressure on their daily routines:

> The worst time was when Barbara and the boys were in bed and I eventually sat down to the mending, sewing and knitting, often to hours of unpicking cast-offs from friends to make clothes for the children. Still it ended and we survived!
>
> (Quoted in Braybon and Summerfield, 1987: 253)

Many women entered into the paid labour force in the early 1940s in order to help the war effort:

> whereas only 16 per cent of working women were married in 1931, 43 per cent were married in 1943. It was estimated that at least 7,750,000 were in paid work in that year, and it was believed that if part-time and voluntary work were taken into account, fully 80 per cent of married women and 90 per cent of single women were by now contributing to the war effort.
>
> (Braybon and Summerfield, 1987: 168)

One of the anxieties about wearing uniforms, caps and boiler suits for working seemed to be the lack of an expression of individuality: 'young girls used to plaster their faces with thick make-up – anything to look a bit different from the next girl' (Minns, 1980: 157). In contrast, Hollywood stars were remembered by respondents as expressing exactly that – individuality – especially through their physical appearance.

In wartime Britain, there was tremendous anxiety about definitions of femininity, since women's participation in war work, doing so-called 'men's jobs', and in the armed forces, wearing uniforms and handling equipment, contradicted patriarchal notions of femininity as passive and delicate and as 'there to be looked at' and judged by men. Advertisements for 'feminine' products during the war were full of ways to combine being an active patriotic war worker with attractive femininity; skin, hair and nails were of particular concern (see advertisements in *Picturegoer and Film Weekly*, 13 July 1940, p. 18, and 31 August 1940, p. 18, for examples).

With the presence of the American army in Britain in 1942, the luxuries offered by American culture became more visible, and to some, more reachable. Up until then, women had painted stockings on their legs with yellow dye and a seam up the back of the leg with eyebrow pencil. Stockings were a much-sought-after commodity during the war and seemed to signify luxury and femininity. The American GIs 'brought with them flimsy nylons and superior cosmetics, symbols of glamour, prosperity and hope' (Minns, 1980: 157). American consumer goods were envied by British women, who felt excluded from desirable forms of femininity. One WAAF woman recalled:

> At the Anglo-American club we used to watch the American girls putting on face-packs before dances as if they were men from Mars. It was every girl's dream to have one of those leather cases of different make-up bottles.
>
> (Quoted in Minns, 1980: 157)

Apart from glimpses of American affluence through episodes such as this, Hollywood film stars were the main source of images of American culture in Britain during this period. They were perceived as epitomising the abundance of American culture as opposed to the deprivation experienced in Britain. As such they were the focus for particularly intense feelings amongst British women audiences at this time: 'we talked about film stars in terms of . . . "wish I could" . . . all full of envy and admiration . . .' (Millie Mills).

What needs to be emphasised here is that the utopian feelings offered by these stars were clearly both historically and gender specific. The lack of commodities associated with 'feminine glamour' was constantly referred to in the material I received. This lack in Britain was frequently remembered in connection with and in contrast to the desirability of American femininity. Thus it could be argued that in this historical and national location there was a doubling of the desire of the female spectator.

This 'double desire' in the spectator/star relationship, then, needs to be understood within a very specific set of historical circumstances. As I have argued, femininity is conventionally reproduced within dominant culture through the circulation of idealised images, constructed as desirable and yet unattainable. In the context of wartime austerity, however, there was an intensification of the desirability of the feminine ideals represented by Hollywood film stars. Thus, these memories of Hollywood stars of this time focus particularly upon ideals of feminine glamour which were envied and desired.

HOLLYWOOD STARS AS UTOPIAN FANTASIES

In her analysis of popular narratives read by women, Tania Modleski adds to Dyer's categories of utopian sensibilities 'the desire for transcendence (self-forgetfulness)', a major current in Harlequin Romances, and 'the desire for female autonomy', a constant preoccupation of Gothic novels (Modleski, 1982: 112–13). The first of these, the desire for transcendence, is especially relevant here in relation to how these female spectators remembered the pleasures of escapism offered by Hollywood stars during this period. In the final section of this chapter the processes of escapism will be analysed in terms of that familiar pleasure of 'losing oneself'.

Generally escapism is associated with leaving behind one's own life and participating in another imaginary world for a short period of time. Many respondents wrote about this process in terms of escaping their lives, their worlds and, indeed, themselves:

> It was something completely different to what my life was. I used to put myself in their place, pretend for an hour or two.
>
> (Mary Williams)

> I wasn't attractive or had a good figure, I wore glasses and didn't have any money to buy glamorous clothes and the cinema was escapism away from a rather dull life.
>
> (Geraldine Crick)

> [I enjoyed] the usually happy crowd – the cinemas were always full – and the special 'Saturday night out' kind of excitement – of living in another more glamorous kind of life for a few hours.
>
> (Mary Marshall)

The cinema, then, was remembered as offering spectators the chance to be part of another world and participate in its glamour in contrast to their own lives. Many respondents remembered Hollywood's appeal in terms of 'fantasy':

one was looking for escapism – into perhaps a fantasy world and removed from the sometimes austere world of reality.

(Betty Cole)

The cinema offered escape into a fantasy world for only 9 old pence. I found the cinema restful and relaxing – it gave me vigour to face my daily life. . . . I went to escape into a world of fantasy, wealth and above all glamour.

(Elizabeth Rogers)

The realm of fantasy helped with wartime restrictions.

(Anon)

The significance of such fantasy worlds is also, importantly, written about in relation to the spectator's own worlds, in many cases a world of wartime or postwar austerity, routine and lacking glamour. It is the difference between these worlds that produces the fascination and the desire for movement from one to the other. Thus the pleasures of transcendence offered by Hollywood cinema took specific forms in relation to the particular contexts of reception.

The differences between these fantasy worlds which the stars inhabited and those of the spectator provide the possibility for the spectator to leave her world temporarily and become part of the star's world:

Then along came Hollywood and we soaked it up like a sponge. It took people out of themselves and transported them to a place where they didn't need to think or worry. All they needed to do was to sit and stare.

(Kathleen Lucas)

I was only a girl, but I could be transported from the austerity and gloom of that time to that other world on the silver screen.

(June Thomas)

Hollywood in general presented a fantasy world in the eyes of young people whose own lives were devoid of romance and adventure.

(Norah Turner)

Several respondents wrote of being 'transported' to another world, suggesting the pleasure of the process of giving up one's own world for a fantasy one on the screen. However, rather than simply participating in the star's world on the screen, it is the movement from one world to the other which the feeling of being 'transported' conveys.

Age difference here clearly had a strong role to play in the importance of fantasy for cinema spectators. The second two examples here are concerned with the delight of escaping to the Hollywood fantasy worlds in relation to their youth: Hollywood stars thus represent the tempting ideal of adult femininity and sophistication.

All these respondents write of the pleasures of imagining oneself in a different world of Hollywood glamour. As I argued in the previous section, the pleasures of escapism are strengthened by the national differences between Britain and the United States. This national difference provided space for particular forms of fantasy.

The feeling of lack of familiarity with American culture clearly contributed to the pleasures Hollywood offered. Several respondents referred to Hollywood screen worlds in the language of magic and make-believe:

> Escapism – from the everyday world – into magical make believe where good always (nearly) prevailed. . . . America at that time to me (as a child and a teenager) might as well have been on another planet – and I enjoyed seeing the country, the house interiors, the beautiful women and their hairstyles and clothes.
>
> (Pamela Done)

Here the difference between America and Britain is represented by an exaggeration of the distance between them: America is not just 'the other side of the world', but 'might as well have been on another planet'. This reference emphasises the 'other worldness' of America to many female spectators in Britain at this time which facilitated pleasures of escapism. The feelings of 'losing oneself' were thus intensified by the unfamiliarity of American culture and its *difference* from British culture during this period.

The processes of retrospection are also important here. For many respondents American culture will have become more familiar than it was in the 1940s. Television has increasingly brought representations of American culture into the domestic space of most British households; the expansion of tourism has transformed perceptions of distances and differences between continents; and the continuing expansion of American economic and cultural imperialism has contributed to the breakdown of such fixed national boundaries between Britain and America. Thus, memories of times when America 'might as well have been on another planet' contrast starkly with the everyday presence of American culture in Britain today in which MacDonald's, baseball hats and 'Cagney and Lacey' are part of everyday life.

One respondent wrote of the ways in which Hollywood reminded her of her childhood fairy stories:

> The musical stars gave me the feeling of going back to being a child again and having all the fairy story characters and principal boys and

118

Figure 4.4 'America at that time to me . . . might as well have been on another planet – I enjoyed seeing the country, the house interiors, the beautiful women and their hairstyles and clothes.' (Publicity still of Joan Crawford.)

girls rolled into one. They took you into another world and another time. Just for a short while.

(Anon)

Indeed, this sense of magic is often drawn upon to convey the extraordinariness and uniqueness of Hollywood cinema for some respondents at this time:

I think in those eras we were more inclined to put stars on a pedestal. They were so far removed from our everyday lives, they were magical. These days stars are so ordinary – the magic has gone. Hollywood will never be the same again!

(Kathleen Sines)

Hollywood stars were also written about in the language of dreams: 'To me it was like a dream come true to see these lovely people'; 'The main reason for our choice of film was to dream and enjoy the luxury as a change from our Brummy slum' (Millie Mills). Indeed, Hollywood generally, with its wealth and glamour, is frequently likened to a dream world:

The cinema fulfilled the dream I know could never come true but watching the big screen anything was possible.

(Betty Cruse)

I was a great dreamer in those days. . . . I suppose the cinema provided an outlet – you could be in another world for a while.

(Phyllis Knight)

The cinema was escapism for me, as I was born in the 30s and from a very poor background, the depression also meant no work was available and then the war years . . . so I lived in a dream world I suppose and by having the cinema, one could see places and lovely people.

(Jean Forshaw)

Watching films has been compared to the process of dreaming for several reasons. The process of sitting in a darkened room in front of larger-than-life images on a screen has been likened to a dream-like state. Here, dreams are significant in terms of the projected desires of better things, and also in terms of the suggestion of inhabiting another world which offered those things lacking in everyday life.

That dreaming involves loss of consciousness is significant here in terms of Modleski's category of transcendence. Clearly women in the audience do not lose consciousness when watching films, but they do write of the pleasures of being completely caught up in this fictional world:

I just found total absorption in the cinema . . . a complete change from everyday 'doings'.

(Mrs M. Caplin)

Transportation – a seat in the dark where I could become entirely engrossed in a situation or music.

(Marie Burgess)

This complete absorption in another world involves the temporary loss of self in that world. This is also remembered as one of the pleasures of Hollywood cinema:

[If stars were unlike women in everyday life] it did one good to think and fantasize oneself in such a situation . . . one could enter into the situation more easily and lose oneself in it – a form of escapism, I suppose, which everyone indulges in at times.

(Anon)

It was something to look forward to, to lose yourself from everyday worries.

(Mary Williams)

I enjoyed the escapism from reality and you could lose yourself in the story.

(Anon)

Dad was a commissionaire at the old Londesborough. So I had films right from the 1930s, but later I think it was because I was a rather retiring teenager and whilst I loved dancing etc., I was much happier lost in a film in the dark cinema.

(Jean Davison)

This loss of self enabled women to hide from the stresses of everyday life, from their own feelings of inadequacy, and to imagine themselves in the utopian world of Hollywood stars for a short time.

However, the pleasure of fantasy is not necessarily purely in terms of its content which compensates for everyday drabness, but also, as Ien Ang has argued in relation to contemporary soap operas, it may be the experience of fantasising, of playing with fictional worlds and selves, which is itself pleasurable. Ang argues that 'the "flight" into a fictional fantasy world is not so much a denial of reality as playing with it. A game that enables one to place the limits of the fictional and the real under discussion, to make them fluid' (Ang, 1985: 49). Thus, the desire for transcendence is not only a self-forgetfulness, but is also generative of fantasy selves: a pleasure in the fluidity between experienced and imagined selves. As Ang argues:

One dimension of life in which the distance between a (pleasurable) absent and an (unpleasurable) present can be eradicated is that of fantasy. . . . It is not a matter of the content of the fantasy, but mainly of the fact of fantasizing itself: producing and consuming fantasies allows for a play with reality, which can be felt as 'liberating' because it is fictional, not real.

(Ang, 1985: 134)

Ang somewhat underestimates the interdependence of the content and context of producing and consuming fantasies which has been emphasised in this chapter; the pleasures of escapism are historical ones, as I have demonstrated. Nevertheless, Ang's argument is important, highlighting, as it does, the importance of the process of transcendence in terms of its fictional dimensions.

Thus the desire for transcendence was articulated in a variety of ways; be it magic, make-believe, fantasy or dreamworld, spectators' desire for a temporary loss of self in their ideals emerges as one of the significant pleasures of Hollywood cinema. This relationship between spectators and their ideals is discussed further in the next chapter on cinematic identification.

CONCLUSION: FEMININITY AND ESCAPISM

In the introduction to this chapter I raised the question of the meaning of the commonsense category of 'escapism' in relation to Hollywood cinema. Instead of using it to dismiss women's pleasures in popular culture, I have reversed its negative connotations and used it as a starting point for taking such pleasures seriously. Indeed, escapism has been here investigated as one of the central pleasures of Hollywood cinema for the female spectators in this study.

Much of the work on pleasure in film studies has focused exclusively upon the psychic pleasures of textual mechanisms. This is, of course, an important aspect of cinematic pleasure, but it is only one of many, if spectators' accounts are taken seriously by film theorists. By analysing the question of cinematic pleasure in terms of Dyer's model of entertainment's utopian sensibilities, I have extended the usual parameters of the 'pleasure debate' to include the emotional dimensions of such pleasures. This aspect of popular culture has remained a rather neglected one in the context of the preoccupation with the unconscious pleasures of spectatorship which has so frequently dominated film criticism.

Indeed, extending Dyer's emotional focus, I have argued that escapism involves a multi-dimensional set of processes, rather than one single mechanism of appeal. The memories I have analysed have highlighted the many levels at which escapism provided pleasures for female spectators: material, sensuous, emotional as well as psychic. For example, the cinema interiors provided a utopian space and numerous sensuous luxuries; the feelings of being in an audience offered a sense of belonging and togetherness; and the stars were enjoyed as utopian, transcendent fantasies. Thus, it was not simply the visual pleasures of film texts that operated, but rather a whole range of appeals which encouraged the feelings of complete absorption in another world.

Furthermore, the interconnectedness of these different dimensions proved significant to their appeal. The different pleasures reinforced each other, contributing to the intensity of cinematic escapism; the luxury of the cinema interiors, for example, provided a complementary context for the pleasures of abundance associated with Hollywood glamour and female stars' costumes. As well as the 'pleasures of the text', then, the pleasures of the context produced lasting, and detailed, memories. Thus the whole cinema-going experience, rather than one aspect of it, was shown to create the meanings of cinematic escapism for these female spectators.

The exclusively textual focus of so much film studies work has further limited our understanding of cinematic pleasures through its inability to address crucial questions about how and why the cinema is popular at different times and to particular audiences. The analysis of what women remembered escaping *from* as well as what they remember escaping *into* has demonstrated the importance of historical and cultural location to an understanding of the specific pleasures of escapism.

The Second World War proved to be a constant reference point in relation to the question of escapism. The stresses and hardships of wartime Britain were remembered in contrast to the escape of the cinema and the feelings of abundance offered by the luxury of Hollywood and its stars. Thus an analysis of cinematic escapism needs to be situated within a consideration of the historical influences on spectators at a particular time.

In this chapter the focus has mainly been on the 1940s, since it was particularly in relation to the war that spectators wrote about escapism. This is not to suggest that they no longer enjoyed the utopian feelings offered by Hollywood cinema in the 1950s, but rather that escapism had a specific appeal for female spectators in 1940s Britain. Thus, these utopian feelings have different meanings in different contexts which cannot be fully understood through textual analysis alone.

Wartime Britain, for example, framed women's memories of escapism in very significant ways; wartime and postwar austerity and trauma provided the context for particular emotional investments in certain forms of utopian-ism. In particular, I have argued that the cinematic pleasure of utopian feelings may differ according to historical and cultural locations. Indeed, three categories of utopian sensibility were shown to be particularly signifi-cant in these memories of cinema-going in wartime and postwar Britain: those were abundance, community and transcendence. Whilst Dyer con-cludes that entertainment forms have in common certain utopian sensibili-ties, then, I have argued that, in terms of the audience, the significance of escapist pleasures varies according to historical circumstances. At another time, these three categories may be less significant than some of those not found to be relevant to memories of this period.

National location was also found to be important in terms of the significance of Hollywood stars as utopian fantasies. Americanness clearly featured strongly in the popular British imagination as a signifier of difference. Hollywood stars were seen as offering forms of femininity unavailable, unfamiliar, and even inappropriate in Britain. The geographical distance seemed to reinforce the difference between Americanness and Britishness, and contribute to the feelings of escapism offered by Hollywood cinema. Some elements of American culture were introduced into Britain by the presence of US troops, but it was not until the 1950s that American femininity could be successfully imported through the consumption of consumer goods (see Chapter 6). Memories of the 1940s, then, focused specifically on the unattainable differences represented by the utopian fantasies of female Hollywood stars.

In addition to the importance of the historical and national specificities, I have also analysed the previously unexplored gendered dimensions of escapism. The appeal of certain utopian feelings related to the specific construction and organisation of femininity at this time. All three of the utopian categories – abundance, community and transcendence – can be seen to have specifically gendered meanings. In wartime Britain, women's experiences of the double burden of productive and reproductive labour, of having few resources at their disposal, and of the constant fear or experience of loss of friends and family are repeatedly remembered in contrast to the pleasures of Hollywood escapism. Besides the importance of their everyday lives outside the cinema to women's memories of their pleasure within it, cinematic consumption was itself feminised in particular ways. The feelings of abundance and community were both shown to be gendered cultural processes: the glamour of the interior and the shared intimacy of the collective identity of the audience both connote femininity as constructed within dominant cultural forms. The desire for transcendence can be summed up as 'the pleasure in the temporary loss of self in a utopian other'. This desire for loss of self can be connected in particular ways to the cultural construction of femininity in so far as the desire was articulated in terms of escaping into a more ideal femininity.

Thus utopianism had a particular significance in relation to femininity. In a culture saturated with images of desirable femininity, the desire to submerge oneself in an imagined ideal is constantly being reproduced. Hollywood stars offered female spectators such utopian ideals and the fantasy of becoming that ideal. The desire for transcendence can thus be fulfilled in cinematic fantasies which offer the female spectator the pleasure of temporarily merging with her star ideal.

Furthermore, utopianism connects with femininity at a more general level, extending beyond the three utopian categories discussed in this chapter. Whilst there are doubtless masculine, as well as feminine, utopias prevalent in this culture, there are nevertheless specific ways in which femininity is closely tied to cinematic utopian ideals as *images*. In other words, because of the ways in which femininity itself is defined and judged as image, and because, to be successfully feminine, women have to produce themselves as visually attractive to others, the utopian feminine images on the screen have a particularly deep-rooted significance. There is thus an intensification of the importance of utopian ideals, such as Hollywood stars, to female spectators precisely because of the centrality of image-making to dominant constructions of femininity. In other words, the appeal of Hollywood's female stars to female spectators has a specific utopian dimension, given that producing oneself as an appealing image is central to the definition of femininity.

However, the relationship between feminine selves and their ideals in terms of cinematic spectatorship takes many different forms, not all of which involve the denial of self. Indeed, respondents wrote of a complex set of processes through which they remembered their relationships to Hollywood stars. It is these which are the subject of investigation in the next chapter.

5

FEMININE FASCINATIONS
A question of identification?

I talked to friends and colleagues, mainly about their [favourite stars'] style, hair-dos etc., and to family about their singing and acting. I preferred stars with whom I could identify as being like women in everyday life – but I also enjoyed it when their lives became more exciting than everyday. . . .

I liked to be able to identify with them, but again, I preferred them to have more charm and ability than I did.

(Anon)

I don't think I consciously thought of myself *looking like* any particular star – it was more the semi-magical transformation of screen identification! I adored Ava Gardner's dark magnetism, but knew I wasn't like that.

(M. Palin)

Both these statements capture well the complexity of the pleasures of cinematic identification. They raise questions about the relationship between stars and spectators and the processes of the formation of feminine identities through cinematic modes of address.

In the first statement, the respondent comments on the enjoyment in the recognition of familiar aspects of everyday life, and yet also describes the possible fantasy of something better. Similarity between self and star is combined with the memory of a pleasure in a more successful femininity: 'more charm and ability'. In the second example, the star is adored, but the spectator recognises the impossibility of being like her ideal. Despite the recognition of the fixity of their differences, however, the spectator remembers 'the semi-magical transformation of screen identification', suggesting that her own identity is indeed transformed through processes of spectatorship. Thus, whilst recognising the difference between herself and her favourite Hollywood star, the fixity of the difference is open to temporary fluidity, and yet there is a conscious knowledge that the difference will indeed be reimposed after the magic of Hollywood wears off. Both these examples introduce the contradictions of similarity

126

Figure 5.1 'I adored Ava Gardner's dark magnetism, but knew I wasn't like that.'

and difference, recognition and separateness which characterise the relationship of female spectators to their star ideals.

Many respondents described their pleasures in Hollywood stars in terms
of 'identification': this term was used in numerous ways to refer to a whole
range of spectator/star relations. As these two examples demonstrate, what
is meant by such a term is complex and difficult to put into words: hence,

127

the description of the process as 'semi-magical'. The difficulty of representing the feelings remembered in relation to Hollywood cinema is expressed here through a common characterisation of Hollywood itself: both are described as magical. This highlights well the problems of pinpointing the exact processes at stake for spectators in cinematic identification.

One way to think about 'identification' in this context is in terms of the negotiation between self and other, which some have argued characterises all 'object relations' (Benjamin, 1990). At the centre of this negotiation between spectators and their star ideals is the recognition of similarities and differences.

> I preferred stars to be unlike women in everyday life. The stars gave us a lift, took us away from everyday life, from worrying about how to make our meat ration go further, and going stockingless to save some coupons. . . . I preferred female stars who were like me in some way because I could imagine what I would do if I were in a position that happened to them on the screen.
>
> (Vera Barford)

> Because I had auburn hair in my younger days and I related to stars with red hair (dreaming only) I had one thing in common with a movie star . . . but I preferred stars unlike me because you wanted to see stars different from everyday people – it made life more interesting, so it was easy to believe you were in some way like a star and yet you only wanted to be 'in' the movie whilst in the cinema.
>
> (Audrey Westgarth)

> I preferred stars who were like me in some way – I liked to think I was like them – but in fact I was very tall, thin, shy and gangly. So the answer should really be no!
>
> (Anon)

These examples are typical of the contradictory feelings spectators have in relation to Hollywood stars: on the one hand, they value difference for taking them into a world in which their desires could potentially be fulfilled; on the other, they value similarity for enabling them to recognise qualities they already have.

The match or mismatch between self and ideal is constantly reassessed by female spectators. In the first example, the star is appreciated for providing light relief from the burdens and material deprivation of life in 1940s Britain: the spectator's situation is temporarily forgotten as she fills her imagination with the fictional life of the star. Women going 'stockingless' is a striking contrast to images of Hollywood glamour in which the stockinged leg has almost become an icon of desirability; the shot which moves up the female star's leg from ankle towards thigh is a favourite convention within Hollywood to introduce the desirable protagonist. Yet at the same time, this respondent also preferred stars like her in some way so she could imagine herself in their position and decide what she would do if she were. Thus the processes here involve the negotiation between self and other, but also between self and an imaginary self which temporarily merges with the fictionalised feminine subject to test out new possibilities. The recognition of a potential self in the fictionalised situation, based on some similarity between star and spectator, is operating simultaneously with a desire to maintain the difference between self and ideal.

In the second example, the recognition of similarity between spectator and star takes a more concrete form in the common feature of auburn hair: typically the identification is made through similarity of physical appearance. Yet the respondent represents this relation to her favourite stars as 'dreaming only': it is thus only an imaginary point of identification that belongs to the realm of dreams. However, this respondent also expresses contradictory feelings about her star ideals: she prefers them both like and unlike herself. As well as recognising a common feature between herself and Hollywood stars with red hair, she also enjoys the differences between self and idealised other. Indeed, it is this gap between the film star and everyday people that produces the self-transformation to become more like the star. Thus the difference provides the space for the production of a fantasy self more like the ideal, and yet simultaneously the gap is closed as that new fantasy self is produced. This temporary self-transformation is written about as a process that the spectator realises will end as the film does. In this case there is enough difference to affirm the subject, desired self and idealised image: thus self and other are simultaneously held apart and merging in a complex process of recognition based on similarity and difference.

The third example further highlights the complexity of this interplay between spectator and star: the respondent shifts from asserting that she prefers stars like herself to the reluctant realisation that perhaps this connection remains at the level of desire, and thus admits – 'the answer should really be no!' She describes herself, again in terms of physical appearance, in derogatory terms (tall, thin, shy and gangly) to contrast herself with the ideals in which she mistakenly recognised herself. In other words, her desire would be to recognise herself in these ideal feminine images, and yet, upon reflection, she recognises that the gap is too great. However, the preference is stated clearly at the beginning, suggesting that some recognition of similarity did, nevertheless, characterise the spectator/ star relationship in this case. Again the subject and the idealised image produce a contradictory set of negotiations of identities in which similarity and difference between spectator and star are continuously reassesed.

Indeed, what comes across most forcefully from the analysis of spectators' memories of Hollywood discussed in this chapter is the diversity and complexity of processes involved in what might be referred to as 'identification'. Existing theories of cinematic identification have attempted to analyse this 'magical' process. However, in the light of my research, I shall argue that they fail to account for the complexity and diversity of meanings at stake. Specifically, the dominance of psychoanalytic accounts of identification within feminist film criticism has led to the exploration of universal patterns of unconscious processes, ignoring the particularities of forms of cinematic identification, and, indeed, its meaning to cinema spectators. In this chapter some key aspects of these existing theories of identification are reassessed in the light of female spectators' accounts of their relationships to Hollywood stars in 1940s and 1950s Britain.

THEORISING CINEMATIC IDENTIFICATION

In film studies generally, the term 'identification' has been widely used to suggest a rather amorphous set of cultural processes. Drawing on literary analysis, identification has often loosely meant sympathising or engaging with a character. It has also been understood to suggest something analogous to the idea of 'point of view', watching and following the film from a character's point of view. This involves not only *visual* point of view, constructed by type of shot, editing sequences and so on, but also *narrative* point of view, produced through the sharing of knowledge, sympathy or moral values with the protagonist (Perkins, 1972). Identification has thus been used as a kind of commonsense term within some film and literary studies, referring to a set of cultural processes which describe different kinds of connections between spectators/readers and fictional others.

The main body of work on cinematic identification, however, has drawn upon Freudian and Lacanian psychoanalysis. The feminist analysis of the pleasures of the cinema for female spectators has been largely based on a particular reworking of psychoanalytic theories of identification. It is with this work that I shall take issue, arguing against some of its premises and conclusions.

Within psychoanalytic theory, 'identification' has been seen as the key mechanism for the production of identities. Freud analysed the unconscious mechanisms through which the self is constituted in relation to external objects. In her paper 'Identification and the star: a refusal of difference', Anne Friedberg draws upon Freud's theory of identification as follows:

> First identification is the original form of emotional tie with an object; secondly, in a regressive way it becomes a substitute for a libidinal object-tie, as it were by means of introjection of the object into the ego; and thirdly, it may arise with any new perception of a common

quality shared with some other person who is not an object of sexual instinct. The more important this common quality is, the more successful may this partial identification become, and it may thus represent the beginning of a new tie.

(Freud, 1921, quoted in Friedberg, 1982: 48)

The role of vision in identification has always been part of the Freudian formulation; the emphasis on the significance of the moment of the *sight* of sexual difference in the constitution of feminine and masculine identities, for example. For Freud this relationship, between self and ideal other, could be understood within his third example of the narcissist's love objects: 'what he himself [*sic*] would like to be' (Merck, 1987: 6). Freud argued that it was women who were particularly prone to narcissism. Within this framework, narcissism is often a derogatory term, used to suggest a self-love which has yet to mature and be directed outwards towards an external object. Indeed, in commonsense usage narcissism typically has taken on connotations of feminine self-indulgence and vanity.

Lacanian theory could be said to have rescued narcissism from its derogatory connotations. The 'specular role of identification' has taken centre stage, most particularly in Lacan's theories of the mirror phase, through which subjects are constituted through a specular misrecognition of an other. According to Lacan, it is a necessary stage in the development of the human subject. The process is summed up succinctly by Elizabeth Wright thus:

> the child looks in the mirror and is delighted by several qualities of its own image simultaneously. Whereas before it experienced itself as a shapeless mass, it now gains a sense of wholeness, an ideal completeness, and this all without effort. This gratifying experience of a mirror image is a metaphorical parallel of an unbroken union between inner and outer, a perfect control that assures immediate satisfaction of desire.

(Wright, 1984: 108)

Since all subjects are fascinated by their ideal reflected back to them during the pre-oedipal formation of subjectivity, narcissism is seen to be a necessary part of the development of all subjectivities. As Mandy Merck has pointed out: 'Freud's opposition of ego and object love neglects "the fundamental narcissistic nature of all object relations", if they begin with the child's fascination with its own image in the Lacanian mirror' (Merck, 1987: 6, quoting Penley, 1985).

However, it is important not to lose the gender specificity of such psychic processes which becomes clear when they are analysed within particular social domains. Whilst narcissism may indeed be part of the psychic formations of subjectivity generally, the cultural construction of femininity

131

in terms of physical appearance and 'to be looked-at-ness' shapes the meanings of such narcissistic object relations for female spectators. The early attachment to an ideal image of the self has a different significance in relation to masculinity and femininity, since the latter is so centrally defined in terms of being an image in this culture. Indeed, narcissism takes on a particular social and historical meaning for women in a culture dominated by the endless circulation of idealised visual images of femininity. The relationship between self, ideal self and idealised image of femininity has specific meanings in the female spectator/star relationship.

These models of identification employed within psychoanalysis to explore the developments of unconscious identities have been adopted by some film theorists, such as Christian Metz (1975). Here early psychic processes are seen as analogous to cinematic identification. As Friedberg outlines:

> Primary identification as Metz describes it (as distinct from Freud's 'original and emotional tie') means a spectator who identifies with the camera and projector, and like the child positioned in front of the mirror, constructs an imaginary notion of wholeness, of a unified body. . . . Secondary identification is with an actor, character or star . . . any body becomes an opportunity for an identificatory investment, a possible suit for the substitution/misrecognition of self.
>
> (Friedberg, 1982: 50)

Psychoanalytic film theorists have thus developed a complex analysis of cinematic identification, based on an analogy between the construction of individual identities in infancy in relation to others, and the process of watching a film on a screen.

Following Laura Mulvey's original attack on the visual pleasure of narrative cinema, much feminist work on the process of identification is still marked by a suspicion of any kind of feminine role model, heroine or image of identification. Mulvey's films (such as *Amy!*, 1980), as well as her influential theoretical work, have advocated a rejection of the conventions of popular representations, not simply for the images of femininity constructed, but also for the processes of identification offered to the cinema spectator. 'Identification' itself has been seen as a cultural process complicit with the reproduction of dominant culture by reinforcing patriarchal forms of identity. Anne Friedberg sums up what feminists have seen as the problematic functions of identification thus:

> Identification can only be made through recognition, and all recognition is itself an implicit confirmation of an existing form. The institutional sanction of stars as ego ideals also operates to establish normative figures. Identification enforces a collapse of the subject

onto the normative demand for sameness, which, under patriarchy, is always male.

(Friedberg, 1982: 53)

Identification of any kind is thus criticised for reproducing *sameness, fixity* and the *confirmation of existing identities*.

In her contribution to the *Camera Obscura* retrospective on female spectatorship, Jacqueline Rose affirms these criticisms:

> it was not possible to ask cinema for a positive identification for women, unless at the expense of rendering invisible once again – and this I had thought had been the crucial contribution of film theory in the 1970s – the psychic economy of cinematic process which had generated that image and on which in turn it had seemed so heavily to rely. If I was interested in criticizing a too monolithic image of Hollywood – the idea, for example, that all narrative film effectively ended in some type of oedipal resolution for the man, or that his look was the controlling gaze of the film – it was not in order to insert women as positivity (image on the screen, or spectator off-screen), but because I read this fundamental visual economy of cinema as always prey to its own dissolution.

(Rose, 1989: 275)

This relegation of 'woman' to the position of negativity, absence or lack is typical of the Lacanian framework in which 'woman' can have no positive place in the symbolic order of patriarchy. As Linda Williams argues: 'Lacan's description of castration and female "lack" – though it offered an eloquent statement of the nullity of woman within the symbolic structure – was beginning to seem such an overstatement of the problem as to become a problem itself' (Williams, 1989: 335). Within a Lacanian framework, then, women's pleasure in Hollywood cinema, either through identification with the female protagonist, or otherwise, can only be conceived of as a sign of their complicity with their oppression under patriarchy. Identification, both as a psychic and as a cinematic process, is criticised for fixing the meaning of sexual difference within a patriarchal symbolic order in which femininity functions as the 'other' to the masculine subject of desire.

It is easy to understand the rejection, and indeed condemnation, of cinematic identification within such a framework. However, identification is conceptualised here as a singular and rigid process which fixes the spectator as the subject of the filmic discourse. Although Rose's argument rests on the assumed fragility of the visual economy of patriarchal cinema, it assumes identification itself to be a process with little fluidity of meaning or flexibility for the female spectator. The only pleasure for the female spectator can be that of masochism in her identification with her place as

133

object in the patriarchal order. Within such a reading, the Hollywood cinema is seen as 'a powerful ideological tool, the spectator its gullible victim' (Greig, 1987: 40).

Identification has been seen as the feminine counterpoint to masculine desire in feminist criticisms of popular narrative cinema. The visual economy and narrative trajectory of Hollywood cinema, it has been argued, are typically organised around the masculine desire of the protagonist and the spectator. Feminists have found little space for feminine desire within Hollywood cinema, except the desire to be a passive object of masculine desire. Female desire in the context of cinematic spectatorship, then, has generally been discussed in terms of passivity (taking pleasure in being desired), or masochism (desire to submit to the punishing will of the masculine subject). Both these readings of female desire, whilst highlighting the dominant construction of sexual 'complementarity' in which the man expresses his desire and woman is the object of it, come too close to reinforcing women's place as passive victims of patriarchal culture for comfort.

Through a more flexible model of cinematic spectatorship, based on a notion of fantasy elaborated by Laplanche and Pontalis (1968), Cowie (1984) has attempted to move beyond the rigidities of such problems within feminist film criticism (see Chapter 2). In her analysis Cowie explores the multiple identifications offered to the spectator by a film text and the interchangeability of different subject positions for the spectator. Cowie's model of spectatorship, it has been argued, is one in which the spectator has 'a relative autonomy' from the text and, rather than being positioned mechanistically to identify or not, the spectator is provided with 'a series of possible entries and identifications with characters according to their different roles and functions within a network of character relations' (Greig, 1987: 40). Identification for the female spectator might therefore be conceptualised as something less rigid and less easily dismissed as colluding with the dominant patriarchal order.

Thus, rather than being constrained by the negative construction of feminine identification discussed above, female spectators, like male spectators, are able to make multiple identifications across gender boundaries. As a result, the feminine spectator may or may not be a woman, or only women; or, as Constance Penley puts it, the emphasis on fantasy highlights

> the great range and diversity of identificatory positions in film, and how those positions can be taken up by either the man or the woman watching the film. While there are 'masculine' and 'feminine' positions in fantasy, men and women, respectively, do not have to assume those positions according to their assigned genders.
>
> (Penley, 1989: 256)

However, as I discussed in Chapter 2, such a model of identification and spectatorship would seem to make the task of the feminist critic a redundant one, since this reading of fantasy as the location of sexually undifferentiated, multiple subject positionings suggests that the gender of characters and spectators might cease to be of significance. There is no acknowledgement here of the relationship between 'the social' and 'the psychic'.

Thus, a general problem with psychoanalytic work on cinematic identification is highlighted, namely that the relationship between the unconscious workings of film texts and the identities of actual female spectators in the cinema remains of little or no significance. As Gaylyn Studlar has argued, an engagement with actual cinema spectators' responses may unsettle some of the neater psychoanalytic formulations prevalent within feminist film theory:

> The attempt to analyze gendered spectatorship and the representation of women in film has encouraged generalizing claims centered around the notion of a hypothetical, ideal spectator 'constructed' by coercive textual mechanisms. . . .
>
> It for no other reason than for its theoretically well-behaved nature, the textually constructed spectator is methodologically attractive. Actual spectators' responses are much more unruly, but they obviously demand attention in the debate over spectatorship. . . . I am concerned . . . that feminist film theory is reluctant to mediate theory through the response of real (i.e., nonacademic) spectators.
>
> (Studlar, 1989: 302–3)

My analysis of cinematic identification is based on female spectators' accounts of Hollywood stars. It is therefore necessarily working on a broader level than the psychoanalytic accounts that concentrate primarily on the unconscious processes at stake in identification. Psychoanalytic theory may seem to be the obvious starting point for a consideration of the processes of identification, since it does offer some account of the meaning and significance of these processes. However, as I shall go on to demonstrate, these psychoanalytic theories of identification used within film criticism have led to very narrow conceptualisations of *cinematic* identification, which have ignored the broader meanings of spectator/star relations and indeed have led to some overly pessimistic conclusions about the pleasures of popular cinema.

What, then, does identification mean to female spectators? How might we conceptualise cinematic identification, not solely as analogous to early psychic developments, but as a cultural process with social meanings beyond the cinema? In classifying the material I received from female spectators it was hard to pinpoint a single process and name it 'identification'. Instead I found that these accounts forced me to reflect upon the meaning of such a concept. 'Identification' seemed to include forms of feminine desire, rather than being strictly constituted as their opposite. When women wrote of their love and adoration of a particular star this was in fact a form of identification: because of such devotion to some stars, there remains a kind of bond with favourites. In addition, 'identification' seemed to involve many diverse, if overlapping, processes which could usefully be separated out for the purpose of analysis. Thus, rather than finding a single and fixable process which could be labelled 'identification', I was confronted with a whole range of connections between female spectators and their ideals on the screen. This necessitated moving beyond the narrower psychoanalytic conceptualisations of identification and re-thinking its diverse meanings within an understanding of the social context of the cinema.

A broader framework for conceptualising audience–star relations has been developed by Andrew Tudor. Reworking Leo Handel's audience study (Handel, 1950), Tudor maps out a useful set of possible relations between stars and their audiences within a more sociological framework (see Table 5.1). The model suggests a helpful distinction between the audience–star relations which take place in the cinema itself (context specific) and those which take place outside the cinematic context (diffuse). It also distinguishes between particularly intense connections between star and audience (high) and less intense involvements (low). 'Emotional affinity' refers to a loose attachment to the star, what Tudor calls 'standard involvement' (Tudor, 1974: 80). 'Imitation', primarily found among young members of the audience, involves the audience using film stars as role models for clothes, hairstyles or behaviour. 'Projection' is used to describe processes whereby the audiences' identities become bound up with those of their favourite stars outside the cinema context. Finally, 'self-identification' describes the intense pleasure of taking on the identity of the star whilst watching the film.

Table 5.1 Types of audience–star relation

	Intensity of involvement	*Range of consequences*	
		Context specific	*Diffuse*
Range of star–individual identification	*High*	Self-identification	Projection
	Low	Emotional affinity	Imitation (of physical and simple behavioural characteristics)

Source: Tudor, 1974: 80.

However, in the light of my research, this model remains overly schematic and in need of further elaboration. It ignores the ways in which the 'range of identifications' and 'range of consequences' may vary according to gender: do women develop a particularly strong attachment to their star ideals, and if so, why and under what circumstances? Furthermore, what is the relationship between imitation and projection and do these take on a particular significance at different times and in different contexts? Nevertheless, Tudor's model does provide a useful starting point here, since it introduces the argument that audience–star relations involve a diverse set of practices whose meanings extend beyond the cinema itself.

In the exploration of cinematic identification which follows I examine the multiplicity of processes connecting female spectators to female Hollywood stars. Respondents' memories of Hollywood stars are analysed in relation to the question of what cinematic 'identification' signified to spectators. The categories of spectatorship around which the following sections are organised are thus not psychoanalytic categories (though they may overlap with them considerably), but rather categories through which spectators articulated the pleasures offered by female Hollywood stars in the 1940s and 1950s. In taking spectators' accounts, rather than film texts, as the basis for this exploration, I am clearly focusing on conscious memories, rather than unconscious processes. Indeed, it could be argued that my challenge to the psychoanalytic models is limited by such a focus. However, as we shall see, taking spectators' memories as the material for an exploration of cinematic identification does not exclude the psychic dimensions of such processes, since fantasy is central to these memories, but rather it necessitates a broader analysis which does not exclude conscious practices and spectators' activities.

The first section addresses processes of identification that involve fantasies about the relationship between the identity of the star and the identity of the spectator. On the whole, these forms of identification relate to the cinematic context; in other words, they are processes that take place during the actual viewing of a film. The second section examines forms of recognition that involve practice as well as fantasy, in that spectators actually transform some aspect of their identity as a result of their relationship to their favourite star. These practices extend beyond the cinema itself and thus spectatorship is considered in relation to the construction of feminine identities more generally.

The distinction between fantasy and practice employed here aims to differentiate between the processes of spectatorship that do not involve the spectator in activities or self-transformations in a physical way, and those that do. In other words, the fantasies are processes that only take place in the spectator's private imagination, and may not be evident to others, whereas the practices, which are obviously fantasies as well, involve activities that are perceivable to others, and indeed often rely on the participation of others. Although this is a problematic dichotomy in some ways, some distinction between these different processes of spectatorship is necessary, especially in order to highlight the ways in which the latter categories have been ignored within theories of spectatorship in film studies.

CINEMATIC IDENTIFICATORY FANTASIES

In the first group of categories of spectatorship, 'devotion', 'adoration' and 'worship', the star is at the centre and the spectator only included in so far as she facilitates the construction of the star's image and identity. These memories, then, make little reference to the relationship between self-image and Hollywood ideal and focus instead upon the wonder the spectator remembers feeling in relation to the star.

Devotion

> I wanted to write and tell you of my devotion to my favourite star Doris Day. I thought she was fantastic, and joined her fan club, collected all the photos and info I could. I saw *Calamity Jane* 45 times in a fortnight and still watch all her films avidly. My sisters all thought I was mad going silly on a woman, but I just thought she was wonderful, they were mad about Elvis, but my devotion was to Doris Day.
>
> (Veronica Millen)

The passion for female stars expressed by spectators is striking in its intensity: it is difficult to see *Calamity Jane* (1953, David Butler) forty-five times in a fortnight! In this example, the adoration of female fan for female star is commented upon in contrast to her sisters' attachments to Elvis, the epitome of smouldering heterosexual masculinity. They disregarded her love for her favourite female star which did not fit into the conventional heterosexual model. Her sisters describe her devotion as 'going silly on a woman', suggesting an important attachment to her favourite star, but denigrating it as immature and lacking the seriousness of adult, heterosexual love. Another way to describe such an attachment, which again has had rather dismissive connotations, is in terms of a crush: 'Then stars had far more mystique and . . . one tended to look up to them and yours truly was still at the age of "crushes"' (Jo Keen). Here the respondent draws attention to her age, indicating that 'crushes' belong to adolescence or schoolgirl years, where adoration of feminine ideals is more acceptable.[1] Numerous memories of favourite female stars included accounts of such devotion. In this example, the contrast to heterosexual devotion is made by the spectator herself, but the homoerotic connotations of such attachments are left implicit.

138

Adoration

Such feelings, however, continued into adulthood for many female spectators, though there may have been an intensification of attachment to
feminine ideals at the time of transition into adulthood (see Chapter 6); as
the following respondent says this was 'no passing fancy'. Her elucidation
of her adoration for Deanna Durbin is worth quoting at length to capture
the narrative elements of the description:

> In the late 1930s, when I was about nine or ten, I began to be aware
> of a young girl's face appearing in magazines and newspapers. I was
> fascinated. The large eyes, the full mouth, sometimes the wonderful
> smile, showing the slightly prominent but perfect teeth. I feel rather
> irritated that I do not recall the moment when I realised that the face
> belonged to a very lovely singing voice beginning to be heard on the
> radio record programmes.
>
> The face and the voice belonged to Deanna Durbin. . . .
>
> In 1940 at the age of twelve, I was evacuated from my house in
> South London to Looe in Cornwall, and it was there that I was taken
> to the pictures for a special treat. There at last I saw her. The film, a
> sequel to her first, was *Three Smart Girls Grow Up*. The effect she
> had upon me can only be described as electrifying. I had never felt
> such a surge of admiration and adoration before.
>
> Even if Deanna had not possessed her beautiful soprano voice, I
> believe that she would still have been a favourite of mine. But the
> singing was of course the reason for such adoration. . . . When she
> sang the most simple melody it became so beautiful and moving that
> it moved me to tears.
>
> My feeling for her was no passing fancy. The love was to last a life-
> time. Over the next few years, we watched as Deanna grew into a stun-
> ningly lovely woman. Her voice matured and completely fulfilled its
> earlier promise, and we eagerly awaited every film. To the four hundred
> or so members of 'the Deanna Durbin Society', she remains the love-
> liest Hollywood film star of all time. She keeps in touch with us. Our
> meetings and our newsletter bring us all such a great deal of pleasure.
>
> I feel it quite extraordinary that Deanna can inspire such devotion,
> as it is now forty years since she made a film or any kind of public
> appearance.
>
> I must just add that the members of our society seem to be about
> equal in number male and female. I think perhaps that it would be
> considered a bit of a giggle today, if a large number of women
> confessed to feeling love for a girl. Nobody seemed to question it
> then. Just in case; I have been married since 1948! Have two sons and
> a daughter, one grandchild.
>
> (Patricia Robinson)

Figure 5.2 'The face and the voice belonged to Deanna Durbin . . . The film . . . was *Three Smart Girls Grow Up*. The effect she had upon me can only be described as electrifying.'

Deanna Durbin is introduced here within the discourse of romance. The memory of the first 'meeting', or rather 'sighting', is retold within the structure of a romantic narrative whose sequence of events culminates in the moment of seeing her favourite star on the cinema screen. Its structure is built around a series of gaps, enigmas or absences which is typical of the romance narrative (see Stacey, 1990). The story begins with her fascination with an anonymous female face, the details of which are easily reconjured. Then a beautiful singing voice is heard on the radio. In a forgotten moment the beauty of the face and of the singing voice of this Hollywood star are coupled to produce a tantalising combination for the young female spectator. This lost moment interrupts the smooth flow of the narrative and draws attention to the processes of recollection at work. The memory of the star's face is crystal clear, but a magical moment of realisation is frustratingly lost in the past. Its loss, however, foregrounds its importance to this respondent and it thus becomes a 'treasured moment' (rather than a treasured memory) by its absence. This lost moment of realisation is the only (apparent) missing link in the story, and yet its absence becomes part of the narrative structure.

It is only at this point in the narrative that the repondent introduces her favourite star by name – Deanna Durbin – and yet the picture continues to remain incomplete since the moving image of this Hollywood star on the cinema screen remained out of reach. The anticipation of finally seeing the star on screen is recreated through the gradual build up to the moment when 'there at last I saw her': the picture is thus completed – face, voice, name and, finally, the 'real thing'. Magazines and radio could only offer partial pleasures, preliminaries to the excitement of the moment of seeing her on screen. Only the cinema could offer that combination of 'reality' and intimacy which gave a sense of meeting the star of your dreams. Far from being the closure of this narrative, however, this moment signifies the beginning of a lifetime's devotion to Deanna Durbin.

This recreation of the step-by-step movement towards the moment of seeing Deanna Durbin offers a structure for the articulation of increasingly intense feelings for the star. At the beginning of the story the respondent describes herself as being 'aware of a young girl's face' when she first saw it in magazines; she then becomes 'fascinated' by her, and finally, on seeing Deanna on screen she recalls: 'the effect she had upon me can only be described as electrifying'. This rhetorical device – 'can only be described as' – draws attention to the singularity of the experience. Indeed, she had 'never felt such a surge of admiration and adoration before'. The use of the words 'electrifying' and 'surge' suggest the peculiar intensity and indeed conjure up a sense of the immediate physicality of such emotions, which, in their newness and unfamiliarity, took this young female spectator by surprise. These feelings of 'adoration', 'admiration', and, indeed, 'love', were, we are told, to last a lifetime. The strength of feeling is conveyed in the repetition of words such as 'adoration' and 'devotion'; and the significance of that first moment is reinforced by the continuing membership of Deanna's fan club, fifty years later, given as evidence confirming the intensity and durability of the devotion. Thus the memory is not only structured like a romantic narrative but is also characterised by its use of romantic language.

This respondent conveys a certain amount of surprise herself at the strength of her feelings for Deanna. Interspersed with the story of her devotion are indications of self-reflection about the reasons for her attachment and even some unease about how it might be interpreted. At one point it is Deanna's voice which is given as the reason for such devotion, and yet even without it 'she would still have been a favourite'. 'Feeling love for a girl' is remembered as being all right in the 1940s, clearly suggesting a contrast with today's interpretations of such feelings.

The anxiety about the possibility of homoerotic connotations is here expressed through the respondent's heterosexual identity and confirmed by her marital status and reproductive roles. Heterosexuality is thus invoked to protect against any interpretations, including those which have clearly occurred to this respondent, of such love of another female as containing homoerotic pleasures. The rigid boundary between heterosexuality and homosexuality as two mutually exclusive identities is thus reaffirmed, despite the strength of adoration and love 'for a girl' expressed in this respondent's story. The homoeroticism of such romantic recreations is nevertheless striking in this narrative of 'love at first sight'.

Worship

The feelings of love and adoration towards stars are often represented through the discourse of religious worship in which stars become goddesses and no longer belong to our world:

> Film stars . . . seemed very special people, glamorous, handsome and way above us ordinary mortals.
>
> (June Thomas)

> Rita Hayworth . . . she was just the personification of beauty, glamour and sophistication to me and to thousands of others. Self-assured, wore gorgeous clothes beautifully, danced gloriously and her musicals were an absolute delight. She just seemed out of this world!
>
> (Mary Marshall)

> They were screen goddesses – stars way up in the star studded galaxy, far removed from the ordinary hum-drum lives of us, the cinemagoing fans.
>
> (Dawn Hellmann)

These respondents emphasise the difference between themselves and their ideals by representing stars as 'out of this world' and 'way up in another galaxy' and thus located at a vast spatial distance from the cinema spectator.

The language of religious love is drawn upon to convey the significance of the attachment to favourite stars. This combined with a 'love at first sight' story in which the sequencing of the anonymous star, the film and finally the star's name replicate the conventions of romance narratives referred to above (see section on adoration):

> I'll never forget the first time I saw her, it was in *My Gal Sal* in 1942, and her name was Rita Hayworth. I couldn't take my eyes off her, she was the most perfect woman I had ever seen. The old cliché 'screen goddess' was used about many stars, but those are truly the only words that define that divine creature. . . . I was stunned and amazed that any human being could be that lovely.
>
> (Violet Holland)

> Stars were fabulous creatures to be worshipped from afar, every film of one's favourite gobbled up as soon as it came out.
>
> (Pauline Kemp)

These statements represent the star as something different and unattainable. Religious signifiers here indicate the special status and meaning of the stars, as well as suggesting the intensity of the devotion felt by the spectator. They also reinforce the 'otherness' of the stars who are not considered part of the mortal world of the spectator. The last example, however, does introduce the star into the mortal world by a metaphor of ingestion reminiscent of the act of communion.

Worship of stars as goddesses involves a denial of self found in some forms of religious devotion. The spectator is only present in these quotes as a worshipper, or through her adoration of the star. There is little reference to the identity of the spectator or suggestion of closing the gap between star and fan by becoming more like the star; these are simply declarations of appreciation from afar. The boundaries between self and ideal are quite fixed and stable in these examples, and the emphasis is very strongly on the ideal rather than the spectator. Even in the last statement, where the self is implicit in that the star is to be gobbled up, the star nonetheless remains the subject of the sentence.

In these first three categories, then, spectators articulated their attachments to their favourite stars within the language of love, adoration and worship. The 'identification' here is not a question of similarity with the star, indeed the identity of the spectator remains absent from the equation. Thus, we might ask whether they are in fact forms of cinematic 'identification'. I have included them here because they are forms of spectator/star relations which recurred in accounts of Hollywood cinema of this time and they seemed to me to be representing something rarely considered within theories of identification, yet not entirely separable from it. These memories of Hollywood idols are not straightforward articulations of desire for, or

Figure 5.3 'I'll never forget the first time I saw her, it was in *My Gal Sal* . . . and her name was Rita Hayworth. I couldn't take my eyes off her.'

desire to be, the love object. Rather they express something else, somewhere in between: an intense, often homoerotic bond between idol and worshipper.

In the next group of categories of cinematic identificatory fantasies, the relationship between the star's image and the spectator's identity can be seen as rather more fluid and relational. Instead of the rather static division between mortals and goddesses characteristic of the pleasures expressed in the sections above, here it is the imagined transformation of self which produces the cinematic pleasure. The spectator takes pleasure in escaping into the world of Hollywood favourites, and indeed in taking on the star's identity. This section overlaps considerably with my analysis of escapism in the last chapter. It is repeated here since its absence in either chapter would have left too large a gap. Indeed, the overlap could be seen to be indicative of the important connections between escapism and identification.

Transcendence

Many women wrote of the pleasure in imagining themselves taking on the roles and identities of the stars whilst in the cinema:

> An ultra glamorous star was an awesome sight for us gangly girls. A sight to behold forever in our minds. During these spectacular musicals we were transported to a fantasy land where we were the screen movie queens.
>
> (Gwyneth Jones)

> It made no difference to me if the film was ushered in by a spangled globe, the Liberty Lady or that roaring lion, I was no longer in my seat but right up there fleeing for my life from chasing gangsters, skimming effortlessly over silver ice, or singing high and sweet like a lark. . . . No secret agent served their country more bravely, and no one tilled the earth more diligently.
>
> (Dawn Hellmann)

The movement from spectator to star identity in these examples is more fluid than in the previous categories, and this fluidity provides the opportunity for the well-known pleasure of the cinema, 'losing oneself' in the film, as discussed in the previous chapter: 'no matter how bad things were around you, you could lose yourself even for one moment in time' (Betty Cunningham); 'Growing up was difficult (even in those days); the films were where I could sit and lose myself and imagine it was me up there and they usually had happy endings too! I suppose they were really the "Mills and Boon" of the age for us girls' (Anon).

This temporary loss of self in an ideal other is reflected upon here as

145

being akin to the pleasures of contemporary romance fiction for women. In retrospect, this respondent suggests she now sees how Hollywood 'really' functioned which she sums up with the gloss 'Mills and Boon' – typically considered to be 'dope for the dopes'.[2] This kind of 'put down', often accompanied by a kind of embarrassment about the escapist pleasure of cultural forms such as romances, soaps and Hollywood, emerged occasionally when respondents began to reflect upon their enjoyment of Hollywood cinema. However, the point here is not to deny that Hollywood is escapist, but rather, as I argued in the previous chapter, to analyse the processes of escapism in relation to Hollywood cinema in wartime and postwar Britain.

In contrast to the distinction between self and ideal maintained in the processes of spectatorship discussed above, in this version the spectator's identity merges with the star in the film, or the character she is portraying: 'I always put myself in the heroine's place' (Anon). The pleasure this fantasy transformation offers is frequently associated with particular stars:

> my favourite was Bette Davis. Her films always held me in thrall, always dramatic, the sort of film with a real good story that one could lose oneself in.
>
> (Mrs G. Adams)

> In the 40s it was Betty Grable for me, I loved musicals – she was so bubbly, so full of life it took you out of yourself, you could bury yourself in her parts.
>
> (Betty Cunningham)

> Joan Crawford could evoke such pathos, and suffer such martyrdom . . . making you live each part.
>
> (Marie Burgess)

It is the intensity, here of narrative, personality and emotion respectively, which spectators remember as bonding them to their favourite stars. Another respondent writes of 'getting high' on Hollywood stars:

> I was enraptured by any star who appeared in a Hollywood musical. I was completely lost – it wasn't Ginger Rogers dancing with Fred Astaire, it was me. My going to the movies in the forties and fifties was akin to the high young people get now by doing drugs.
>
> (Kay Barker)

There is a striking intimacy between spectator and star in these moments of intense feelings. Some respondents remembered particular moments in films in which they had become one with the star and had shared her emotions:

> Jennifer Jones made a great impression in *Duel in the Sun* – her sheer beauty – her voice – magnetic eyes and the merest trembling of her

Figure 5.4 'Joan Crawford . . . could evoke such pathos.'

chin could convey so much feeling and emotion. I'll never forget the last crawl towards Gregory Peck over the rocks. I was with her every inch of the way and my heart was bursting to reach him.

(Yvonne Oliver)

Processes of spectatorial identification are articulated in relation to both

147

Figure 5.5 'It wasn't Ginger Rogers dancing with Fred Astaire, it was me.' (Seen here in *Top Hat*.)

similarity and difference between self and ideal. Some respondents imagined themselves as their ideals because of some similarity with the star with whom they identified. For example:

[My favourite star was] Dorothy Lamour (I don't want to be big

Figure 5.6 'Jennifer Jones made a great impression in *Duel in the Sun*.'

headed, but my mother thought I looked like her). . . . The stars in the 1940s and 1950s were really beautiful and at that time I suppose we felt we were the characters we were watching.

(Mrs P. Malcolmson)

Figure 5.7 'My favourite star was Dorothy Lamour (I don't want to be big headed, but my mother thought I looked like her).'

Others clearly found that the difference facilitated their shift in identity. For example, one respondent remembers:

I preferred stars who were unlike everyday women because I went to the cinema to escape into a world of fantasy, wealth, and, above all, glamour. I preferred those unlike me because I could put myself in their place for a short while and become everything I wasn't – beautiful, desirable and popular with the opposite sex.

(Elizabeth Rogers)

In many cases these processes of identification involve a complex interplay of similarity and difference as this example demonstrates:

If they were like women in everyday life, one could associate one-self with them in their film parts. On the other hand, if they were sometimes unlike real life it did one good to fantasize and think of oneself in such a situation. . . . One could enter into the situation more easily and lose oneself in it – a form of escapism I suppose.

(Anon)

The pleasures of becoming part of the fantasy world on the screen thus take many different forms. However, all these examples demonstrate the importance of the pleasure of shifting identity during the film screen-ing. What is remembered here, albeit in a variety of ways, is the temporary loss of self and the adoption of a star persona, especially in terms of shar-ing emotional intensity with the star. Thus the boundary between self and ideal is not fixed in these examples, since there is a temporary fantasy self which takes over, and yet the star's identity is still primary here. In other words, the forms of identification articulated here involve a one-way movement towards the star, with little mention of the spectator, except by way of poor comparison (such as 'the gangly girls', see p. 145). The boundary between the self and ideal is therefore relatively stable, being crossed during the film viewing in terms of the spectator entering her fantasy world and becoming her fantasy self, but this temporary, one-way movement leaves the spectator's own identity apparently unchanged by the process.

Aspiration and inspiration

In this next section, the processes analysed involve the spectator's identity more centrally. Here the star's identity is written about more in relation to the desire for transformation of the spectator's identity. The discourses through which the star is remembered, then, are ones which centre on the feminine identity of the spectators, as opposed to the other way around, as in the previous sections.

In some examples the relationship between star and spectator is articu-lated through the recognition of an immutable difference between star and spectator:

Hollywood stars in the roles they depicted were all the things we'd

151

have liked to have been, wearing glamorous clothes and jewels we had no chance of acquiring and doing so many wonderful things we knew we would never have the nerve to do – even given the opportunity . . . Bette Davis was the epitome of what we would like to be, but knew we never could!

(Norah Turner)

Yet here the desire to move across that difference and become more like the star is expressed, even if this is accompanied by the impossibility of its fulfilment (see Stacey, 1987a). The distance between the spectator and her ideal produces a kind of longing which offers fantasies of transformed identities. 'The cinema took you into the realm of fantasy and what you as a person would like to be and do' (Anon).

These desires to become more like the stars occur on several levels. Many of them are predictably articulated through the discourse of glamour. Stars offer ideals of feminine appearance:

I finally kept with Joan Crawford – every typist's dream of how they'd like to look.

(May Ross)

And of course her [Betty Grable's] clothes – how could a young girl not want to look like that?

(Sheila Wright)

Joan Bennett – not so much for her acting, I can't even remember her films. I just thought she was gorgeous. The star I would most like to look like.

(Joyce Lewis)

We liked to think we were like them, but of course, we couldn't match any of the female stars for looks or clothes. It was nice to have them as role models though!

(Valerie Channell)

Not surprisingly, stars serve a normative function to the extent that they are often read as role models, contributing to the construction of the ideals of feminine attractiveness circulating in the culture at that time. Stars were variously referred to as 'role models', 'someone to emulate' and 'the epitome of what every woman should be'. Spectators often felt 'unattractive', 'dowdy', 'plump' and 'gangly' by comparison. Stars are remembered through a discourse of feminine glamour in which ideals of feminine appearance (slim, white, young and even-featured) were established and in comparison to which many spectators felt inadequate.

Successful physical attractiveness also signifies successful romantic conclusions:

152

Figure 5.8 'I think my favourite was Rita Hayworth, I always imagined if I could look like her I could toss my red hair into the wind . . . and meet the man of my dreams.'

Although I wished to look like a different star each week depending on what film I saw, I think my favourite was Rita Hayworth, I always imagined if I could look like her I could toss my red hair into the wind . . . and meet the man of my dreams.

(Rene Arter)

153

Furthermore, glamour is linked to wealth and property, as the following example demonstrates:

> my enjoyment of going to the pictures was my way of imagining myself one day going somewhere equally lovely and being able to wear lovely gowns and meet a rich handsome man and have a big house with servants, especially when I had seen a colour film!
>
> (Jean Forshaw)

Thus Hollywood stars function as role models encouraging desire for feminine 'attractiveness', attachment to a man and possession of property (and even servants!). This encouraged traditional forms of aspiration among women whose lives were very unlike anything they saw on the Hollywood screen.

However, star glamour was understood not only in terms of appearance, but also as signifying confidence, sophistication and self-assurance, which were perceived by female spectators as desirable and inspirational:

> Maureen O'Hara seemed to me, a teenager, the type of person I would have liked to be as she was the complete opposite of me. Her fiery beauty and nature, and the way she handled situations in her films were magical to me. The same applies to Marilyn Monroe. I was a shorthand typist-cum-secretary; life was rather run of the mill, the lifestyles they portrayed were something we could only dream about.
>
> (Brenda Blackman)

What is interesting here is that it is not only the 'beauty' which was admired, but also 'the way she handled situations', suggesting a kind of ability and confidence in the world which the spectator herself felt she lacked:

> I liked seeing strong, capable and independent types of female characters mostly because I wished to be like them.
>
> (Joan Clifford)

> Likening myself to women who portrayed characters I would have liked to have been or had the courage to have been.
>
> (Mrs P. McDonald)

> I think I admired the ones I would like to have been like and considered myself uninteresting, being quiet and shy.
>
> (Anon)

Thus the courage, confidence and independence of feminine stars is aspired to by spectators who saw themselves as unable to enjoy such admirable qualities.

Some female stars, such as Bette Davis, Joan Crawford and Katharine Hepburn, were frequently referred to as representing images of power and

Figure 5.9 'I liked seeing strong, capable and independent types of female characters . . . because I wished to be like them.' (Publicity still of Joan Crawford.)

Figure 5.10 'We liked stars who were most different to ourselves and Katharine Hepburn, with her self-assured romps through any situation, was one of them.'

confidence. These were frequent favourites because they offered spectators fantasies of power outside their own experience:

> We liked stars who were most different to ourselves and Katharine Hepburn, with her self-assured romps through any situation, was one of them. We were youngsters at the time, and were anything but self

156

Figure 5.11 'Bette Davis took the other pedestal. She could be a real "bitch" without turning a hair, and quelled her leading men with a raised eyebrow and a sneer at the corners of her mouth.' (Seen here in *All About Eve*.)

confident, and totally lacking in sophistication, so, naturally, Bette Davis took the other pedestal. She could be a real 'bitch', without turning a hair, and quelled her leading men with a raised eyebrow and a sneer at the corners of her mouth.

(Norah Turner)

Bette Davis . . . was great, I loved how she walked across the room in her films, she seemed to have a lot of confidence and she had a look of her own, as I think a lot of female stars had at that time.

(Anon)

Powerful female stars often played characters in punishing patriarchal narratives, where the woman is either killed off, or married, or both, but these spectators do not seem to select this aspect of their films to write about. Instead, the qualities of confidence and power are remembered as offering female spectators the pleasure of participation in qualities they themselves lacked and desired.

Again, the age difference between the star and the younger fans is central here, and stars provide ideals of femininity for adolescent women in the audience who are preoccupied with attaining adult femininity:

Doris Day . . . seemed to epitomise the kind of person, who with luck, I as a child could aspire to be.

(Betty Cole)

I favoured stars I could identify with – romantic, adventurous, glamorous, strong minded – all the things I hoped to become 'when I grew up'.

(M. Palin)

Thus female stars represented not only ideals of feminine glamour in terms of appearance, but also a mature femininity which was a source of fascination to younger spectators. Stars were envied for their confidence and their capabilities in the fictional worlds of Hollywood cinema.

These examples demonstrate not simply the desire to overcome the gap between spectator and star, but a fantasy of possible movement between the two identities, from the spectator to the star:

I preferred stars who were unlike women I knew. They were better dressed and looked much more attractive. They gave me the ambition to do more for myself.

(Anon)

Hollywood stars can thus be seen as offering more than simple role models of sexual attractiveness (though clearly they offered this too!). However, they were also remembered as offering female spectators a source of fantasy of a more powerful and confident self:

158

I think everyone needs an inspiration or aspiration. Some of the stars I liked because they were down to earth, but they usually became something quite different in their films, making one feel that the unattainable could be reached.

(Marie Burgess)

So far, then, I have discussed processes of spectatorship which involve negotiating the difference between the star and the spectator in various ways. These all overlap to some extent, but what can be seen clearly is that these processes of spectatorship involve distinct relations between self and ideal. First, the processes of spectatorship which involved the denial of self in favour of praising the screen goddesses were analysed. Second, there was a discussion of those relations involving the loss of self in the fantasy world of the star ideal and thus the merging of self with ideal. In the final section, the desire to transform the self and become more like the ideal were explored. Thus, the early examples in which the difference between the star and the spectator remained fixed, and was itself a source of pleasure, contrast increasingly with those in which the boundary between self and ideal is more fluid and relational. This boundary dissolves further in the following sections, in which aspects of the star's identity are taken on by the spectator in a variety of practices that take place outside the cinematic context.

EXTRA-CINEMATIC IDENTIFICATORY PRACTICES

In this section, the processes of spectatorship that concern what I shall call 'identificatory practices' are discussed. I have called these 'extra-cinematic' to indicate that they relate to forms of identification that take place outside the cinematic context. These processes also involve the spectators engaging in some kind of practice of transformation of the self to becomes more like the star they admire, or to involve others in the recognition of their similarity with the star. This transformation does not only take place at the level of fantasy, but also involves activities in which the star becomes part of discourses of the spectator's identity outside the cinema. This is not to suggest that practices do not involve fantasies, or that fantasies cannot be seen as practices, but rather to distinguish between those categories of spectatorship that involve the spectator in some kind of social practice outside the cinema, and those in the previous section, which remained within the spectator's imagination during the viewing of a film. These examples provide the opportunity to explore the meaning of stars for spectators in their everyday lives beyond the spectatorial fantasies of the viewing situation. This is an area of film reception which has been largely ignored within film studies in the past.

Pretending

[T]here was a massive open-cast coal site just at the tip of our estate –
there were nine of us girls – and we would go to the site after school,
and play on the mounds of soil removed from the site. The mounds
were known to us as 'Beverly Hills' and we all had lots of fun there.
Each of us had our own spot where the soil was made into a round –
and that was our mansion. We played there for hours – visiting one
mansion after another and each being our own favourite film star.

(Mary E. Wilson)

Here the familiar childhood games of make-believe are played out through
an imaginary transformation of a physical place into the Hollywood resi-
dence, constantly written about in film magazines at that time, called
'Beverly Hills'. Many young spectators would have seen pictures of stars'
mansions in magazines such as *Picturegoer*, which most of these respondents read frequently; it regularly featured articles about particular stars'
mansions, showing interiors, gardens, swimming pools and so on. The
wealth of Beverly Hills, the affluent world of Hollywood stars, contrasts
here especially strikingly with the image of the open-cast coal site next to
this respondent's housing estate.

The adaptation of their physical surroundings enables each girl to take
on a different identity of a Hollywood star. This game of pretending to be
famous film stars visiting each other's mansions was clearly a favourite one
– 'we played there for hours' – and indeed proved to be a treasured
memory of lasting significance for these women who continued to call each
other by their Hollywood names some fifty years later: 'it was such fun and
your letter brought back all these things – I've had such a laugh about
them. I often bump into Betty Grable in Morpeth – I'll mention your letter
to her next time I see her' (Mary E. Wilson).

The durability of the significance of particular stars is very striking.
Again, fifty years later another spectator remembers the significance of
Loretta Young, whom she used to pretend to be in childhood games,
despite having only ever seen her in one film:

Loretta Young was probably the first star that I was aware of. I think
it was her hair that I remember most – very long and glossy with a
heavy fringe over her forehead. I always wanted hair like that! I also
remember wishing that she could be my mother. (My real mother was
very nice, I hasten to add.) Childhood games were often played using
film star's names. I was always Loretta Young. . . . I probably only
saw Loretta Young in one film – but she must have made a lasting
impression on me because when I think of '40s films, she's the first
person that comes to mind.

(Molly Frost)

Stars' names prompted an obvious source of recognition between self and ideal. A number of respondents wrote of their connection to particular stars because of sharing their name:

> I really loved the pictures, they were my life, I used to pretend I was related to Betty Grable because my name was Betty, and I used to get quite upset when the other children didn't believe me.
>
> (Betty Cunningham)

> Esther Williams would fascinate me always. This was only vanity on my part. I was quite a good swimmer in those long ago days. I belonged to a swimming club and the young men there used to call me 'Esther'.
>
> (Audrey Lay)

Pretending to be particular film stars involves an imaginary practice, but one where the spectator involved knows that it is a game. This is rather different from the processes of entering a fantasy world or taking on a fantasy self in the cinema discussed above, whereby the spectator feels completely absorbed in the star's world and which thus involves a temporary collapsing of the self into the star identity, discussed in the section on 'transcendence'. The first example given above is also different in that it involves a physical as well as an imaginary transformation. Furthermore, pretending does not simply involve the privatised imagination of individual spectators, as in the processes which take place in the cinematic context, but also involves the participation of other spectators in the collective fantasy games. It thus becomes a social practice in so far as the stars are given meanings through activities with others outside the cinema. This kind of representation of the relationship between star and fan is based more on similarity than difference, since the fan takes on the identity of the star in a temporary game of make-believe, and the difference between them is made invisible, despite the recognition of the whole process as one of pretending.

Resembling

The connection between the spectator and the star established through childhood games of pretending to be one's favourite star is also remembered as a consequence of shared physical appearance. There are numerous points of recognition of similarities between the spectator and the star. These are not based on pretending to be something one is not, but rather selecting something which establishes a link between the star and the self based on a pre-existing part of the spectator's identity which bears a resemblance to the star. This does not neccesarily involve any kind of transformation, but rather a highlighting of star qualities in the individual spectator. In some cases, a general physical resemblance connected spectator and star:

> I have *many many times*, both then and since, been told that I could be Bette Davis' double – I never argued. And I can assure you, I do not look like her now!
>
> (Mary May)

Clearly being taken to resemble a Hollywood star by other people was perceived as flattering and complimentary ('I never argued'), but in some cases the resemblance with Bette Davis was perceived as more threatening:

> Bette Davis – her eyes were fabulous and the way she walked arrogantly. . . . I have dark eyes, those days I had very large dark eyebrows . . . and my Dad used to say . . . 'Don't you roll those Bette Davis eyes at me young lady. . . .' Now Doris Day, that's a different thing – we share the same birthday.
>
> (Patricia Ogden)

Bette Davis was of course known for the use of her eyes as part of her performance style: they signified intensity and passion at key moments of dramatic tension in the narrative.[3] Her star image was also associated with confidence and power. Thus the significance of particular features, such as 'Bette Davis eyes', seems to exceed physical likeness, to suggest a certain kind of femininity, in this case a rebellious one which represented a challenge to the father's authority.

The perceived personality types of Hollywood stars were also a point of connection for some spectators:

> Monroe appealed to me deeply and desperately, little girl lost with the body of a desirable woman. She lit up the screen with her performances, the glamour, her movements were so exciting. Watching her made me feel she was in some way lonely and vulnerable, she was my cult figure, I felt like me, she was running away from herself.
>
> (Betty Cruse)

Here the spectator recognises aspects of herself – vulnerability and fear – in Marilyn Monroe, despite her glamour and the excitement of her performance. Thus resemblance involves connecting to a favourite star through the name, looks or personality of the spectator.

Imitating

Unlike the above process of recognising a resemblance to a star, which involves selecting an already existing common quality with the star, many respondents wrote about imitating their favourite star. This is different

Figure 5.12 'My Dad used to say . . . "Don't you roll those Bette Davis eyes at me young lady."'

from the fantasy of becoming the star whilst viewing a film, or even expressing the desire to become more like the star generally, since it involves an actual imitation of a star or of her particular characteristics in a particular film. In other words, this identificatory practice involves a form of pretending or play-acting, and yet it is also different from pretending,

163

since pretending is represented as a process involving the whole star persona, whereas imitation is used here to indicate a partial taking on of some aspect of a star's identity.

Several respondents gave examples of imitating the singing and dancing of favourite stars after the film performance:

> My favourite female star was Betty Grable. The songs she sang in the film, I would try to remember, I would sing and dance all the way home.
>
> (Pam Gray)

> My favourite star was Deanna Durbin. I absolutely adored her voice when she sang it was like an angel's, and so was her face, she was such a sweet girl and her acting too was always so appealing. I've often tried to sing like her, but of course couldn't ever reach her top notes.
>
> (May Nuckley)

The singing and dancing associated with Hollywood cinema in the 1940s and 1950s also offered a sense of community (see Chapter 4). A favourite cinema experience from the 1940s is remembered as:

> in a village cinema, a group of teenagers, we filled a row. Lena Horne sang 'Paper Doll' and our row of seats rocked. We sang all the way home.
>
> (Jean Barrett)

Groups of friends were frequently remembered as recreating Hollywood scenarios:

> Deanna Durbin had such a beautiful voice. I too loved to sing and my friends and I used to put on shows singing her songs.
>
> (June Thomas)

> We used to go home and do concerts based on the songs and dances we had seen in the films, and one of my friends had an auntie who was a mine of information on the words of songs from films.
>
> (Jean Forshaw)

> The films we saw made us sing and sometimes act our way home on the bus.
>
> (June Thomas)

These performances often involved others in the judgement of success or failure of the imitation:

> I adored Judy Garland. She was just a couple of years older than me. Her face and her voice were pure magic to me. I saw almost every one of her films from the early days, right to the end of her life. I always longed to meet her, but of course knew I never would. I would

164

Figure 5.13 'Lena Horne sang "Paper Doll" and our row of seats rocked. We sang all the way home.'

even try to sing like her, thought I could, but the family thought different!

(Anon)

The imitation of stars was not limited to singing and dancing, but was

165

Figure 5.14 'I adored Judy Garland. . . . Her face and her voice were pure magic to me.'

clearly a pleasure in terms of replicating gestures, speech and star personalities:

I had my favourites of course. . . . One week I would tigerishly pace about like Joan Crawford, another week I tried speaking in the

166

staccato tones of Bette Davis and puffing a cigarette at the same time.

(Dawn Hellmann)

The types of stars who were most frequently imitated in terms of posture, movement and gesture tended to be those associated with the more 'confident', 'powerful' feminine identities, such as Bette Davis and Joan Crawford:

> I remember seeing Bette Davis, and, as nobody had cars then, strutting home a mile and a half flashing my eyes pretending I was Bette, lovely days, and for the next few days, using the same move-ments around the office until everyone got sick . . . until my next good film came out.
>
> (Patricia Ogden)

Copying

Although imitation and copying are very closely linked as practices, I want to use them here differently to distinguish between audiences *imitating* behaviour and activities, and *copying* appearances. As the attempted replication of appearance, then, *copying* relates back to the desire to look like stars discussed above. However, it is not simply expressed as an unfulfillable desire or pleasurable fantasy, as in the earlier examples; it is also a practice which transforms the spectators' physical appearance.

Copying is the most common form of cinematic recognition outside the cinema. Perhaps this is not surprising given the centrality of physical appearance to femininity in general in this culture, and to female Hollywood stars in particular (see Chapter 6). Here individualised fanta-sies become practices aimed at the transformation of the spectator's own identity:

> I was a very keen fan of Bette Davis and can remember seeing her in *Dark Victory*. . . . That film had such an impact on me. I can remember coming home and looking in the mirror fanatically trying to comb my hair so that I could look like her. I idolised her . . . thought she was a wonderful actress.
>
> (Vera Carter)

This process involves an intersection of self and other, subject and object. The impact of the film on the spectator caused her to desire to resemble the ideal physically. In front of a reflection of herself, the spectator attempts to close the gap between her own image and her ideal image, by trying to produce a new image, more like her ideal. In this instance, her hair is the focus of this desired transformation.

Indeed, hairstyle is one of the most frequently recurring aspects of the star's appearance which the spectators try to copy:

167

My friends and I would try and copy the hair styles of the stars, sometimes we got it right, and other times we just gave up, as we hadn't the looks of the stars or the money to dress the way they did.

(Anon)

Now Doris Day . . . I was told many times around that I looked like her, so I had my hair cut in a D.A. style. . . . Jane Wyman was a favourite at one stage and I had my hair cut like hers, it was called a tulip. . . . Now Marilyn Monroe was younger and by this time I had changed my image, my hair was almost white blonde and longer and I copied her hairsyle, as people said I looked like her.

(Patricia Ogden)

These forms of copying involve some kind of self-transformation to produce an appearance similar to that of Hollywood stars. Some spectators clearly have a stronger feeling of their success than others: the first example includes a sense of defeat whilst the last seems to be able to achieve several desired likenesses, especially bearing in mind that this respondent is the one who had 'Bette Davis eyes'! The difference, then, between the star and the spectator is transformable into similarity through the typical work of femininity: the production of oneself simultaneously as subject and object in accordance with cultural ideals of femininity.

Copying the hairstyles of famous film stars can be seen as a form of cultural production and consumption. It involves the production of a new self-image through the pleasure taken in a star image. Many examples of copying intersect with the consumption of commodities other than the Hollywood star image. The construction of women as cinema spectators overlaps here with their construction as consumers (see Chapter 6).

I have separated hairstyles from other aspects of this process, since changing hairstyles does not necessarily involve the actual purchasing of other products to transform the identity of the spectator, although bleach and so on may have been bought. The purchasing of items such as clothing and cosmetics in relation to particular stars brings into particularly sharp focus the relationship between the cinema industries and other forms of capitalist industry. This is discussed more fully in the chapter which follows but a few examples are given here, since copying is such a central identificatory practice.

Stars are consumable feminine images which female spectators then reproduce through other forms of consumption:

and I bought clothes like hers (Doris Day) . . . dresses, soft wool, no sleeves, but short jackets, boxey type little hats, half hats we used to call them and low heeled court shoes to match your outfit, kitten heels they were called. . . . as people said I looked like her (Marilyn

Figure 5.15 'People said I looked like her (Marilyn Monroe). I even bought a suit after seeing her in *Niagara*.'

Monroe). I even bought a suit after seeing her in *Niagara*.

(Patricia Ogden)

Stars are thus identified with particular commodities which are part of the reproduction of feminine identities. The female spectators in these examples produce particular images of femininity which remind them of their favourite stars. In so doing, they produce a new feminine identity, one which combines an aspect of the star with their own appearance. This is different from imitation, which is more of a temporary reproduction of a particular kind of behaviour which resembles the star. It transforms the spectator's previous appearance, and in doing so offers the spectator the pleasure of close association with her ideal.

> As teenagers and young girls we did not have the vast variety of clothing and choices of make-up that is available today, so hairstyles and make-up were studied with great interest and copied. . . . I seem to remember buying a small booklet by Max Factor with pictures of the stars, M.G.M. mostly, with all the details of their make-up and how to apply it.
>
> (Anon)

> Their make-up was faultless and their fashion of the forties platform shoes, half hats with rows of curls showing at the back under the hat. . . . We used to call the shoes 'Carmen Miranda' shoes. . . . I felt like a film star using Lux Toilet soap, advertised as the stars' soap.
>
> (Vera Barford)

Through the use of cosmetic products, then, as well as through the purchasing and use of clothing, spectators take on a part of the star's identity and make it part of their own. The self and the ideal combine to produce another feminine identity, closer to the ideal. This is the direct opposite of the process of identification I began with in the first section, in which the spectator's own identity remained relatively marginal to the description of the pleasure taken in female Hollywood stars. In this final process, the star becomes more marginal and is only relevant in so far as the star identity relates to the spectator's own identity. As has been noted by other commentators, these latter practices demonstrate the importance of understanding Hollywood stars and their audiences in relation to other cultural industries of the 1940s and 1950s.[4]

CONCLUSION: RETHINKING CINEMATIC IDENTIFICATION[5]

Having outlined the different forms of identification in spectator/star relations, it is now important to reconsider some of the earlier models of identification and spectatorship in the light of this research. First, the *diversity* of the processes of identification and desire evident in these examples is striking. Within psychoanalytic film theory, the multiplicity of its formations in relation to the cinema have been ignored. The idea of a singular process of identification, so often assumed in psychoanalytic film theory, is unsatisfactory, and indeed reductive in the light of the range of processes discussed above.

Besides categorising the many different kinds of identification in the relationships between spectators and stars, I have drawn attention to the broad distinction between two different forms of identification: *identificatory fantasies* and *identificatory practices*. As I have stressed this is not to suggest that the practices do not also involve fantasies, or that fantasies cannot also be considered as practices. The analytic distinction has been used here to highlight the fact that identifications do not take place exclusively within the imagination, but also occur at the level of cultural activity. It is thus important to extend our understanding of cinematic identification, previously analysed solely at the level of fantasy, to include the practices documented by these spectators, in order to understand the different forms of overlap between stars' and spectators' identities.

Another significant distinction is that between *cinematic identification*, which refers to the viewing experience, and *extra-cinematic identification*, referring to the use of stars' identities in a different cultural time and space. So far, film studies have, not surprisingly, been concerned with the former. However, the importance of these extra-cinematic forms of identification to these female spectators came across very forcefully in their accounts of their relationship to Hollywood stars. Not only was this one of the most written-about aspects of the relationship between stars and spectators, but the pleasure and force of feeling with which they recalled the details of the significance of stars in this context was also striking.

All the above forms of identification relate to a final distinction which I have used to frame the sequence of the quotations: identification based on difference and identification based on similarity. The early categories of identification concern processes where the differences between the star and the spectator produce the sources of pleasure and fascination. The representations of these processes tended to emphasise the presence of the star and de-emphasise the identity of the spectator. The later categories concern processes where the similarity between stars and spectators, or at least the possibility of closing the gap produced by the differences, is the source of pleasure expressed. In these examples the reproduction of the spectators' identities tended to be the focus of the commentary. Thus identifications do not merely involve processes based on similarity, but also involve the productive recognition of differences between femininities.

Indeed, the processes of identification articulated most strongly in terms of difference seem to be those relating more directly to the cinematic context where the image of the star is still present on the screen. The processes, and practices, which involve reproducing similarity seem to be those extra-cinematic identifications which take place in the spectator's more familiar domestic context, where the star's identity is selectively reworked and incorporated into the spectator's new identity. Even in these cases, identification involves not simply the passive reproduction of exist-ing femininities, but rather an active engagement and production of chang-ing identities.

The assumption behind much of the psychoanalytic work discussed earlier is that identification fixes identities: 'identification can only be made through recognition, and all recognition is itself an implicit confirmation of existing form' (Friedberg, 1982: 53). Many of the examples I have dis-cussed contradict this assumption and demonstrate not only the diversity of existing forms, but also that identification involves the production of desired identities, rather than simply the confirmation of existing ones. Many forms of identification involve processes of transformation and production of new identities, combining the spectator's existing identity with her desired identity and her reading of the star's identity.

Furthermore, Friedberg's critique is symptomatic of the psychoanalytic attack on identity itself typical of some feminist film theory. Any cultural process which is productive of identities is seen as confirming the fixed place of the subject within discourse and thus reinforcing dominant culture; it further offers the subject the pleasure of illusory unity, it is claimed. The implied corollary of this is the claim that cultural forms which fragment and deny identity are necessarily radical and transgressive of bourgeois, patriarchal norms. However, this research challenges the assumption that identification is necessarily problematic because it offers the spectator the illusory pleasure of unified subjectivity. The identifications represented in these examples speak as much about partial recognitions and fragmented replications as they do about the misrecognition of a unified subjectivity in an ego ideal on the screen. Thus, the cultural consumption of Hollywood stars does not necessarily fix identities, destroy differences and confirm sameness.

Identificatory and ideal love

One of the central arguments in this analysis of cinematic identification is that there is a complexity of relationships between stars and spectators, between self images and screen images, and between identification and desire, which cannot be accounted for within many of the existing frame-works of feminist film theory. As I argue in Chapter 2, in much of this work there is a misplaced assumption that 'desire' in the cinema can be straight-forwardly conceptualised within the psychoanalytic model of 'erotic object choice' and, as such, is necessarily the opposite to 'identification'. Within this framework, 'desire' involves wanting to 'have' and identification in-volves wanting to 'be'.

What I hope to have shown in this chapter, and indeed throughout this book, is that the spectator/star relationship significantly concerns forms of *intimacy between femininities*. These forms of intimacy are not direct

172

articulations of 'erotic object choice'; nevertheless, there is an obvious homoeroticism to some of the spectator/star relationships discussed here. The 'love' and 'devotion' which are expressed repeatedly by these respondents do not suggest an overt lesbian desire, but neither can they be described as mere expressions of 'identification' devoid of erotic pleasure. The intensity and the intimacy found in these memories repeatedly strike the reader as signifying more than simply 'the desire to become'. Instead they involve some forms of homoerotic pleasure in which the boundary between self and ideal produces an endless source of fascination. So much feminist film criticism has focused on sexual *difference* as the key cinematic signifier, ignoring the importance of differences between femininities to the meaning of popular cinema for female spectators. Within existing theories of spectatorship there are few possible ways of understanding these forms of fascination between femininities in the cinematic context.

In the final section of this chapter, then, I shall suggest some new directions for the theorisation of these forms of female spectatorship by drawing on Jessica Benjamin's theory of 'identificatory and ideal love' (1990). This needs to be situated briefly before I go on to discuss its relevance to the spectator/star relationship. Using object relations theory,[6] Benjamin develops an argument about identity formation in which she seeks to combine what she calls the 'intrapsychic' – 'the inner world of fantasy, wish, anxiety and defense; of bodily symbols and images whose connections defy the ordinary rules of logic and language' – with the 'intersubjective' – the 'capacities which emerge in the interaction between self and other' (Benjamin, 1990: 20).

Central to the intersubjective theory of identity formation proposed by Benjamin is the concept of *recognition*. The need for recognition, based in early infancy, continues to inform self-perception throughout adult life. Benjamin's theory of recognition extends beyond the pre-oedipal phase of the Lacanian mirror stage, and differs from it further in its emphasis on the exchange between self and external other, rather than the internal (self and imagined self, or self and internalised other) structures of the individual psyche:

> Recognition . . . appears in so many guises that it is seldom grasped as one overarching concept. There are any number of near-synonyms for it: to recognise is to affirm, acknowledge, know, accept, understand, empathize, appreciate, see, identify with, find familiar, love.
>
> (Benjamin, 1990: 12)

Within the concept of recognition Benjamin includes many of the pleasures of spectatorship described by my respondents; identification here is one of the many forms of recognition at work in the constitution of the subject in relation to others involved in the social and cultural processes of cinematic spectatorship.[7]

173

The relationship between stars and spectators involves many of the processes of recognition which Benjamin analyses in her work. In particular, Benjamin introduces the concepts of 'identificatory love' and 'ideal love' which involve the relationship between the self and its ideal. In separating from the mother, the first bond, the child develops an attachment to the father, or rather to the ideal of the father:

> The boy's identificatory love for the father, his wish to be recognised as like him, is the erotic engine behind separation. The boy is in love with his ideal, and through his ideal he begins to see himself as a subject of desire. Through this homoerotic love, he creates his masculine identity and maintains his narcissism in the face of helplessness.
>
> (Benjamin, 1990: 106)

What Benjamin calls identificatory love is the prototype for ideal love, being in love with one's ideal, and underlying both, she argues, is the need for recognition. Ideal love refers to 'a love in which the person seeks to find in the other an ideal image of himself' (Benjamin, 1990: 107). What is crucial here is that the homoeroticism of the self/ideal relationship is central to the processes of identity formation.

Unfortunately, a similar analysis of the place of homoeroticism in the girl's identificatory and ideal love in the development of her feminine identity remains somewhat absent from Benjamin's model. Instead, Benjamin focuses on the father/daughter relationship and offers an account of the girl's desire for identification as thwarted by difference and typically resulting in 'submission' to an ideal in defeated envy and feelings of failure.[8]

If we focus on the development of femininity in relation to the ideals explored in this chapter, however, then a parallel analysis can usefully be developed. These spectator/star relationships all concern the interplay between self and ideal. Such an interplay involves forms of 'identificatory' and 'ideal' love. The spectator in many cases may be described as being 'in love with' her screen ideal. The homoeroticism of such attachments comes across clearly; indeed, it is commented upon by one of the respondents recollecting the intensity of her past passions when she realises how this might appear in a contemporary light.[9] The love of the ideal, then, may express a desire to become more like that ideal, but this does not exclude the homoerotic pleasures of a love for that ideal. Thus, forms of identificatory and ideal love in the spectator/star relationship can be seen to articulate homoerotic desires.

This kind of claim suggests the need to rethink the concept of narcissism. If all object relations contain a form of narcissism (Merck, 1987), then narcissistic love is not to be dismissed as a mere form of reflective self-appreciation. Not only can it be argued that narcissism is part of all object relations, but, furthermore, that narcissism can also be seen as a type of object choice itself. Merle Storr demonstrates how, even within psycho-analytic terms, narcissism does not lack an object choice, but rather is seen as one of the two types of sexual object choice, the other being 'anaclitic' (Storr, 1992). However, as Storr goes on to argue, homoerotic desire between women requires a complete rethinking of these psychoanalytic distinctions. After a thorough assessment of the ways in which psycho-analytic theory has failed to account for same-sex desire between women, Storr criticises psychoanalysis for trying to define it 'in terms of the anaclitic/narcissistic divide at all . . . since it is both, and yet at the same time not really either' (Storr, 1992: 17).

Recognising oneself as different from, yet also as similar to, a feminine ideal other produces the pleasure between femininities which has been referred to as the 'intimacy which is knowledge' (Frith, 1989). Thus, the self and ideal are not collapsed into one, in a narcissistic self-love, but rather there is 'enough difference to create the feeling of reality [so] that a degree of imperfection "ratifies" the existence of the world' (Benjamin, 1990: 47). This difference produces a distance which is desirable both as something to overcome and as something to maintain. As I argue in Chapter 7 the relationship of star and spectator to similarity and difference changes significantly depending on the specific temporal and spatial loca-tions. However, across this specification, the continual negotiation of self and ideal involves the mediation of similarity and difference across the multiple meanings of cinematic desire and identification.

Cinematic identificatory fantasies and practices do indeed contain forms of desire, thus demanding a deconstruction of this dichotomy. Can pro-cesses of spectatorship such as those discussed within the categories of 'devotion' and 'adoration', for example, really be dismissed as devoid of desire? My argument is that cinematic 'identification' does include some forms of desire. However, I am not suggesting the de-eroticisation of 'desire', but rather the eroticisation of some forms of 'identification'.[10] By this I do not mean to suggest that there is never any distinction between desire and identification. Clearly the two processes may be usefully seen as distinct in certain contexts. Rather, my argument is that the insistence upon the rigid dichotomy between these two processes within feminist film criticism has made it very difficult to conceptualise the complexity of spectator/star relationships. My analysis of these respondents' accounts of the cinema introduces processes of spectatorship which require a rethink-ing of the conceptualisation of 'identification' as completely extricable from erotic desire. Whilst desire and identification may be separate pro-cesses in some instances, then, in others, such as the attachment of female spectators to their female star ideals, identification may involve erotic pleasure. Indeed, it is precisely in same-sex relations that the distinction between desire and identification may blur most easily and, moreover, it might be suggested that therein lies their particular appeal.[11]

6

WITH STARS IN THEIR EYES
Female spectators and the paradoxes
of consumption

Since the mid-1980s there has been a definite turn towards the study of consumption within cultural studies. In her critique of much of this work Meaghan Morris challenges the tendency which might lead us to the banal conclusion that: 'people in modern mechanized societies are complex and contradictory; mass cultural texts are complex and contradictory; therefore the people using them produce complex and contradictory culture' (Morris, 1988: 15). Replying to this charge, David Morley argues that the point is to move beyond such banalities to understand 'just *how* "complex" or "contradictory" it is, for *which* types of consumers, in *which* social positions, in relation to *which* types of texts or objects' (Morley, 1991: 3). In order to do this, Morley suggests, what is needed is closer attention to *empirical* details of the 'distinctions' involved in the consumption of culture (see Bourdieu, 1984). Rejecting Morris's argument as 'overly- abstract', Morley argues instead for the usefulness of approaches that return to the broader questions via a 'necessary detour into the detail of domestic consumption' (Morley, 1991: 4).[1]

This chapter considers the ways in which female spectators related to Hollywood stars through consumption in 1940s and 1950s Britain. In an attempt to challenge some of the work which assumes this relationship to be one of totally successful domination, tying women tightly into positions of subordination, I shall argue for a more 'complex and contradictory' model of the female spectator as consumer. Stating this at the outset does not rob the reader of the rewards of the conclusion, nor, hopefully, of the pleasures of argument throughout, precisely because, as Morley points out, such a statement constitutes only the beginning of the necessary investigation of cultural consumption. Indeed, my aim here is to explore some of the questions set out by Morley above in terms of how and why the relationship of female spectators to consumption might be considered complex and contradictory in this specific instance. The central concern of this chapter, then, is how Hollywood stars are connected to the consumption practices of female spectators in the production and reproduction of particular formations of female subjectivity at this time.

Consumption can be a confusing term since it has been used to refer to many different things within sociology, cultural and film studies. Sociological studies have tended to use the term to refer to the purchase and use of commodities, particularly in the domestic sphere; whilst in cultural studies consumption has usually referred to the 'making sense' of cultural texts (generally popular ones) such as adverts, music, television programmes or films which sometimes, but not always, involves commodity purchase. In film studies, where the term consumption has probably been used the least, it has often referred to the place of cinema in consumer culture and the ways in which the film industry promotes the purchase of other commodities. It is this final conceptualisation which I adopt within this chapter. Thus, whilst this whole book could be seen as being about consumption, in the sense of how female spectators consume (make sense or use of) Hollywood images, this chapter extends this broader interest to look specifically at the question of the selection, purchase and use of other commodities.

SPECTACLE AND SPECTATORSHIP: HISTORIES OF FEMININE CONSUMPTION

Hollywood's address to women as consumers, touched upon as an identificatory practice at the end of the previous chapter, needs to be understood within the historical discourses of femininity and consumption more generally. There is a growing body of work on the histories of feminine consumption demonstrating the links between Hollywood and other industries, which offers invaluable commentary on the relationship between women as spectators and consumers of cultural forms and commodities.[2] Before offering a brief outline of their conclusions, however, it is important to draw attention to what kind of history is being evoked in these accounts. What are the objects of its focus and how might this influence its conclusions? Such questions are rarely the subject of discussion within film studies, thus confining these methodological issues to other disciplines whose concerns more easily accommodate them (see Chapter 3). They remain, though, crucial to this study.

The historical accounts of consumption have tended to focus on the developments of capitalist industries in order to chart the ways in which women's roles as consumers have emerged. Thus the focus of much historical analysis has been at the level of production. My study differs from these in focus, source and, possibly, therefore conclusions, since it is consumers' accounts that form the basis of my material. However, to my knowledge, there is very little work on the history of consumption based upon consumer practice. Indeed, in the British context, there is little enough on the history of consumption at all and this is certainly an area warranting further research. What follows is thus a discussion of existing accounts of the convergence of the histories of female consumption with those of spectatorship which are based primarily on the study of the industries.

The feminisation of consumption

It has been argued that women's relationship to consumer culture has been a central one since its emergence (Stuart Ewen, 1976). Towards the end of the nineteenth century, changes in the organisation of capitalism positioned women as key subjects in commodity exchange. As the home increasingly became a place of consumption rather than production, it has been argued, women's role within it was also transformed as they became the managers of consumption (Ewen, 1976). By the time women attended cinemas in the 1940s and 1950s, then, their position as consumers had already been shaped in specific ways through other forms of consumption.

This gendered division of labour in relation to consumption has been investigated by Rachel Bowlby in *Just Looking* (1985). As the processes of commodification developed and there was an intensification in the volume of products and a diversification in the range and types of goods sold in stores, it was women, and not men, who were chiefly responsible for purchasing them. In addition to the responsibility for the purchasing of commodities, middle- and upper-class women were involved in the beautifying of their homes and themselves with 'luxury' products; these practices thus linked consumption to femininity. Bowlby concludes that:

> on both counts – women's purchasing responsibilities and the availability of some of them for extra excursions into luxury – it follows that the organized effort of 'producers' to sell to 'consumers' would, to a large measure, take the form of a masculine appeal to women . . .
>
> . . . the making of willing consumers readily fitted with the available ideological paradigm of a seduction of women by men, in which women would be addressed as yielding objects to the powerful male subject forming, and informing them, of their desires.
>
> (Bowlby, 1985: 19–20)

The emergence of the department store, Bowlby argues, can be seen to mark the beginning of consumer culture, and furthermore the beginning of a particular connection between looking, desiring and buying. Department stores, using new glass technology and electricity to create a space characterised by openness, light and visibility with large expanses of display windows, became the new palaces of consumption offering women the pleasures of escape from dull domesticity. The display of commodities as spectacles, offering the female shopper pleasure in looking, contemplation and the fantasy transformation of the self and her surroundings through consumption thus prefigured similar pleasures to be offered to the female spectator in the cinematic context:

> The transformation of merchandise into a spectacle, in fact, suggests an analogy with an industry that developed fifty years after the first department stores: the cinema. In this case, the pleasure of looking, *just* looking, is itself the commodity for which money is paid.
>
> (Bowlby, 1985: 6)

The cinema screen as shop window

The fact that the cinema developed in the first half of this century as an integral part of the expansion of consumer capitalism is thus not insignificant in understanding the construction of cinema spectators as consumers. The cinema screen has thus been likened to a 'display window . . . occupied by marvellous mannequins' (Eckert, 1978: 4), in which goods and stars are on display to spectators as desirable spectacles. The luxury and abundance of cinemas from the 1930s onwards (discussed in Chapter 4) provides the context for the consumption not only of Hollywood films, but also of the luxury items on display in them. Hollywood cinema, Eckert argues, acted as a showcase for fashions, accessories, cosmetics, furnishings and other manufactured items to American and many other foreign markets:

> at the turn of the century Hollywood possessed one clothing manufacturer (of shirts) and none of furniture; by 1937 the Associated Apparel Manufacturers of Los Angeles listed 130 members, and the Los Angeles Furniture Manufacturers Association listed 150, with an additional 330 exhibitors. Furthermore, 250 of the largest American department stores kept buyers permanently in Los Angeles.
>
> (Eckert, 1978: 7)

In a radio broadcast in 1930 the commercial value of Hollywood as a consumer showcase was boasted of by Will Hays, whom Eckert refers to as 'the most prominent spokesman for celluloid imperialism' (Eckert, 1978: 5). Hays announces proudly:

> Motion pictures perform a service to American business which is greater than the millions in our direct purchases, greater than our buildings. . . . The industry is a new factor in American economic life and gives us solid basis of hope for the future by creating an increased demand for our products. The motion picture carries to every American at home, and to millions of potential purchasers abroad,

179

the visual, vivid perception of American manufactured products.

(Eckert, 1978: 5)

In exchange for the national, and later international, display of commodities to vast cinema audiences, Hollywood studios frequently received free props. Films included scenes which facilitated such display, such as DeMille's bedroom and bathroom scenes, and the exhibition of the latest feminine fashions in films such as *Cover Girl* (1944, Charles Vidor) in which the models on magazine covers 'come to life' and perform a kind of fashion show for the female spectator in the cinema.

According to Allen (1980), women were seen as a key target for Hollywood commodities, including films, magazines and annuals, through their obsessions with film stars and fascination with their looks, lifestyles and romances, and clothes. Thus they were targeted by Hollywood industries, and also by other industries through the cinema. Cinema chains were built near shopping areas, and the matinée screenings encouraged women to combine shopping with a visit to the cinema.[3] The cinema shaped consumer habits through the influence of sets, costumes and images of Hollywood in fan magazines. For example:

> Features, like a forecast of spring fashions designed exclusively for Paramount Pictographs and a description of the way in which fashionable women derive ideas for interior decoration by copying sets presented in films, linked a tradition of imitating theatrical stars to their cinematic descendants.

(Allen, 1980: 487)

The display of the female star as commodity, as well as with other commodities, is important here in understanding the particular address of films to women as consumers:

> Such exposure of properties was frequently tied to a similar exposure of a woman's body as model or property itself. The bold vamp replaced the demure virgin in scenarios that tied the loosening of sexual mores to glamorous consumer styles. Ritualistic moments of narrative stasis permitted voyeuristic access to women bathing and sleeping in the midst of luxurious surroundings.

(Allen, 1980: 488–9)

Press Books were prepared by the studio's publicity department and sent to cinema exhibitors with advice and information on how to market the film as a commodity, and frequently used other commodities in their marketing suggestions. Importantly, the key industries involved in tie-ins were those aimed mainly at female consumers such as cosmetics, fashion, domestic appliances and interior furnishings (Eckert, 1978).

Now Voyager (1942, Irving Rapper), for example, as Maria La Place has demonstrated, was packaged as a woman's film which offered the female spectator not only the pleasures of looking at its 'beautiful clothes, glamorous stars, and romantic locales – but also [of fulfilling] their function as consumers' (La Place, 1987: 142). In the *Now Voyager* Press Book, suggestions for publicity included features with headlines such as 'Bette Shows How Not To Be Glamorous in New Film', and photographs accompanied by 'Proper Coiffure is Key to Beauty Success' (La Place, 1987: 141). It is suggested that the film as a commodity should be tied in with local businesses:

> Window displays in shops catering to femme clientele should be a must in your campaign: Clothing Shops: special windows showing travelling ensembles and accessories – Banner line, 'Now Voyager, Buy Wisely . . . Now!' Beauty Shops: for window displays and newspaper ad, 'Now Voyager, Sail Thou Forth to Seek and Find . . . Beauty'.
>
> (Quoted in La Place, 1987: 142)

Now Voyager concerns the transformation of a 'dowdy, plump spinster' into an 'elegant and sophisticated heroine', and would therefore lend itself to commercial connections with fashion and cosmetic industries. Women audiences were encouraged to see such films just to view the costumes of the female stars. However, it was not only films which accommodated such moments of product display that were linked to wider commodity circulation; Jane Gaines (1989) has documented the commodity tie-ins in conjunction with *Queen Christina* (1933, Mamoulian). This may seem unlikely, as Gaines herself points out: 'how easily does a film about a 17th-century monarch who wears trousers translate into retail merchandising ideas? What is the logic in producing a line of women's fashions to co-ordinate with a film featuring a star who reputedly hated clothes?' (*ibid.*: 38). Yet Gaines goes on to analyse the 'dissemination of a visual aesthetic, its spread from screen to department store display, its tapering off from bold, arrogant design and combative statement to trendy accent, and its "comeback" as camp' (*ibid.*: 38).

By the 1940s, then, the links between the cinema and other industries, especially fashion and cosmetics, were already highly developed (Doane, 1989a; Gaines, 1989). Hollywood stars were linked to women's fashions in a number of ways. In attempting to militate against the perishability of stars by turning them into a cultural phenomenon (Gaines, 1989: 38), the star fashion tie-in was particularly significant. This exchange between motion picture advertisers and fashion retailers produced a mutually profitable connection whose sales advantage is difficult to ascribe to one or other of the industries. The cinema provided display windows for women's fashions, and manufacturers and retailers of women's clothing 'transformed ready-to-wear clothes into star imagery' (Gaines, 1989: 38; see also Gaines and Herzog, 1990).

Hollywood's influence on the cosmetics industry was considerable, and has been documented by Eckert in his work on Hollywood cinema and commodity tie-ins. Hollywood's Max Factor and Perc Westmore were two large cosmetics companies amongst many others, but, Eckert argues, Hollywood seemed to dominate the cosmetics industry 'because its stars appeared in the hundreds of thousands of ads that saturated the media' and the tie-ins between the films, the stars, the fashion articles and the advertisements produced a formidable 'cycle of influence' (Eckert, 1978: 9–10).

Fashion and cosmetics industries in particular, then, developed close connections with female stars in Hollywood: star styles displayed on the screen were quickly reproduced as a line of clothing in department stores, and the establishment of commodity 'tie-ins' with brand manufacturers offered a mutually beneficial system of advertising and promotion of products, of both stars and other commodities: 'One store employed uniformed Roxy ushers as its floor managers. Another advertised for sales girls that looked like Jane Gaynor' (Eckert, 1978: 8).

Fashion manufacturers and wholesalers secured copyright of Hollywood styles and opened exclusive stores in Los Angeles in the late 1920s: 'twelve cloak and suit manufacturers banded together to form Hollywood Fashion Associates. In addition, the Associated Apparel Manufacturers began to co-ordinate and give national promotion to dozens of style lines' (Eckert, 1978: 7). Female stars served as mannequins in publicity for new fashions and the sale of these fashions was boosted by the appearance of these photos in magazines such as Sunday supplements and film fan magazines, for example *Hollywood*, *Picture Play*, *Photoplay* and many others. The female readers of these magazines were thus addressed simultaneously as consumers and spectators: 'in a 1934 *Shadowplay* caption for a dress modeled by Anita Louise: "You will see the dress in action in Warner's *First Lady*". Occasionally one was informed that the fashions were "on display in leading department stores and ready-to-wear stores this month"' (*ibid.*: 9).

The use of commodities in Hollywood film, or in their advertising and promotion of a film, then, highlights the links between spectatorship and consumption very clearly. Studios displayed particular brand name commodities in films themselves, or used commodities to promote or advertise the film.

> After a long soak in a bubble bath (Lux), she prepared herself to meet the critical stares of Fifth Avenue. She applied successive coats of cleansing (Ponds), lubrication (Jergens), and foundation creams (Richard Hudnut) . . .
>
> Stepping out of her dressing gown she lightly dusted herself with a body powder (Luxor). Then following a hint from Edith Head, taped her ever-so-slightly too large breasts so that they were separated as

widely as possibly. A Formfit bra, Undikins, a Bonnie Bright Frock (the Frances Dee model from *Of Human Bondage*, RKO 1934), silk stockings (Humming Bird) and a pair of Nada White Buck shoes (Enna Jettick) completed her outfit. Donning her Wittnauer watch ('Watches of the Stars') and a simple necklace (the Tecla worn by Barbara Stanwyck in *Gambling Lady*, Warner's 1934), she picked up her metallic-sheen purse and left.

(Eckert, 1978: 10–11)

Such is Charles Eckert's playful description of the ideal consumer as conceptualised by those selling Hollywood stars and their associated commodities in America in the 1930s.

Some commodity tie-ins were not specifically concerned with feminine attractiveness or even the beautification of the home. Cars, office furniture, watches and so on were also displayed in the Hollywood showcase. However, as Eckert argues, women made 80 to 90 per cent of all purchases for family use, and thus female spectators were addressed as consumers, even in the cases where the products were not associated with femininity.

Femininity and consumption have thus been historically linked in the cinematic context, it has been argued, through a chain of commodification in which at least three distinct, but interrelated, instances can be isolated: the commodification of the female image; the use of commodity tie-ins in Hollywood cinema (the display of products in films and of stars in advertisements); and the purchase of films as a commodity, 'promoting a certain mode of perception which is fully adequate to a consumer society' (Doane, 1989a: 25). The female spectator is thus a consumer of idealised images of femininity on the screen, and is also invited to recognise herself in that commodified image which she may be able to recreate through the consumption of particular goods. Thus, according to Doane, by consuming (commodities, and female stars as commodities), she prepares for her own consumption.

These accounts of the historical construction of the female spectator as consumer demonstrate the connections between the cinema and other industries. In particular they foreground the ways in which the cinema spectator has been addressed as a consumer of particular commodities; since consumption has been considered the responsibility of women, it could be argued that there has been a feminisation of the cinema spectator, an argument which contradicts the notion of the 'masculinised' spectator discussed in Chapter 2. However, the production of such subject positions for the female consumer does not necessarily contradict the objectification of woman on the cinema screen for the pleasures of the male gaze. Indeed, to pursue Doane's argument briefly, these two processes may be more compatible than is at first apparent.

183

THE FEMALE SPECTATOR AS CONSUMER:
SUBJECTIVITY AS SUBJECTION?

In our social order, women are 'products' used and exchanged by men. Their status is that of merchandise, 'commodities'. . . . So women have to remain an 'infrastructure' unrecognized as such by our society and our culture. The use, consumption, and circulation of their sexualized bodies underwrite the organization and reproduction of the social order, in which they have never taken part as 'subjects'.

(Irigaray, 1985: 84)

Women's relationship to commodities has frequently been conceptualised in terms of their being the objects, and not the subjects, of exchange (Doane, 1989a). The analysis of women as commodities of exchange within patriarchal culture, of their 'being' rather than 'having' commodities, has been developed within feminist film theory in terms of the specific processes of objectification, fetishisation and display of the female body as sexual spectacle within Hollywood cinema (Mulvey, 1989).

The simultaneous positioning of women as subjects and objects of consumption took a specific form in relation to female spectatorship and Hollywood cinema in the 1940s. In a rather Foucauldian reading of women's relationship to image consumption, Doane argues that the very discourses through which female subjectivity is constructed tie women in even more tightly to forms of subjection.[4] Despite their roles as subjects, Doane argues that:

the woman's ability to purchase, her subjectivity as a consumer, is qualified by a relation to commodities which is also ultimately subordinated to that intensification of the affective value of sexual relations which underpins a patriarchal society.

(Doane, 1989a: 24)

Thus the fact that women are both the objects and subjects of commodity exchange is only *apparently* contradictory. The forms of female subjectivity produced through consumption simultaneously reproduce forms of female subjection within patriarchal culture. Thus Doane concludes:

The feminine position has come to exemplify the roles of consumer and spectator in their embodiment of a curiously passive desiring subjectivity. . . . In her desire to bring the things of the screen closer, to approximate the bodily image of the star and to possess the space in which she dwells, the female spectator experiences the intensity of the image as lure and exemplifies the perception proper to the consumer. The cinematic image for the woman is both shop window and mirror, the one simply a means of access to the other. The mirror/window, then, takes on the aspect of *the trap whereby her*

184

subjectivity becomes synonymous with her objectification. . . . The female subject of the consumer look in the cinematic arena becomes, through a series of mediations, the industry's own merchandizing asset. One must ask at this point, 'Whose gaze is ultimately addressed?' and 'Who profits?'

(Doane, 1989a: 31–2, my emphasis)

This reading of the female spectator's relationship to consumption suggests that popular cinema represents the ultimate site of women's subordination. The combination of the spectator/consumer role for women traps them into a hopeless position of passivity in which even their role as subjects in consumer society is ultimately subsumed by the inevitable processes of objectification: commodities are purchased in order to produce the self as object of the male gaze. The female spectator prepares to be 'consumed' herself in the processes of consuming cultural commodities (stars and other products). The cinema might thus be seen as the physical and imaginative space serving the needs both of heterosexual masculine desire and of consumer capitalism.

The problem with such a conclusion, in which women are tied into these mutually reinforcing relations of powerlessness, is that it robs women of any agency in the reproduction of culture, and may even contribute to dominant notions of female passivity. What hope is left for change, for diversity or for resistance in this rather monolithic and functionalist account of female consumption and Hollywood cinema? After all, forms of control and subjection are never fully successful, otherwise none of us would be writing about them.

It is the question of the *inseparability* of subjectivity from objectification that I wish to challenge in the light of my own research. I argue that whilst Doane may have successfully identified the meaning of femininity within cultural production, this is not synonymous with the uses and meanings of commodities to *consumers*. Following existing cultural studies work on consumption I shall suggest that women are subjects, as well as objects of cultural exchange, in ways that are not entirely reducible to subjection (Winship, 1981; Partington, 1990; Nava, 1992).

In contrast to Doane's position, this work emphasises women's agency as consumers and highlights the contradictions of consumption for women. Although this work does not deal directly with consumers' accounts of consumption, it does open up questions of women's active role as agents of consumption in postwar Britain. These historical accounts suggest that such roles are not completely subsumed within the dominant discourses of production.

Women's place as subjects of consumer discourses has been emphasised in Janice Winship's work on the importance of modes of consumer address to women's 'individuality' in postwar Britain. She offers an important

185

analysis of the ways in which consumption in the 1950s and 1960s constructed women as individuals through particular modes of address. What is crucial here is the sense of agency produced by such discourses. Through, what Winship calls, the 'work' of femininity, women were addressed as individuals and encouraged to reproduce their 'individuality' through the consumption of clothes, make-up and household goods:

> The ideological construction of 'individuality' for women through consumption and the *work* of femininity was, at one and the same time a move towards *independence* from men and, in its display in an ultimately feminine mould, a repetition of traditional dependence on, and subordination to, men.
>   . . . women's involvement in the process of consumption . . . has ideologically constructed them as 'individuals' . . . however woman is a feminine individual whose individuality and implied independence are only *in part* recuperated by patriarchal relations.
>
> (Winship, 1981: 2, 10, my emphasis)

For Winship, then, there is something 'in excess' of patriarchal control which is produced through the discourses of consumption at this time. Thus, the needs of patriarchy and of capitalism may be seen to be in conflict, rather than working harmoniously to further control women.

> For woman her individuality is, then, subjected to femininity and patriarchal relations . . . and yet . . . paradoxically, even such an oppressive construction – as it was articulated through an ideology of consumption in the 50's and 60's – potentially contributed to foundations for a *political* move forwards for women, and didn't just constitute a mere shift in ideological gear.
>
> (Winship, 1981: 36)

Whilst acknowledging the double bind of consumption for women, Winship argues that the new forms of femininity produced by the expansion in consumption during the 1950s had consequences which extended beyond their own objectification and, importantly, beyond the sphere of consumption itself.

Another challenge to the passive construction of women as consumers evidenced in much feminist film criticism discussed above has been the analysis of women's use and appropriation of commodities. Following Miller (1987) and Bourdieu (1984), Angela Partington offers an analysis of women's consumer competences, skills and knowledges in 1950s Britain. She argues that:

> The practices (skills and rituals of consumption) which produce culture have consequences which are heterogenous and open to contestation.
>
> (Partington, 1990: 180)

186

Challenging the privileging of the film text within film studies, Partington argues that the analysis of spectator/consumer competences, rather than the expressive meaning of film, leads to very different conclusions about women's consumption of popular culture. Her argument highlights the discrepancy between professional and commercial discourses of consumption and women's own consumption practices. According to Partington, professional discourses attempted to confine working-class women's consumption practices to the realm of economic necessity, function, practicality and utility, separate from the decoration, display, excess and form that defined middle-class femininity.

Looking at consumption as the site of both self-fulfilment and regulation, Partington argues that the exercise of state and professional surveillance and legislation over consumption practices conflicted with the libidinisation of objects and the encouragement of expression through commodity purchase:

> the marketing industries' incitement to 'look' (e.g. advertising and retailing) may sometimes (though not always) tend towards libidinization (encouraging the consumer to identify with objects), and the cultural leadership's incitement to look (e.g. in the promotion of 'good design') tend towards regulation (discouraging identification).
>
> (Partington, 1990: 5)

Through an analysis of three case studies of consumer culture in 1950s Britain (homemaking, fashion and Hollywood melodrama) Partington demonstrates how working-class women 'disavowed economic necessity (as defined by professionals and experts) through a "sampling" and mixing of the functionalist and decorative, thereby insisting on relating to objects in a way that the professional élites attempted to monopolise' (Partington, 1990: 179). Thus by looking at consumer competences, Partington is able to see consumption practices as acts of appropriation: 'working-class women refused to separate the pleasures of efficiency from the purely aesthetic, therefore their consumption of goods constituted an act of appropriation' (*ibid.*: 177).

Neither Winship nor Partington denies the power of hegemonic forces in the definition of woman's role as consumer. Unlike Doane, however, they do not assume such forces to be totally successful. Both are more useful models for my analysis of female spectatorship and consumption because they address the ways in which consumption is a site of negotiated meanings, of resistance and of appropriation as well as of subjection and exploitation. Such work, however, falls short of offering an analysis of consumers' accounts of such processes. There continues to be very little historical evidence of what sense consumers made of different commodities, based on *their* accounts of their practices.

187

STUDYING CONSUMPTION:
FROM PRODUCERS TO CONSUMERS

In film studies much of the work on consumption has retained a focus on production (Eckert, 1978; Allen, 1980; Doane, 1989a). Whilst importantly broadening the focus of textually dominated film studies (see Chapter 2) to include an analysis of the cinema in relation to other industries, film studies work on consumption has tended to perpetuate a very narrow, production-led approach to the subject. Following previous Marxist analyses of consumption (such as Ewen, 1976), much of the work that looks at Hollywood cinema in terms of consumption takes as its object of study the ways in which the film industry produces cinema spectators as consumers of both the film and the products of other industries. It is with this approach and its conclusions that I aim to take issue in the rest of this chapter. I shall argue that because of their exclusive focus on production, such studies fail to address the question of what consumption means to consumers. Indeed the consequence of this exclusivity has often been misleadingly pessimistic conclusions about the powerlessness of consumers and the success of producers. This is not to deny that Hollywood is tied to other industries through a profit motive, and that to satisfy this spectators are addressed as consumers and need to be convinced to purchase certain commodities; certainly such claims will be reinforced in part by women's memories of consumption in this study. However, this is only half the story. By analysing what consumption means to consumers it is possible to highlight the differences between the discourses of production and the meanings of commodities in people's lives. My analysis thus deals with precisely the 'complexities and contradictions' of these relationships so often ignored by the 'production studies'.

To find substantial consideration of what consumption means to consumers rather than producers it is necessary to turn to some anthropological and sociological literature (see Miller, 1987; Campbell, 1987; and Bourdieu, 1984). This work moves beyond the economic to analyse what goods, tastes or material culture might mean to the people selecting, buying and using them. In contrast to the Marxist account of the successful manipulation of consumer needs by capitalist industry, for example, Colin Campbell's account of modern consumerism and its relationship to the 'Romantic ethic' (Campbell, 1987) argues for the notion of the 'active consumer' and the relative autonomy of the sphere of consumption which cannot be simply read off from production. Bourdieu's influential work (Bordieu, 1984) details the classificatory devices through which cultural tastes and judgements are produced. Although connected to education and occupation, the notion of 'cultural capital', used by Bourdieu to explain distinctions made between cultural objects by consumers, extends beyond the purely economic to include the symbolic meaning of commodities in

188

people's lives. He argues that distinctions in aesthetic taste define different groups' relationships to cultural commodities.[5]

Daniel Miller's study of material culture and mass consumption (Miller, 1987) continues the investigation of consumer goods beyond their economic function for capital, analysing them instead in terms of their cultural significance for consumers. Highlighting the significance of the materiality of cultural artefacts, so often ignored in cultural theory, Miller analyses the specific appropriation of objects by consumers in terms of creating identities, affiliations and 'lived everyday culture'. Reworking the much criticised process of 'objectification' through a more positive (Hegelian) lens, Miller argues for a re-evaluation of people's appropriation of mass goods through consumption.

The importance of mentioning these studies here is to introduce briefly the ways in which consumption might be theorised in relation to the consumers rather than the producers of culture. A detailed consideration of their strengths and weaknesses would constitute a major detour, since it is necessary to move on to consider my research material in more detail. However their inclusion is significant in terms of suggesting possible avenues for the exploration of the meanings that consumers, rather than producers, give to consumption.

Significantly, and not unusually, gender is rarely mentioned in the above studies of cultural consumption. My argument concerns the specificity of gendered forms of consumption in relation to Hollywood cinema. Femininity is constructed within a very particular set of paradoxes within discourses of consumption – the feminine subject being the object of cultural consumption. By drawing on female spectators' memories of Hollywood stars in the 1940s and 1950s, this chapter continues the investigation of the meanings of consumption to a particular group of consumers. My research aims to extend and rethink the conclusions of much work on the female cinema spectator as a consumer which approaches the subject at the level of production (Eckert, 1978; Allen, 1980; Doane, 1989a). My aim is not to refute their conclusions completely, since such studies have produced important critiques of the femininity and consumer culture. They have also provided the only available *historical* accounts of the female spectator of Hollywood cinema as consumer; they are thus drawn upon in order to analyse the historical dimensions of Hollywood cinema and consumption. However, in addition to these accounts I shall consider the material I received from respondents in this study which do indeed complicate the picture by highlighting women's active agency in the consumption process. Thus, I shall argue both that female spectators are successfully constructed as consumers by Hollywood cinema *and* that they also used commodities connected with stars in ways that do not conform to the needs of the market (both in its marital and in its economic senses).

189

SHARED INVESTMENTS

An analysis of female spectators' memories of Hollywood stars in 1940s and 1950s Britain demonstrates the significance of the discourse of consumption to the spectator/star relationship. In addition to escapism and identification (discussed in the previous two chapters), consumption appeared frequently in spectators' accounts of their attachments to Hollywood stars at this time. That female spectators and film stars were closely connected through commodity purchase, then, can be established through the study of *both* commodity production and consumption. But the question here is what conclusions can be drawn from such connections. How do female spectators remember the significance of consumption practices and how might their accounts highlight a more contradictory relationship between spectatorship and consumption than that presented by the production studies? Did consumption simply tie women more tightly into forms of subordination, and if so, what is to be made of their pleasure and delight in such cultural practices?

In this section I examine spectators' memories of their consumption practices in terms of the importance of feminine cultural competence. The knowledge and expertise involved in such competence forms the basis of intense bonding with, and emotional, as well as financial, investment in, particular stars. In addition, connections between female spectators are formed through such shared knowledges and the use to which they may be put.

> I favoured Lauren Bacall most of all during the 1940s and 1950s and still have an interest in her. . . . My colouring was the same as hers, I wore my hair in a similar style and wore the same type of tailored clothes. In the early 1940s . . . matching shoes, gloves and handbag were a 'must'. I remember Lauren Bacall always kept to this unwritten rule, and I identified with her because of that, they were my 'trademark' for years. It was surprising how quickly fashions from the films caught on. In *To Have and Have Not* Lauren Bacall wore a dogtooth check suit and small round pill-box hat, black gloves and shoes and handbag – I can remember I had one very similar with a tan pill-box . . . and my hair in a page-boy like hers. The only difference was that she wore hers without a blouse.
>
> (Kathleen Lucas)

Here Lauren Bacall is written about within the language of product selection: she was 'favoured' above others. She is also appreciated for her enduring value: 'I still have an interest in her'. In turn, the female spectator, through her identification with the star, becomes a product herself, using the language of commodities to describe what characterised her particular personal style: her 'trademark' was the same as Lauren Bacall's

Figure 6.1 'In *To Have and Have Not* Lauren Bacall wore a dogtooth check suit . . . I can remember I had one very similar . . . and my hair in a page-boy like hers.'

in that they both shared the knowledge that matching shoes, gloves and handbags were a 'must'. Interestingly, the term 'trademark' is set in inverted commas by the respondent, as if to suggest a self-awareness, even irony, about this process of self-commodification: it is inappropriate for a woman to have a trademark, since this usually signifies a commodity, and yet it captures very well that production of self as image that is being described here.

The star is selected because of a recognition of resemblance with the spectator (Lauren Bacall had similar colouring); thus star selection involves female spectators looking for themselves (in every sense) in their star ideals. However, differences are also remembered as significant: the style and pattern of the suit is a mimetic representation, but the colour of the hat is different and Bacall's lack of blouse was obviously striking enough to be remembered. The more sexualised star is significant both in terms of national difference and in terms of the licence of Hollywood stars to present a more sexualised image than would have been acceptable for most women in 1940s Britain. Despite this difference, however, there is a strong memory of recognition and similarity. Indeed, this particular example suggests the importance of a shared feminine culture during this period based upon knowledge, expertise and 'unwritten rules'. The shared recognition in the conventions of feminine appearance produce the basis for pleasure and appreciation for this female spectator: 'I remember Lauren Bacall always kept to this unwritten rule, and I identified with her because of that'. Consumer taste, linking star and spectator, is based upon the recognition of shared feminine expertise, invisible to the 'outsider' since these rules are felt to be 'unwritten'.

Female spectators remember Hollywood stars through their connection with particular commodities and the ways in which they were worn or displayed. Typically, this association is made in relation to clothes, hairstyles, make-up and cosmetics, and other fashion accessories. It is the commodities associated with physical attractiveness and appearance that are especially remembered in connection with female stars: clothes and accessories in this case, as in most others.

The speed with which the images on the screen become images 'on the streets' is commented upon here: replications of outfits and styles are remembered as taking place swiftly after the viewing of a particular film. Another respondent offers a similar account of purchasing an outfit to copy a star after seeing a particular film:

> and I bought clothes like hers [Doris Day] . . . dresses, soft wool, no sleeves, but short jackets, boxey type little hats, half hats we used to call them and low heeled court shoes to match your outfit, kitten heels they were called . . . as people said I looked like her [Marilyn

Figure 6.2 'Doris Day was a natural star to me, when she did anything it was always 100% – everything about her is perfect, the clothes she wore and everything.'

Monroe]. I even bought a suit after seeing her in *Niagara*.

(Patricia Ogden)

The detail of the memory of particular fashions and how stars wore them in films is part of the specificity of feminine cultural competence: the colours,

193

patterns, cut and design of clothes remains a vivid memory some fifty years later. This attests to the significance of this connection for female spectators and demonstrates the intensity of their emotional, as well as financial, investments in such details of personal appearance. Pride in having an eye for detail and the ability to recall it so many years later is expressed in the following example:

> The female stars of my major film going period made a big impact on me. I can see a short clip from a film and know instantly whether I've seen it before or not – and as like or not, be able to add – 'then she moves off down the staircase' or 'the next dress she appears in is white, with puffy net sleeves'.
>
> (M. Palin)

The extraordinarily vivid memories here demonstrate the intense emotional investment in Hollywood at this time. This intensity may be because of the heightened emotional investment many young women make in feminine ideals and thus is explicable in terms of life stages. This might also be reinforced by the process of looking back and reminiscing about youthful pleasures and thus be explained in terms of nostalgia (see Chapter 3). Finally, this intensity could also be due to the feelings of recognition of the significance of Hollywood stars in the lives of respondents, after many years of little external recognition and indeed, in many cases even ridicule for their fandom.

It is worth pausing for a moment to reflect upon the forms of memory used by female spectators here. In Chapter 3 I introduced the concept of iconic memory to refer to the 'frozen moment' as a form of memory. Iconic memory can be seen here to be connected to the reconstruction of the star image through a knowledge of the details of her appearance. Indeed, iconic memories of female stars, extracted from the narrative action, depend upon detail for their reconstruction of past images. Such knowledge constitutes the shared cultural competence of female spectators and connects them to each other and to their favourite female stars. The centrality of 'being an image' to definitions of femininity is thus manifest in the forms of memory employed here.

What is striking about the two examples given by M. Palin (above) is the way in which the memories selected both, though in different ways, focus on particular icons of femininity. The woman descending the staircase is an image from Hollywood in which female stars are typically displayed to onlookers below, and to cinema spectators, often at moments in the film when their costumes are of crucial significance. This female icon is also significant to another respondent quoted elsewhere who remembered replicating such movement after the film screening: 'Our favourite cinema was the Ritz – with its deep pile carpet and double sweeping staircase. Coming down one always felt like a heroine descending into the ballroom' (Anon).

The second image selected to exemplify the endurance of this particular respondent's memory also draws upon a particular feminine iconography: the whiteness of the dress signifies purity and virginity, the puffy sleeves an abundance of material and the net material a semi-transparency to display the female body.

Although these examples do establish a clear link between formations of female subjectivity and processes of self-commodification through consumption, they also demonstrate that this is by no means the only significance of consumption practices to female spectatorship. Within the world of female knowledge and expertise, consumption also importantly involved processes of (mutual) recognition between spectators, and between them and their favourite stars, and a passionate connection to feminine ideals. Thus although the end product of such emotional and financial investments in ideal and self image may be the patriarchal institution of marriage, it is important not to deny the intense pleasure and delight in forms of feminine culture reproduced between female spectators and stars in the process.

'THE INTIMACY WHICH IS KNOWLEDGE'[6]

There are important forms of intimacy involved in these shared feminine identities, between spectator and star ideal, and between female spectators. The recognition of shared knowledge forms the basis for such intimacy between femininities which has tended to be ignored in existing accounts of feminine consumption.

Hollywood stars in the 1940s and 1950s were strongly remembered by female spectators for their connection with fashion, and many stars became favourites because of this association:

> The Doris Day films I used to watch mainly for the clothes – she was always dressed in the latest fashions.
>
> (Mrs D. Delves)

> The clothes and the make-up were of great interest. Bear in mind 'teenagers' had not been invented in the late 1940s, so clothes were not on the market for that age group. We seemed to go from school children to grown-ups. The fashion scene was nothing like today's mass market. We had a few outfitters and the chainstores. What was worn on the screen was of importance.
>
> (Anon)

> I loved the cool charm of stars such as Deborah Kerr . . . my childhood dream was to become like her and I used to spend hours shop window gazing and selecting what she would wear.
>
> (Judith Ford)

In these statements the role of film stars as fashion models, advertising the

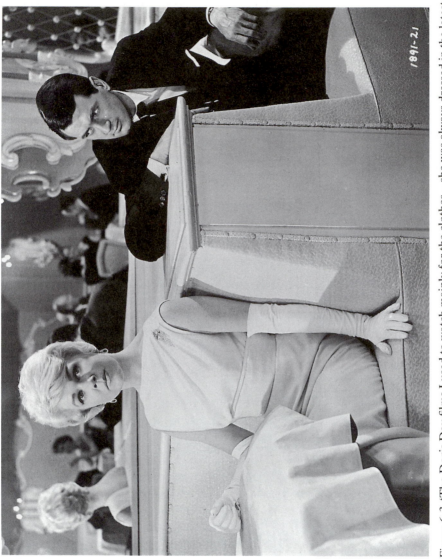

Figure 6.3 'The Doris Day films I used to watch mainly for the clothes – she was always dressed in the latest fashions.' (Seen here in *Pillow Talk*.)

latest styles to female spectators, comes across clearly. In the first example, a particular star is appreciated for her up-to-date clothes in her films. The selection of Doris Day in this role occurred frequently amongst respondents: 'Doris Day was a natural star to me, when she did anything it was always 100% – everything about her is perfect, the clothes she wore and everything' (Shirley Thompson). Clothes and fashion are central here to the attainment of feminine ideals: 'clothes and everything' could be read here as clothes are everything; if you can get them right your femininity is established. There is a delight expressed here in the star who always 'got it right' which again exemplifies a shared cultural competence. Consumer taste is thus based upon forms of recognition between women which constitute a shared cultural competence (see Bourdieu, 1984).

The second example highlights the importance of 'what was worn on the screen' in relation to the transition to adult femininity. Hollywood film stars seemed to play a key role in this rather nerve-wracking and treacherous journey, typically full of potential pitfalls and failures. Transition from childhood to adult femininity is signified through the transformation of the body and how it is clothed and presented. Given the centrality of physical appearance to cultural definitions of femininity, the stakes are high in this process of transformation. Film stars, representing cultural ideals of feminine beauty and charm, played a key role in these processes of identity formation. This memory draws attention to the contrast between contemporary consumer markets and those of the 1940s and 1950s. The significance of stars to spectators' knowledge of consumer fashion is reconstructed as particularly focused in the light of the expansion and diversification of fashion markets since that time.

In the final example, the spectator takes on the imaginary position of her favourite star in relation to consumption of female attire. The spectator's own identity is replaced through her imaginary identification with her ideal. This replacement of self with ideal subject position is effected through the fantasy of consumption; thus the spectator and star are linked, not through the purchasing of clothes, but through the gazing and desiring of the female spectator/consumer who imagines her ideal's choice of commodities. Cinema screen and shop window both display their spectacles: respectively, the female star and her imaginary outfits. Hollywood stars are thus linked to other commodities by the desiring female spectator/consumer who fantasises an ideal feminine self-image through imaginary consumption. The desire to clothe your favourite star, to predict her taste and style and to imagine her in the outfit of your choice suggests an intense intimacy between female spectators and stars. Indeed, it further points to a recognition of 'self-in-ideal' in being able to predict what the star would consume.

All three examples point to the personal investments of spectators in particular stars in terms of commodities associated with female appearance. As the final one suggests, this investment may not be financial, but often took the form of fantasy and imagined identities.

> But Doris Day wore some beautifully cut clothes in some wonderful colours . . . this was in the 1940s when I first became aware of Doris Day – 'My Dream Is Yours' – need I say more!
>
> (Marie Burgess)

Here the spectator and a favourite star are linked through a common dream in which clothes are the currency of a shared femininity. The language of dreams is used frequently by respondents to describe their longings and desires in relation to Hollywood stars. The dream metaphor not only suggests the star ideal is unreachable, but also indicates a state of blissful happiness. Here the title of Doris Day's second film, *My Dream Is Yours*, is used as a self-explanatory statement in which the respondent hopes to encapsulate the exchange between spectator and star, an exchange involving particular commodities, in this case 'beautifully cut clothes in some wonderful colours'. Thus spectators are linked to stars through imagined intimacy with the Hollywood ideal; what more intimate than a shared dream?

STAR STYLES

In this section the connection between Hollywood stars and spectators is examined through an analysis of the construction of feminine style. The national differences between American and British femininity are especially significant to the attachment of fans to particular Hollywood stars. Differences of taste are articulated in relation to the meanings of British and American femininity at this time. Conforming to star styles in some cases could be seen as the successful reproduction of ideals of feminine appearance through consumption. This would certainly reiterate the claims made in the production studies of mutually beneficial collaboration between Hollywood and other industries (Eckert 1978; Allen, 1980; and Doane, 1989). In other cases, however, American feminine ideals are clearly remembered as transgressing restrictive British femininity and thus employed as strategies of resistance:

> Joan Crawford looked good in suits with big shoulder pads; Barbara Stanwyck shone in diaphanous creations (it always intrigued me how dressed up they were in ordinary everyday situations).
>
> (Marie Burgess)

Many respondents used discourses of fashion to write about their favourite Hollywood stars. Some appreciated the 'fit' between fashion style and star: the semi-transparent nature of the outfit allows the star quality to shine through, for example, in the above statement: 'Barbara Stanwyck shone in

Figure 6.4 'Barbara Stanwyck shone in diaphanous creations.'

diaphonous creations'. Similarly, Joan Crawford's star image as a fierce and powerful woman, rivalled only by Bette Davis, is constructed partly through her more 'masculine' costumes: 'suits with big shoulder pads'. The final comment here suggests a fascination with the incongruity of the narrativised situations and the costumes of Hollywood stars, pointing to a use of films to display women's fashions at the expense of 'realism'.

199

As well as remembering favourite stars through a variety of different styles of femininity, some respondents associated Hollywood stars with particular items of clothing:

> I'd like to name Deanna Durbin as one of my favourite stars. Her beautiful singing voice, natural personality and sparkling eyes made her films so enjoyable, and one always knew she would wear boleros; in one film she wore six different ones. I still like wearing boleros – so you can see what a lasting effect the clothes we saw on the screen made on us.
>
> (Jean Davis, Member of the Deanna Durbin Society)

In this case an item of clothing, the bolero, is remembered as Deanna Durbin's 'trademark'. The spectator takes pleasure in the fulfilment of the expectation that Deanna Durbin would appear in her films wearing this particular item of clothing. The spectator is connected to one of her favourite stars through her own purchase and wearing of this distinctive clothing sign. Again the enduring quality of these investments in star styles, replicated through commodity consumption, is striking: some forty years later the same item is worn with pleasure.

Some items of clothing were associated with Hollywood generally:

> We copied whatever we could from the stars we saw in the films. We even sent off by post to Malta and Gibraltar for Hollywood Nylons. And we got them by post.
>
> (Mary Wilson)

The use of Hollywood as an adjective here connects the cinema to the fashion industry. In particular, 'nylons' were a luxury item in Britain at this time, much sought after and extremely scarce; the connection to America would have been reinforced through the presence of American troops in Britain and their easier access to such products. In addition, nylons signify a specific form of display of the female body: the translucent covering of the leg with a fine material which emphasises smoothness and shapeliness. The display of particular parts of the female body, as I shall go on to discuss, is something which connects female spectators and stars, often a connection cemented through commodity consumption.

The connection between Hollywood and the women's fashion industry is made especially clear in the way that certain products were named after stars, not by the industries, but by the female spectators:

> I had a pair of Carmen Miranda platform shoes with ankle straps.
>
> (Vera Barford)

> The earliest film star I remembered was Shirley Temple, because I was the proud owner of a Shirley Temple style dress.
>
> (Mrs M. Breach)

200

Figure 6.5 'One always knew [Deanna Durbin] would wear boleros; in one film she wore six different ones. I still like wearing boleros – so you can see what a lasting effect the clothes we saw on the screen made on us.'

Products are thus named after the stars associated with them, and female spectators purchase styles which give them a feeling of connection with their ideal:

It was fun trying to copy one's favourite stars with their clothes, hats

201

Figure 6.6 'Hats were very much in vogue at that time and shops used to sell models similar to the styles the stars were wearing. . . . Naturally I bought . . . a Rita Hayworth one.'

and even make-up, especially the eyebrows. Hats were very much in vogue at that time and shops used to sell models similar to the styles the stars were wearing. I was very much into hats myself and tried in my way (on a low budget) to copy some of them. Naturally I bought a

Deanna Durbin model hat and a Rita Hayworth one.

(Vera Carter)

Stars are inextricably linked to consumption in these examples in that their commodification extends beyond the cinema and into spectator's purchasing practices of female fashions. Stars are thus commodities within the Hollywood film industry and, in addition, their names become commodities in the fashion industry in Britain as they are used to describe particular styles.

This naming and copying of star styles was remembered in relation to hairstyles, as well as clothes and shoes:

> Now Doris Day. . . . I was told many times around that I looked like her, so I had my hair cut in a D.A. style. . . . Jane Wyman was a favourite at one stage and I had my hair cut like hers, it was called a tulip. . . . Now Marilyn Monroe was younger and by this time I had changed my image, my hair was almost white blonde and longer and I copied her hairstyle, as people said I looked like her.

(Patricia Ogden)

Physical resemblance here links the spectator to Hollywood stars and the replication of stars' hairstyles affirms this connection further. Self-image is infinitely transformable, mirroring Hollywood ideals with new colours and styles of hair. Recognition of self in ideal shifts from star to star in an endless chain of commodification. Public recognition is crucial here; it is through other people's recognition of the spectator/star resemblance that this respondent presents her connection to particular stars (see Chapter 5; see also Benjamin, 1990).

Hairstyles were an important part of the physical transformations which took place in the attempt to become more like one's ideal: whether the more 'masculine' short crop of Doris Day's down-to-earth tomboyishness or the seductive 'peek-a-boo' hairstyle of Veronica Lake:

> Doris Day is the greatest and in the 50's she had a haircut called the 'Butch cut' which I had to be like her.

(Shirley Thompson)

> I think we all liked to identify with our favourite entertainers. Why else did we copy their styles and clothes. During the forties there were thousands of Veronica Lakes walking about. Girls who copied her peek-a-boo hairstyles – long and waved over one eye.

(Mrs Patricia Robinson)

Hollywood star styles and fashions are frequently referred to in the British context in terms of representing something different, something better and often something more sophisticated or even risqué. The impact of star styles on women in Britain was so strong that it was recognised as a problem by the state, which introduced safety regulations about women's hairstyles in factories during this period (Braybon and Summerfield, 1987). It also meant frequent conflict or power struggles with authority figures such as parents: 'Girlfriends talked incessantly about stars. . . . We discussed film star fashions – we were clothes mad. We wanted to dye our hair and copy the stars but we couldn't get permission from our parents' (Anon).

'Dyeing one's hair' clearly represented some kind of act of transgression or rebellion against the codes of respectable femininity in Britain at this time, since dyed hair suggested sexuality, independence and even prostitution. But it was not only sexuality that was seen as threatening, it was also the imitation of images of powerful femininity associated with stars such as Joan Crawford or Bette Davis: 'My father used to say "don't you roll those Bette Davis eyes at me young lady"' (Patricia Ogden).

The conventions of feminine appearance are remembered not only in terms of the reassuring conformity and predictability of Hollywood stars, however, but also in terms of stars breaking with certain fashion codes:

> We were quick to notice any change in fashion and whether it had arrived this side of the Atlantic. We were pleased to see younger stars without gloves and hats – we soon copied them. Had it not been wartime we might not have got away with it, because British fashion then was very old-fashioned and rules were rigid.
>
> (Kathleen Lucas)

Hollywood stars represented fashions on the screen which were identified by spectators as transgressing restrictive codes of British feminine appearance. Indeed, Hollywood stars were considered exciting in contrast to images of femininity offered by women in everyday life in Britain:

> I liked the clothes they often wore, we talked about their hair, make-up, figures and dress. I liked stars unlike myself because in my young days they appeared much more attractive. . . . Our mothers were very matronly at quite an early age.
>
> (Anon)

The reference to 'matronly' mothers here in opposition to glamorous Hollywood stars reinforces the familiar pervasive cultural dichotomy between motherhood and sexuality. The two main sources of information about femininity in the 1940s and 1950s, kinship and the cinema, are thus understood as being in opposition to each other and further reinforced by stereotypical national difference, American glamour versus British respectability (see Chapter 4).

The negotiation of idealised Hollywood femininities with mothers led to memories of intense emotional struggles:

I was fascinated with Shirley Temple . . . she always looked perfect. I loved her curls and as I was about the same age I begged my mother to do my hair like hers with rags or tongs. But I was made to keep my plaits. As for her dresses I was envious of them. However I remember my mother receiving a second-hand dress for me which was very much like the ones she used to wear. I was thrilled and told everyone it was my Shirley Temple dress.

(Muriel Breach)

The language used here suggests a strength of feeling in the attempt to copy the star ideal: this respondent felt love, fascination and envy towards her childhood idol, 'begged' her mother to copy Shirley Temple's hairstyle and was 'thrilled' when she had a Shirley Temple dress. These examples from childhood demonstrate the breadth of the impact of Hollywood stars on women in Britain during this period: it was not only regular cinema spectators with purchasing power who were addressed as consumers by Hollywood, but young girls, too, who relied on second-hand clothes for their star-like replications.

As well as being vehicles to encourage female spectators to become consumers, and to improve their appearances, then, Hollywood stars were also contested terrains of competing cultural discourses of femininity. As I have shown, they were central to challenges to what was perceived as restrictive British femininity, be it 'the dowdiness' of women in wartime Britain, the restrictions of factory regulations about hairstyles or the perceived lack of glamour of motherhood. Many respondents had vivid memories of Hollywood stars as representing an alternative to what they perceived to be these constraining forms of British femininity. In the 1950s particularly, when the purchase of fashions and cosmetics increasingly became a possibility for many women in Britain, the reproduction of self-image through consumption was perceived as a way of producing new forms of 'American' feminine identity which were exciting, sexual, pleasurable and in some ways transgressive.

THE BODY BEAUTIFUL

Since women enter the market place as commodities, they are under pressure to make themselves externally presentable – to use attractive packaging to bump up their market price, or to make themselves saleable in the first place. Implicit in the image of the carefully groomed woman is an assumption that the exchange value of woman is open to manipulation, that it may be added to to give use value as an external appendage. . . . Women's particular mode of socialization centres on the female body and through it the whole range of women's skills and potential competences unfolds within pre-given constraints.

(Haugg, 1986: 131)

Hollywood sold its stars as icons of feminine attractiveness, whose beauty could be replicated through the purchase of particular commodities. One of the most frequent discourses through which female Hollywood stars were sold to spectators was that of the body. It is through the body that feminine identity is constructed (Haugg, 1986), and the fragmentation and commodification of the female body has been a source of much feminist debate about the specificity of women's alienation and oppression. However, as well as exploring these processes of fragmentation in the replication of ideals of feminine beauty, I shall analyse the ways in which the focus on the body, especially the face, had a different significance for female spectators in terms of the personalisation of the female star. Close-up displays of parts of the female may have functioned, not to alienate and objectify, but to produce a fascination which was remembered as a form of intimacy by female spectators. Thus, ironically, the very fetishism and fragmentation criticised within feminist film theory seems to have had a rather different meaning for spectators whose memories of such effects can be understood as a form of personalisation of the Hollywood star otherwise kept at a distance on the screen.

One striking characteristic of consumption practices amongst my respondents in relation to Hollywood stars, then, is the centrality of the female body as a key site of consumption during this period. The body was a central topic in the articulation of the relationship between female stars and spectators. Female stars were not only bodies on display providing ideals of feminine beauty – they were also used to sell products to female spectators for their self-improvement. Thus the female body was both sexual spectacle and the site of consumption:

> Rita Hayworth was a joy to watch dancing. She had a lovely square face and beautiful hair. I grew my hair as long as hers and put it up and made it bounce when I walked as hers did. . . . I always bought the highest heels I could find and always copied Rita Hayworth in them.
>
> (Doreen Gibson)

Here the purchase of 'the highest heels' is closely connected to the movement of the star, and in particular the 'bounce' of her hair. Thus the purchase of a certain design of shoe produces the kind of walk which displays the hair to the best advantage: star style is copied in terms of movement and posture emphasised by high-heeled shoes.

The transformation of the body, through consumption, emerged as one of the key consumption practices that connected spectators with their

206

favourite stars. Respondents recognised or desired a particular look or style in their favourite star which they sought to replicate in their own self-image by purchasing certain commodities:

> My colouring was the same as hers [Lauren Bacall's], I wore my hair in a similar style . . . in a page-boy like hers . . . and wore the same type of tailored clothes.
>
> (Kathleen Lucas)

> [Deanna Durbin's] . . . beautiful singing voice, natural personality and sparkling eyes made her films so enjoyable, and one always knew she would wear boleros. . . . I still like wearing boleros.
>
> (Jean Davis)

The female body here is written about within the discourse of consumption in which little distinction is made between commodities and parts of the body: hair, eyes and 'colouring' are all parts of the female body which make up the whole star image, but can also be consumed autonomously, especially through the purchase of certain commodities. The whole body of the female star is a commodity, but the parts of her body (hair, legs, face) and the parts of her face (eyes, nose, mouth) and the parts of her eyes (colour, lashes, eyebrows) are also commodified. The female star's body is thus infinitely commodifiable, and, as has been illustrated above, spectators attached immense significance to particular body parts of Hollywood stars. Spectators clearly remember stars in terms of body parts they admired and, through the consumption of products, attempted to replicate their ideal through the transformation of particular body parts. The fragmentation of the female body is further commodified through the purchase of products in order to become more like star ideals.

It has been argued that the fetishisation of the female body characterised the representation of female stars in Hollywood (Mulvey, 1989). Fetishism can be related to the reproduction of feminine images both in the Marxist sense of commodity fetishism, in terms of the female body as object of patriarchal exchange, and in the more psychoanalytic sense, in terms of the fragmentation and sexualisation of parts of the female body in relation to castration anxieties, though these are not necessarily all analogous.[7] It has been argued that fetishism on the screen, in terms of the visual conventions of Hollywood during this period which fragmented and sexualised the 'woman as body', was reinforced by the kinds of consumption encouraged by female stars. The fetishised body image was accompanied by the corresponding narcissistic forms of consumption which were centred upon the improvement of self through products related to the female body.

Doane argues that women's new role in production in the 1940s 'was masked by an insistent emphasis on narcissistic consumption' (Doane, 1989a: 28). She highlights:

the overwhelming intensity of the injunction to the female spectator-consumer to concern herself with her own appearance and position – an appearance which can only be fortified and assured through the purchase of a multiplicity of products.

(Doane, 1989a: 29)

The female body is fragmented by the market, as well as by the camera, and women's bodies are broken down into component parts for the purposes of consumption:

Commodification presupposes that acutely self-conscious relation to the body which is attributed to femininity. The effective operation of the commodity system requires the breakdown of the body into parts – nails, hair, skin, breath – each one of which can be constantly improved through the purchase of a commodity.

(Doane, 1989a: 31)

The female body, in particular, can always be guaranteed to be at fault (Ewen, 1976: 39). The achievement of feminine ideals is always, to a large extent, reliant on men's approval. Since desirable ideals are always changing with new fashion trends, and feminine ideals are actually never fully realisable, the one is always contradicted by the other. Feminine insecurities about the attainment of bodily perfection are a reasonably sure bet for the endless reproduction of commodities for feminine self-improvement. The association of stars with particular products functions as the promised guarantee of the successful fulfilment of such desired progress towards feminine ideals. Thus female spectators can attempt to close the gap between self and desired feminine other through the consumption of commodities for the improvement of the female body.

However, attributing the term 'narcissistic' to forms of feminine consumption discussed above suggests a kind of passive self-indulgence which is misleading. This is particularly true when contrasting it with 'women's new role in production', as Doane does above: the suggestion seems to be that women's role as consumers was typically passive whilst their role as producers was more active. Narcissism has had derogatory connotations in a number of ways within psychoanalytic and other cultural discourses because of its association with femininity: it tends to be associated with a 'curiously passive desiring subjectivity' typical of femininity (Doane, 1989a: 31).

In contrast to this condemnation of consumption as mere feminine self-indulgence and vanity, I would argue that consumption, like female spectatorship, also theorised for some time in terms of its curious passivity, involves the active negotiation and transformation of identities which are not simply reducible to objectification. As I argued in Chapter 5, narcissism needs to be rethought through in relation to its meaning as 'love of self in the ideal' and the kind of homoerotic love this may involve (see

Benjamin, 1990). The gap between self and ideal, between spectator and star, continuously reproduces female subjectivity, the differences between the two endlessly deferring the fulfilment of desire. These are not just processes of objectification and self-commodification; they also (paradoxically) give rise to new and different images and identities through the selection, appropriation and conversion of feminine ideals as self-image. Forms of recognition of the self in the idealised other, or indeed recognition of the desired self in the idealised other, inform the choices and selection of favourite stars made by spectators. What is at stake is the love for an ideal which literally embodies the desired self in an intimate negotiation between feminine images involving forms of expertise and knowledge firmly based within the culture of femininity.

Furthermore, the processes of commodification, objectification, fragmentation and fetishisation are not identical and neither are they always neatly mutually reinforcing. To regard them as unproblematically so is to construct a rather monolithic model of power and to ignore the complexity of negotiations between the production and consumption of popular images of femininity. This perspective may also underestimate the disjunctures and mismatches between the needs of the marriage market and of the commercial markets.

It is also important to point out that the female body on the screen was not only remembered through discourses of consumption. Furthermore, the forms of objectification and fragmentation were clearly not always read in ways which can be used as evidence of female self-commodification. Here too we may need to rethink the significance of the fragmentation of the body of the female star in the light of the ways in which such processes had significance for spectators. Respondents repeatedly offered detailed memories of their favourite stars' bodies and what they liked about them in ways which personalised the stars. Although the rest of the female body was occasionally commented upon, at the general level of 'enviable figures', it is the face and its features which are repeatedly the source of this feminine fascination: eyes, eyelashes, teeth and hair:

> Susan Hayward had beautiful eyes, hair and voice. Rita Hayworth was vivacious – flashing white teeth and beautiful red lips.
>
> (Anon)

> My two favourite female film stars were Loretta Young – because she had very large eyes and such lovely long lashes and a beautiful voice, and the other was Rita Hayworth – because of her ginger hair and super figure.
>
> (Mary E. Wilson)

> Technicolour was the in thing then and it couldn't have been kinder to Rita, that glorious mahogony coloured hair was shown to perfec-

tion. . . . I was stunned that any human being could be that lovely.

(Violet Holland)

June Allyson always appealed to me because she had a lovely smile which always looked natural and the way she crinkled her eyes. . . . She had a husky voice which always fascinated me.

(Muriel Breach)

Cinema technology is remembered here as highlighting Rita Hayworth's 'glorious mahogany hair': thus changes in technology enabled new forms of feminine display and encouraged new forms of fascination. Another kind of technology which is important here is the close-up shot. The use of close-ups in Hollywood cinema emphasised the details of facial features and expressions. The details of eyebrows, lashes, teeth and so on could not have been seen by female spectators were it not for the close-up shot offering the possibility of detailed scrutiny and cataloguing. Thus the perception of stars in terms of their body parts or facial features was, in part, made possible and encouraged through particular cinematic and representational forms.

However, the technology did not only encourage the fragmentation of the female body, it also, again paradoxically, enabled a personalisation of Hollywood stars. Numerous respondents read off the type of personality of particular stars through bodily signifiers, and most especially facial details. The close-up shot has conventionally been used within cinematic practice to signify intimacy between characters within film narratives: the close-up is typically on the face and by convention encourages heightened emotional connections between stars and spectators. Respondents frequently referred to stars as friends, companions, people who have always been there. Thus, the personalisation of female stars ironically often stems from images which might also be read as depersonalising and objectifying. The same processes at the level of production that can be read as both fragmenting and objectifying the female body for consumption by the spectator can, therefore, also be seen to have produced particular forms of intimate reception in the exchange of feminine expertise about bodily appearance.

Copying a star's bodily movement, posture or gesture, as well as appearance, was frequently remembered through a bodily connection with the star:

I was a very keen fan of Bette Davis and can remember seeing her in *Dark Victory*. . . . That film had such an impact on me. I can remember coming home and looking in the mirror fanatically trying to comb my hair so that I could look like her.

(Vera Carter)

Moving from cinema screen to mirror, this spectator sits in front of her own reflection trying to copy Bette Davis through this bodily connection, the

Figure 6.7 'June Allyson always appealed to me because she had a lovely smile . . . [and because of] the way she crinkled her eyes.'

hair. The replication of this gesture is clearly loaded with emotional intensity.

These forms of feminine fantasy involve intense forms of intimacy between star and spectator. The bodily connection between star and spectator, which may or may not involve consumption, is one such form of

wasn't. . . . Surrounded as a child by the politics of class consciousness, she became a working-class Conservative, the only political
form that allowed her to reveal the politics of envy.

(Steedman, 1986: 7)

Envy and longing recur throughout Steedman's account of the structures of
feeling specific to feminine subjectivity in working-class early 1950s
Britain. The stories she remembers her mother telling her, which she
recreates for the reader: 'were stories designed to show me the terrible
unfairness of things . . . [the] subterranean culture of longing for that
which one can never have. These stories can be used now to show my
mother's dogged search, using what politics came to hand, for a public
form to embody such longing' (Steedman, 1986: 8).

Steedman's stories can be used here to highlight some of the limits of the
accounts of the relationship between Hollywood cinema and consumerism
referred to previously in this chapter (Eckert, 1978; Allen, 1980; Doane,
1989a). These accounts emphasise the successful connections between the
film industry and other industries, such as the women's fashion industries.
Whilst they offer important analyses of the ways in which the female
spectator is addressed as consumer by the various forms of overlap and
commodity tie-ins between these different commercial concerns, they tell
us little about how female spectators negotiated these modes of address in
their lives. Although these studies deal with questions of consumption,
they do so at the level of production: in other words, the consumption
practices of the female spectator remain unexplored.

In addition to this general limitation, there is the problem of national
difference: women in Britain in the 1940s and 1950s are likely to have had
rather different constraints on their consumption activities from those of
women in the United States:

> I preferred stars who were glamorous as in the 1940s – there were
> not many women in England who were glamorous as we all had too
> much to do to help with the war effort. Clothes and cosmetics were in
> very short supply.
>
> (Kathleen March)

The impression arising from the 'production studies' of consumption is of
the mutually reinforcing workings of multiple industries, successfully con-
vincing female spectators to leave the cinema and go and 'spend, spend,
spend'! Indeed many respondents I quoted earlier confirmed the impact of
Hollywood stars on women's consumption practices at this time. However,
many women remembered the constraints of the material circumstances in
Britain at this time which shaped not only their desires, but also their
purchasing powers:

So we grew up with Hollywood stars, but it was not really till the war

214

started, when we were teenagers, Hollywood female stars became models for us, to copy hairstyles, clothes, whenever possible with clothes rationing. I distinctly remember my friends and I knitting the beanie hats, mitts and scarf in rabbit wool as worn by Deanna Durbin in her film. . . . I was enchanted by Deanna Durbin, she had the loveliest singing voice, so pretty, and in all her films seemed to be my age and wearing the sorts of clothes I would have given my eye teeth to have worn.

(Anon)

An important, and often neglected, component of female spectatorship is the feeling of envy. The fascination with Hollywood stars is articulated repeatedly in terms of the commodities associated with the stars which respondents themselves were denied, but longed for. In this example, the respondent would have given her 'eye teeth' to have worn Deanna Durbin's clothes, and in another example, a respondent was envious of Shirley Temple's dresses. Rationing in Britain during the war (see Chapter 5) and for some years after limited women's purchasing powers considerably. Most respondents mentioned clothes rationing with regret because of the constraints this imposed on their ability to copy star styles:

I preferred female stars unlike women in everyday life. Women's clothes and lifestyles were dull during the war, so it was lovely to go to the films . . . when I bought clothes (on coupons), I tried to get something really nice. As near as I could to something glamorous.

(Joyce Blackburn)

I was always interested in dressing up – though during the war we were of course restricted as clothes were rationed. Clothing coupons were very precious. It was lovely to admire the clothes of the stars.

(Vera Carter)

However, women did not have to purchase clothes in order to copy their favourite star's styles; some made their own, some adapted existing possessions and others played 'make-believe':

I talked to my sisters about our favourite stars. The conversation was mostly about stars' looks and clothes. Being handy with a needle, we used to make dresses copied from stars.

(Vera Barford)

[What I enjoyed most was] watching glamorous actresses in lovely dresses, when I got home, I would play dressing up as a child and make out I was wearing these lovely gowns even if I only had a couple of scarves draped around me.

(Geraldine Crick)

There is little doubt that one of the main ways female stars are remembered is indeed through their appearance and their clothes; however, the kinds of purchases that could be made depended very much on specific contexts:

> The lovely glamorous clothes of the stars also appealed to me – this interest is still with me today. I have watched 'Dynasty' for the same reason. But naturally, none of the working-class and lower middle-class women I knew ever wore the sharply-cut suits of Joan Crawford and Bette Davis, or the floating, feathery, chiffon dresses of Fred Astaire's dance partners.
>
> (M. Palin)

In the 1950s more women were able to spend more on these kinds of commodities, and thus stars could be copied more easily through commodity consumption:

> The 1950s – [it] has to be Doris Day and Jane Wyman – both wore similar girl-next-door type clothes and hairstyles, I used to copy them both and they certainly had a great influence on my life at that time. Hairdressers were, as they are today, asked to copy the styles and you spent most every Saturday around the town looking for clothes to match theirs . . . even dyeing our canvas shoes to match our outfits.
>
> (Patricia Ogden)

However, class differences between female spectators made consumption more of a possibility for some than others even during the 1950s. When consumer markets began to proliferate in Britain and clothes rationing had ended, many working-class women could not purchase the kinds of commodities that they longed for and which they desired, and envied, on the cinema screen:

> During my teenage years I also loved to watch the style of dress and hairstyles of the stars; my friends and I would try to copy their hairstyles, sometimes we got it right, and other times we just gave up, as we hadn't the looks of the stars or the money to dress the way they did.
>
> (Anon)

Many respondents wrote of *trying* to copy star styles and of giving up, of failing. Achieving the perfect feminine image was left to the screen goddesses whose images were reproduced within a studio system by a multi-million dollar industry. Much pleasure was expressed in the attempts to copy these Hollywood ideals, but disappointment, failure and frustrated longing were also important components of the spectator/star relationship in the 1940s and 1950s.

Feelings of envy, failure and frustration highlight the mismatch between ideals and self-image. The negotiations of feminine identities in terms of everyday practices is crucial here: some women purchased commodities, others used knitting, playing or pretending to negotiate their relationship with their feminine ideals. Recognitions and identifications were always partial and incomplete, partly because of the limits that material constraints put on women's identity production, and because of the impossibility of feminine perfection in a culture where there is always room for improvement.

As I stated at the beginning of this section, processes of identification and recognition are always partial, if we accept the Lacanian model of subjectivity as fundamentally split.[9] However, female subjectivities are formed within particular sets of historical relations which give specific meanings to those processes. Thus, the cultural construction of feminine identity involves failure, not only at the psychic level, but also at the material. Indeed, rather than being strictly separable, these are mutually informing aspects of identity. Hence, the production of particularly intense forms of feminine desire came through the experience of material constraint in the case of the New Look.

Thus, female spectators in Britain in the 1940s and 1950s may have been addressed within the unified category of the female consumer by Hollywood and other industries, but class differences, economic circumstances and changes in the organisation of commodity consumption played key roles in shaping how women negotiated their consumption practices in the reproduction of their feminine identities. In the 1940s, for example, the difference between star and spectator was reinforced because of the difficulties of purchasing the desirable commodities and images displayed on the Hollywood screen. During the 1950s, expanding consumer markets facilitated the increasing 'consumerability' of the female star and the possibility of self-transformation to become more like one's ideal through the purchase of commodities. What I am suggesting is that there was an intensification of the link between female subjectivity and commodification as consumer markets expanded in 1950s Britain. The production of oneself as image became an increasingly important part of feminine subjectivity during the 1950s. However, this is not to return to Doane's position which sees subjectivity as completely synonymous with objectification, since, as I hope to have shown, the production of self as image through consumption produced its own paradoxes and its own excesses.

CONCLUSION: CONSUMING AND PRODUCING THE SELF – FEMININITY AND COMMODIFICATION IN POSTWAR BRITAIN

My argument draws rather different conclusions from those found in the 'production studies' of the relationship between femininity and consumption discussed at the beginning of this chapter (Eckert, 1978; Allen, 1980; Doane, 1989a). When considered in terms of its relationship to the production of consumer commodities, Hollywood cinema has often been seen as the ultimate site of the successful combination of the dominant interests of the marriage and the commodity markets in 1940s and 1950s Britain. The cinema space has been seen as a key site for heterosexual courtship and romance, reinforced by the Hollywood message that happiness for women lay in catching a man and keeping him. It also offered the physical and imaginative space in which captive audiences, surrounded by luxury and abundance, were introduced to new styles and commodities on the screen. Female stars offered spectators ideals of feminine desirability which, through the purchase of certain commodities, they tried to recreate for themselves.

However, as I have shown, the dominant discourses of Hollywood producers are not necessarily equivalent to consumer practices of female spectators in specific contexts. This is not to argue for the supremacy of the consumer as determining her relationship to femininity through commodities, nor to champion the pleasures of consumption as inherently transgressive.[10] Rather, it is to argue for the importance of maintaining a theoretical understanding of the space between dominant discourses of consumption and female spectators' consumer practices in different locations. Whilst the forms of pleasure taken in Hollywood stars are often centrally concerned with appearance and image and involve self-transformation in terms of commodities sold to women to improve their appearance and their bodies, the forms of spectatorship that I have explored in this chapter involve a complex negotiation of subject and object, and of self-image and ideal image. Challenging the rather functionalist model of the relationship between female spectators and consumption found in the production studies discussed earlier, I have offered an account which analyses the very contradictions of the relationships between Hollywood film stars, female spectatorship and consumption practices.

The contradictions of consumption for women have been importantly highlighted in Janice Winship's work discussed at the beginning of this chapter. She argued that consumer discourses addressed women in mid-1950s Britain as individuals and that this may have produced forms of desire and identity in excess of the needs of the market (Winship, 1981). Such forms of subjectivity are clearly offered to women in order to encourage commodity purchase, and, often, the production of self as a commodity for others. However, consumer practices demonstrate well the contradictory effects of such an address.

One example, to refer back to the first example discussed in this chapter (see p. 190), is the feeling of having a trademark, something which singles you out from others, distinguishes you from those who do not recognise the appropriate codes of feminine appearance as you do, and suggests a sense of individuality; and yet, ironically it is precisely by recognising oneself in the idealised other that this sense of individuality is achieved. Moreover, the trademark is itself based upon a self-proclaimed conformity to certain conventions of fashion at that time: 'matching shoes, gloves and handbag were a "must"'. Such are the contradictions of modes of consumer address: one is at once unique and yet also part of a mass audience, at once original and yet conforming to existing codes of femininity. For women, however, this contradiction has particular resonance. In a culture where women are denied the status of the subject, modes of subject address within discourses of consumption may affirm identities and offer forms of recognition, even as they encourage women to produce themselves as commodities.

I have argued for an understanding of the specificity of the relationship between female spectators and consumption in wartime and postwar Britain. This might be characterised by the negotiation of being both subjects and objects of a discourse of consumption which is fundamentally reshaped within the postwar British context. In wartime and early postwar Britain, for example, the desire to be more like one's ideal frequently remained at the level of fantasy, with only the exceptions being able to purchase the commodities which enable the difference between self-image and ideal to be reduced. Wartime Britain, as I argued earlier in Chapter 4, was a place of shortages, rationings and restraint, in which female spectators had severe limits on their purchasing powers. Despite these limitations, however, I have shown how female spectators transformed their images and identities through borrowed or second-hand clothes, self-made copies of star styles, or simply playing make-believe.

In addition, where spectators did purchase commodities, which clearly some managed despite the constraints, ideal star images were nearly always partially replicated, and rarely felt to have been fully achieved. The consumption of Hollywood ideals on the screen, then, remained a far cry from the production of self for consumption through the purchase of commodities, suggested by Eckert's analysis or Doane's conclusions. Fantasies of more desirable forms of femininity remained unattainable for most spectators until the expansion of consumer markets in Britain in the mid-1950s.

The 'consumer boom' in Britain happened much later than in the United States. The transition from 'austerity' to 'affluence' was slow and uneven in 1950s Britain (see Hopkins, 1963; Lewis, 1978; Wilson, 1980). The typical account of the 1950s as a decade of prosperity for all, consensus and optimism has tended to smooth over the national, ethnic and class specificities of such developments. Britain's consumer markets never expanded to the same extent as American ones did from 1950 onwards. In the first two years of the 1950s, rationing of food products continued and, in some cases, was more severe than during the war and in the immediate postwar period. In addition to food shortages, fuel shortages and housing shortages contributed to the continuing difficulties of everyday life in Britain well into the 1950s and the so-called age of affluence (Lewis, 1978).

As rationing ended and consumer markets began to proliferate in Britain from 1953 onwards, however, the consumption of commodities associated with Hollywood was more widely accessible. Some women began to be able to consume commodities which enabled them to look and feel more like their Hollywood ideals. The possibility of producing oneself as image at this time meant that Hollywood ideals could be copied more closely and images replicated through consumption. The viewing of films meant something rather different in a context where an attempt to replicate one's screen ideal through consumption became more imaginable. Increasingly during the mid- to late-1950s the difference between star and spectator became a mutable dividing line in spectators' imaginations. The increasing availability of certain commodities offered the fantasy of realisation of the endless possibilities of star-replication through consumption practices.

By the mid-1950s, then, there were substantial changes in the number and variety of commodities available on the market. Mass market 'Fordisation' did have an enormous impact on the British economy, albeit a delayed one. Statistics detailing this consumer boom, from increases in household spending, the extent of purchases of new commodities, to the growth in profits and the development of advertising, marketing and display, demonstrate the rapidity of these changes. Such details rarely offer accounts of the consumption of clothes, cosmetics and other items connecting female spectators with their star ideals; there is a clear necessity for further research in this area of the construction of femininity and commodity consumption. This lack of historical work on these particular consumption practices of women in Britain in the 1950s contrasts with the knowledge available about the role of women as consumers for the domestic benefit of others (such as husbands and children). Indeed this disparity replicates, in part, some of my general conclusions about the ways in which the consumption of commodities connected to Hollywood stars can be seen as a rejection of, or an opposition to, the domestic roles of self-sacrificing wife and mother.

The extent and rapidity of consumer expansion in Britain may have been less dramatic and less immediate in the postwar years but was nevertheless striking in contrast to previous decades. There was a rise of 50 per cent, for example, in the amount of money passing across shop counters between 1950 and 1956; between 1951 and 1959, the average consumption per head rose by 20 per cent, as large a rise in those nine years as in the twenty-six between 1913 and 1939 (Hopkins, 1963: 309, 311). The income group receiving £500 to £750 per annum after tax grew from 1.9 million in 1949 to 5.8 million in 1954 (Hopkins, 1963). Advertising expanded and pioneered a more glamorous image: advertising expenditure grew at an average annual rate of 13 per cent from 1950 onwards. Shops were redesigned and shop fronts extended and new purchasing schemes launched. In 1956, one survey showed that half the television sets and one-third of vacuum cleaners were being bought on higher purchase. By 1957, one in every three middle-class and one in every five working-class homes in Britain had an electric washing machine (Hopkins, 1963: 309). There was a shift from the department store to the new chain stores which proliferated throughout Britain from the mid-1950s onwards. With an emphasis on quality control and accurate specifications, rather than the palatial surroundings and aristocratic luxury of the department store, chain stores such as Marks and Spencer's saw a quadrupling of profits between 1948 and 1958 (Hopkins, 1963: 316).

This expansion of consumption which has come to characterise the 1950s demanded a particular role of women in Britain. As I discussed at the beginning of this chapter, it was women who were seen as the key consumers. As the editor of *Woman* wrote in 1957:

> In her function as a consumer an immense amount of a woman's personality is engaged. Success here is as vitalising to her as success in his chosen sphere to a man.
>
> (Mary Grieve, quoted in Hopkins, 1963: 320)

Typical of the 1950s belief in the inevitability of 'separate spheres', this statement demonstrates the importance of women's roles in the new consumerism in Britain. Women's magazines were one source of advice and information about these new duties and indeed about changes within the 'family' and the organisation of the domestic sphere. The increase in the sales of magazines such as *Woman* is another indicator of the expansion of consumer markets: in 1938 the circulation was 75,000, in 1952 it had risen to 2,225,000 and by 1957 it had reached 3,500,000 – one in every two women between the ages of 16 and 40 in Britain. In such magazines of the period debates about women's new role in the postwar, consumer society were rife. Here, and in government reports and academic studies (see Finch and Summerfield, 1991), the new discourse of 'companionate marriage' as a partnership of equals, of women and men as 'equal but different' was emerging.

Many of these new commodities, such as washing machines, vacuum cleaners, refrigerators, and all kinds of new kitchen equipment, already part of the mass market of the American economy, were designed for the home of the 1950s-style married 'partnership'. Part of the 'equal but different' discourse was an emphasis on the importance of the new responsibilities of the housewife: management of the household required skill and 'knowhow'. In an attempt to value women's unpaid labour in the home the housewife was addressed as an important expert on the most crucial room in the home: 'The kitchen, not long ago synonymous with woman's subjugation, now became the shining badge of her triumph' (Hopkins, 1963: 324).

The home thus became the focus for a great number of new commodities. The availability of television and the emergence of 'Do It Yourself' commodities were amongst important influences which contributed to the notion of the home as the key site of leisure and pleasure in 1950s Britain. As well as, or indeed, rather than, watching images on the screen at the cinema, audiences were able to watch images in the home, offering a kind of proximity previously unavailable to them. Hollywood films began to appear on British television for the first time in the mid-1950s. Thus those distant ideals from the big screen of cinema were brought into the domestic space on the relatively compact and contained screen of the television.[11] Thus female spectators' proximity to idealised images can be understood in two ways: first through the consumption of commodities and second in terms of the presence of the visual technology producing images within the domestic, familiar location of the home.

One popular representation of this consumer boom has been of its equalising effects. Through access to commodities woman were seen as the essential pivot for this 'people's capitalism' (see Wilson, 1980, and Partington, 1990). However, as Steedman's story reminds us, only some women were able to buy new styles and fashions for themselves, whilst others knew their desires had to remain subordinated to the needs of others, usually men and children: '[she looked] across the street at a woman wearing a full-skirted dress, and then down at the forties straight-skirted navy blue suit she was still wearing, and longing, irritatedly for the New Look; and then at us, the two living barriers to twenty yards of cloth' (Steedman, 1986: 29–30). The desire here is not one of self-commodification, but rather one of material possession denied to many working-class women even in the 'egalitarian' 1950s Britain (Wilson, 1980). It is her role as mother that she perceives as preventing her from being an 'individual' who could purchase the New Look for herself. Whereas Doane argues that women's new role in production in the 1940s 'was masked by an insistent emphasis on narcissistic consumption' (Doane, 1989a: 28), Steedman instead presents the frustrations of a woman who is excluded from consumption because of her role within reproduction. Thus, the inability to take up the subject position within the discourse of consumption produces frustration, longing and envy. Consumption here is represented as a potential form of self-assertion and agency for women in contrast to the necessary self-denials of motherhood.

In 1950s Britain, although many women did, in fact, remain in the labour market, despite popular myths to the contrary, women were nevertheless primarily addressed in terms of their positions as wives and mothers in 'the family'. There was a proliferation of professional discourses of motherhood in response to the loss of so many at home and abroad and the falling birthrate during the war (Birmingham Feminist History Group, 1979). Motherhood was primarily defined in terms of self-fulfilment through others. In contrast to this, consumption offered women the possibility of the production of self and of agency in the public sphere. Thus, Hebdige's (1988) argument, that certain American commodities signified the rejection of certain values within postwar Britain, needs to be expanded to include the ways in which this may have been the case in the construction of femininity in postwar Britain. As several of my respondents made clear, discourses of Hollywood glamour, in particular, were often remembered in contrast to those of domesticity and 'dowdy' motherhood.

Thus, although the 1950s has been seen as a deeply conservative period for women in which they were encouraged back into the home after their role in production in the 1940s, and in which the expansion of fashion and other markets invited new and intensified forms of self-commodification, consumption needs to be read during this period as having contradictory meanings for women. Discourses of consumption addressed women as subjects and encouraged their participation in the 'public sphere' which could be seen to have offered new forms of feminine identity in contrast to their roles as wives and mothers.

Of course it could be argued that Hollywood stars and consumer markets merely prepare women for their roles as wives and mothers, in so far as they are encouraged to make themselves desirable and glamorous for the marriage market and for heterosexual male approval. However, I have shown that there is more at stake in consumption than this rather functionalist approach would reveal. This is not to deny the ways in which consumption constructs women as objects within patriarchal culture. Instead, I have argued that the consumption of Hollywood stars and other commodities for the transformation of self-image produces something in excess of the needs of dominant culture – be it through forms of bodily intimacy, the investment of stars with familiar personalities, the frustration of recognising stars as impossible ideals or the sense of individuality produced through consumer address.

Thus I have challenged the view of consumption as unproblematically tying women deeper into the forms of their oppression, and argued instead for a fuller consideration of the contradictions of feminine consumption in 1940s and 1950s Britain. It is precisely these contradictions that shape the modes of feminine perception specific to cinematic spectatorship at this time in Britain. The negotiation of subject and object which is at stake in the reproduction of feminine identities took very specific forms during this period. The shift from a mode of perception characterised more by a fixity of difference between self and ideal in the 1940s to one where similarity became an imaginable possibility through consumption in the 1950s can be said to characterise the significance of consumption to female spectatorship in Britain during this period.

7

RELOCATING FEMALE
SPECTATORSHIP

I began the introduction to this book with a discussion of three images – a snapshot of myself aged seventeen, an image of the Hollywood star Susan Hayward in an advertisement for Lux soap, and a self-portrait of Cindy Sherman. In different ways all three images raise a central question explored throughout the book: how are feminine identities produced and reproduced in relation to idealised feminine images on the Hollywood screen? My commentary upon these three images in Chapter 1 introduced the reader to my primary concern in this study: namely, the cultural inscription of femininity within a complex and contradictory negotiation of the subject and object relations of looking in the cinema.

Each of the images can be read in the light of such an investigation. The 1970s snapshot represents a self-image produced as an imitation of an imagined 1950s Hollywood glamour. In the borrowed clothes of my mother, whose memories of that period structured my fantasies of it, I perform a retrospective masquerade of a femininity of the past. In producing myself as both subject and object of the discourse of glamour, I remain vulnerable to the critical masculine judgement of my success, yet immune to its ultimate authority through the play of imitation. The event, 'the 1950s party', announces imitation in its conception and thus facilitates the denial of the authenticity of the 'desire to be desirable' so fundamental to femininity.

The advertisement for Lux soap presents the image of the Hollywood star Susan Hayward side by side with a sculpture which replicates what is perceived as the beauty of her form. The transformation of the feminine subject into an object for admiration visually replicates the negotiation of the subject/object dichotomy which has been argued to characterise the cultural construction of femininity more generally. The advertisement, then, not only produces Susan Hayward as a desirable object for our consumption, but also simultaneously reinforces such a positioning by reproducing her beauty in the adjacent object of the sculpture. The classical style of the sculpture connotes the permanence of such beauty, its eternal and essential nature. However, the ambiguity of the medium (is it marble or is it soap?) undercuts the stability suggested by the classical style of the sculpture. Indeed, if it is carved from soap, what substance could be more transient and fragile? Unlike marble, soap is a product which literally dissolves and disappears. In this sense, its transience and fragility parallels feminine desirability itself: based so centrally upon appearance, such a definition of desirability couples it with youth which is inevitably temporary. Thus neither feminine beauty, nor the product which promises to sustain it, could guarantee the permanence connoted by the 'eternal feminine' of the sculpture. On the contrary, both are bound to fade with time.

The permanence of the 'eternal feminine', which naturalises the position of woman as object of the gaze, is thereby contradicted by the replicability and dissolvability of the material out of which the sculpture is carved. Paradoxically, it is precisely such commodification that undermines the discourses of 'nature' and the 'eternal', through which ideals of feminine beauty are repeatedly reinforced, whilst simultaneously drawing upon such discourses to sell commodities to women. Femininity may thus be characterised as the constant reproduction of self as object of consumption for others, which is achieved through the consumption of other objects. This process is inevitably endless and unfinished precisely because of the transience of ideals of feminine desirability.

The Cindy Sherman self-portrait underscores the processes through which femininity is endlessly reproduced in a contradictory relation to the subject/object polarity. In drawing attention to the place of woman as image in this culture, Sherman's work highlights the problems posed for women of being subjects and objects of the gaze. Her play with femininity as masquerade pushes feminine glamour to an excess which in turn comments upon it as convention rather than as 'nature'.

What might be seen as specific to feminine identities, then, is the centrality of physical appearance to notions of its successful embodiment. Whereas cultural ideals of masculinity as well as femininity clearly exist, the latter are more closely tied to physical appearance and bodily desirability. Whilst there have arguably been significant changes recently in the commodification of masculinity as image, there nevertheless remain important distinctions between the discursive inscriptions of femininity and of masculinity.[1] Ideals of masculinity may include physical appearance, but this is typically only one amongst many options.[2] Furthermore, it is not usually the most important one; success at work (be it technical, financial, intellectual, organisational or physical) and in leisure (be it sport, other hobbies, drinking or sex) tends to take priority. Ideals of femininity, on the other hand, conventionally include a central emphasis on physical appearance and sexual attractiveness to men.

Importantly, this greater *range* of ideals available within discourses of masculinity operates diachronically as well as synchronically: thus, there is both a greater variety of masculine ideals at one particular moment, and a greater range across a lifetime. In contrast to ideals of femininity, which construct desirable femininity as 'youthful' and thus vulnerable to deterioration with age, ideals of masculinity become increasingly realisable and cumulative with age. Precisely because ideals of femininity are so closely defined through physical appearance and sexual attractiveness, the threat of loss is always inscribed in any sense of its achievement, since, despite fantasies to the contrary, physical ageing is inevitable. The very small percentage of female characters over the age of forty in Hollywood cinema indicates the undesirability of ageing to femininity.[3]

This emphasis on image and appearance means that the fantasy of achieving such feminine ideals is undercut by a sense of its fragility and transience. Recent cultural theory has demonstrated the ways in which 'identity', be it gender, sexuality, nationality or ethnicity, should be seen as partial, provisional and constantly 'in process'.[4] Indeed, such an argument has been crucial to the destabilisation of oppressive identity constructions and to the denaturalisation of inequality. Thus problematising identity itself has been seen as an important political and theoretical move. However, in order not to lose the specificities of forms of oppression which can sometimes fade into relativity with such dispersals of power, it remains equally important to highlight the ways in which identities *are* fixed by particular discourses, however unsuccessfully, temporarily or contradictorily.

My argument here, at a very general level, is one about the specificity of feminine identities as fragile and transient. The centrality of producing oneself as image to cultural definitions of femininity connects to the forms of women's memories of Hollywood cinema discussed in Chapter 3. One form of memory constructed repeatedly by the female spectators in this study is iconic memory. Historically, icons have offered symbolic articulations of religious precepts which have attained a privileged status within specific religious discourses. The icon thus condenses and validates broader cultural beliefs and values. Similarly, icons of femininity condense and validate broader cultural ideals. Significantly, iconic memory reproduces the status of femininity as image by taking the form of a 'frozen moment', thus enabling the thorough examination of the details of feminine glamour represented by a particular star image. In contrast to typical forms of masculinity represented through memories of 'action', 'adventure' and 'hero narratives', which offer ideals of activity and achievement, iconic memory fixes femininity within a symbolic representation of its place as static and visually pleasing.[5]

The research process clearly has a structuring function here. Eliciting memories of female Hollywood stars almost inevitably encourages their reproduction as icons since they were constructed as such by the cinema industries in the 1940s and 1950s. Furthermore, they are memories of visual images and thus likely to take some iconic forms. The gap between the past and the present which structures processes of remembering is also significant here. The past is fixed through certain icons which metonymically represent the meaning of femininity at a different time. Memory constructs the past as a selection of 'treasured' moments (see Chapter 3) which may have become 'fixed' or 'frozen' with the passage of time. Such a fixing may be the result of their repeated recirculation or indeed of the attempt to preserve them.

This guarding against the loss of the past returns us to the question of the pleasures of nostalgia for the female spectators in this study (see Chapter 3).[6] Iconic memories work to restore the lost ideal of femininity, if temporarily. The request for memories of Hollywood in this research offered the chance for the recreation of a past self and its relationship to past ideals of femininity. There are two forms of nostalgic desire articulated here: there is nostalgia both for the past self (younger, healthier, more glamorous?) which is remembered within the possibility of becoming more like the feminine ideal on the screen, and also for a period when a particular relationship between ideals and spectators existed. As I shall go on to discuss later in this chapter, the loss made good by the processes of remembrance is for a time when 'stars were really stars' and remained distant ideals on the Hollywood screen. Thus these nostalgic desires express contradictory forms of longing for the past: one for the possibility of becoming like one's ideal, and the other for the pleasure of the impossibility of crossing such a boundary.

SUBJECTIVITY AND OBJECT RELATIONS

The study of Hollywood stars and spectators, then, raises important questions about the reproduction of feminine identities in relation to cultural ideals; as such, the relative neglect of stardom as a cultural site within feminist analysis is surprising.[7] As I have indicated, this relationship between stars and spectators involves the complex negotiation of self and other, image and ideal, and subject and object. Screen image and self-image are connected through a dialectical interplay of multiple feminine identities.

This interplay of self and other has been a continuing theme within psychoanalytic theory. In this book, whilst I have shown the importance of psychoanalysis to debates about gendered spectatorship and visual pleasure, I have also challenged its limits for a more 'situated' understanding of these cinematic processes. In particular, I have suggested that the psychoanalytic theory employed within film studies has often produced a universal model of cinematic spectatorship which is unable to account for its specific forms and located pleasures.

Traditionally, object relations theory has not been included within the remit of cine-psychoanalysis, despite its continuing significance to psycho-analytic theory and practice. Whilst the debate in film theory has raged between the Freudians and the Lacanians about the meanings of sexual difference in the cinema and the role of the visual in the filmic production of identities, object relations theory has barely been addressed. Frequently rejected for its preoccupation with the pre-oedipal and its focus on the mother (ignoring the Lacanian insights into the structuring 'Law of the Father'), object relations theory never really became 'fashionable' within film studies, as it has elsewhere in feminist cultural theory.[8]

Despite sharing many of the limitations of Freudian and Lacanian psychoanalysis that I discussed in earlier chapters, I shall argue that object relations theory is nevertheless particularly illuminating for the cultural analysis of the spectator/star relationship. Specifically, object relations theory focuses on the production of self in relation to external others, and, as such, may be seen to produce a more firmly rooted *social* theory of the subject (see Chapter 5). However, as I shall go on to argue, such theory needs to be combined with other approaches to produce an understanding of the historical changes in forms of cinematic spectatorship. In the rest of this chapter, then, my aims are twofold: first, to focus upon some aspects of object relations theory which seem to me particularly pertinent to the understanding of spectator/star relations; and second, to rethink the psy-chic processes analysed in object relations theory through the specific location of historical and cultural change identified in this study.

As the term 'object relations' suggests, the theory and practice of this type of psychoanalysis is concerned with the relations of the self to external others or 'objects'. In object relations theory the designation of others (people) as objects does not have the negative connotations of the feminist critique of 'objectification' discussed earlier. Rather, it refers to the process of distinguishing between self and other from infant years onwards. Whereas traditional Freudian psychoanalysis has typically been concerned with the workings within one individual psyche, object relations theorists have emphasised the relationship of one psyche to another and have been interested 'in the psychic processes which mediate the relationship between self and world' (Wright, 1984: 79). As I discuss in Chapter 5, Benjamin distinguishes between these two different psychoanalytic approaches through the terms 'intrapsychic' (the Freudian model) and 'intersubjective' (the object relations model) (Benjamin, 1990: 20).

Although these theories of 'intersubjectivity' have been developed within the therapeutic context and primarily pertain to the relationships between infants and adult others, they can nevertheless shed light upon the spectator/star relationship. Melanie Klein's work is central to object re-lations theories of the development of the self in relation to external ideals. Of particular relevance for my purposes here is Klein's theory of 'projection' and 'introjection'. These two mechanisms, whereby the infant deals with its experience of the world as 'both satisfying and frustrating', involve the splitting of the ego. This splitting functions as a defence: it can, for example, 'deny or repudiate unwelcome reality' (Mitchell, 1986: 19, 29). Klein argues that early bodily infant interaction with the external world (typically with the mother, and initially with the breast) forms the basis for the establishing of 'object relations'. The two key mechanisms of these 'object relations' according to Klein are:

> the structurings 'projected' outwards and 'introjected' inwards which form the pattern of a self's dealings with the world, including other people. Projection is a process whereby states of feeling and unconscious wishes are expelled from the self and attributed to another person or thing. Introjection is a process whereby qualities that belong to an external object are absorbed and unconsciously regarded as belonging to the self.
>
> (Wright, 1984: 80)

The processes of projection and introjection, then, enable the subject to 'expel' the bad and 'absorb' the good through the construction of the other as the particular object that suits the needs of the ego. Thus the infant 'creates an ideal object for itself by getting rid of all the bad impulses from itself and taking in all it perceives as good from the object' (Wright, 1984: 80). The connection between the ideal and the self may be established through 'projective identification' in which 'the ego projects its feelings into the object which it then identifies with, becoming like the object which it has already filled with itself' (Mitchell, 1986: 20).

Object relations theory, then, is concerned with the reproduction of subjectivity through interactions with external others. The external other may be constructed as an ideal, devoid of what are perceived to be any negative feelings or qualities, or, alternatively, the other may be constructed as the bad object who becomes the repository for perceived 'undesirable' qualities. What might at first appear to be a rather neat and functional defence mechanism, however, is complicated by the fact that both good and bad can coexist or alternate within the same object or person. Hence 'the same ambivalence could be claimed to infect all our attempts to apprehend the world in terms of self-favouring images' (Wright, 1984: 80).

These processes of constructing the self through mechanisms of projection and introjection, it is argued, begin in early infancy but continue to structure adult relationships with others and with the world more generally. Within this psychoanalytic model, identity is not seen as a finished product, but rather as a continual, and incomplete, process of formation and reformation throughout adult life. Moreover, these mechanisms are relevant to the analysis of identity construction not only through our interaction with other people, but also through our perceptions of, and relationships to, cultural objects, such as art, literature and the media. Thus, object relations theory has been used to explore questions of aesthetics, pleasure and reader–text relationships. The patterns and mechanisms of identity formation between the infant and the adult 'other' (typically the mother) conceptualised above, then, have been used to analyse the ways in which readers interact with texts through fantasy, idealisation and imaginative transformations (see Wright, 1984: 80–104).

THE PSYCHIC ECONOMY OF CINEMATIC SPECTATORSHIP

How might the cinema, then, be seen to invoke the reenactment of such psychic processes? In what ways are such psychic processes suggestive of the dynamics of spectator/star relationships? Moreover, how might these psychic processes be transformed through the specifically cinematic dimensions of such reenactments? Within this object relations model, Hollywood stars can be read as symbolic 'others' in the processes of subjectivity formation of the female spectator. Both projection and introjection can be identified within the multiple processes of spectatorship analysed in this study.

Projection, for example, usefully describes the ways in which the spectator 'fills the object with some of [her] own split feelings and experience' (Mitchell, 1986: 20). As such, stars might be seen to function as either 'good' or 'bad' objects: either the sum of the desirable qualities projected onto the good object felt to be lacking in the self; or the repository for all the undesirable qualities rejected by the self. Questions of 'taste' in relation to female stardom might be established through such mechanisms. Spectators may make choices between competing definitions of desirable femininity in relation to their feelings about themselves and about particular stars who embody such definitions. In this study there are, of course, many more examples of the star as 'good object' since most of the memories elicited focus on the pleasures offered to female spectators by favourite Hollywood stars. Some stars, however, are popular because they embody the 'bad object' which the spectator dares not: female stars are often narratively set up in opposition to each other and the transgressive or rebellious character is often more popular than the caring or nurturing one.

Similarly, introjection can be seen as the process whereby the spectator 'takes into [herself] what [she] perceives or experiences of the object' (Mitchell, 1986: 20). The parts of the good object which are attributed to the star, for example, are absorbed by the spectator, thus transforming her sense of self and including within it the absent good object. Here the star remains the good object, and the bad object is perceived within the split

230

self which is in need of transformation. Processes of introjection within the cinema are often articulated through the temporary fantasy of taking on the star's identity during the film screening (see Chapters 4 and 5) or through the spectator's connection with a favourite star by integrating an aspect of the star's image into her own identity. This typically takes the form of sharing a name or, more commonly, a physical attribute such as hair, eyes or voice, or movement, gesture, posture, or walk (see Chapter 5). The physicality of the signs of femininity are demonstrated through these repeated forms of bodily connectedness to stars. Furthermore, this introjective connection can be seen to be extended through commodity purchase: styles and brands of shoes, hats, suits and cosmetics form memories of powerful bonds with favourite stars (see Chapter 6). A part of the star image thus metonymically symbolises a desirable form of feminity which can be 'introjected' by the spectator through consumption.

Both projection and introjection involve the negotiation of the self and the star through particular feminine ideals. The construction of the star as 'ideal object', and the production of the imagined ideal of the self, are significant within both projective and introjective processes. Stars frequently symbolise cultural ideals of femininity which may be seen as a distant idol on the screen through projection, or absorbed into the self in either identificatory fantasies or practices (see Chapter 5); or, indeed, both processes may occur simultaneously. As Dyer (1979) argues, the combination of 'specialness' (otherness and difference) with 'ordinariness' (familiarity and similarity) has typified discourses of stardom within Hollywood cinema. Importantly, this highlights the operations of the industry and connects them to questions of pleasure and popularity. Thus, these psychic processes need to be situated within the cultural discourses produced by the cinema industry itself.

What has been referred to as 'projective identification' in object relations theory describes these multiple dialectical replays between spectator and star, between self and ideal other. Hence the female spectator might be seen to project her feelings 'into the object which [she] then identifies with, becoming like the object which [she] has already imaginatively filled with [herself]' (Mitchell, 1986: 20). Thus the spectator/star relationship involves complex forms of 'recognition' of the self in the ideal other and vice versa.[9] As I discussed in Chapter 5, similarity to, and difference from, the star ideal coexist within spectators' often highly contradictory accounts of their cinematic tastes and experiences.

Using object relations theory, then, it is possible to identify a proliferation of projective and introjective interactions with star images. Here lie both its strengths and its weaknesses as a model for analysing spectator/star relations. On the one hand, the multiplicity of such interactions moves beyond the usual choice between 'identification' with the star, or 'desire' for her, found in so much film theory. Thus, the complex interplay of subject and object within projection and introjection precisely relates to one of the aims of this study: to rethink the place of the feminine subject in cinema spectatorship. On the other hand, the productions of these possible interactions in the universal early psychic structurings goes against the grain of my general concern in the book to *situate* female spectatorship and *locate* its pleasures. On its own, object relations theory does not lend itself to such a project; remaining within this deterministic framework it is impossible to delineate any variation, change, resistance or indeed 'deviation'. Do all female spectators, for example, relate to their Hollywood heroines through all the psychic processes described above? How might we distinguish between these multiple processes and their significance to different spectators at different times?

Thus, although object relations theory does indeed develop a model of the subject in interaction with the external other, situating identity formation within a more firmly social location than many other psychoanalytic approaches, it nevertheless remains problematically universalistic and ahistorical in its formulations. Throughout this study, spectator/star relationships have been shown to be articulated through changing historical discourses. My analysis of spectators' accounts of Hollywood cinema has demonstrated the importance of such changes to the significance of stars in spectators' lives. What follows, then, is an attempt to develop an understanding of the psychic processes of female spectatorship in the specific historical and national location of this study – Hollywood cinema in 1940s and 1950s Britain.

CHANGING CINEMATIC MODES OF PERCEPTIONS

In order to do this I shall investigate the changes in what has been referred to as the cinematic 'mode of perception' (Doane, 1989a). This conceptualisation suggests that 'ways of seeing', or 'relations of looking', far from being universal, are actually transformed through particular historical developments. Walter Benjamin's influential essay 'The work of art in the age of mechanical reproduction' (reprinted in Benjamin, 1970) has paved the way for many subsequent arguments about the nature of such transformations and indeed for the notion of a history of 'modes of perception'. Central to his argument is the idea that the transformation of the meaning of art in the age of mass production and consumption involves a change in the spatial location of objects and subjects: the cultural object (the work of art) is brought closer to the subject (the consumer).[10] Thus, according to Benjamin, the 'aura' of art characteristic of previous periods (the specialness or uniqueness achieved through distance) has been eroded and replaced by the proximity made possible by mechanical reproduction.

Benjamin's model has been extended and reworked by theorists concerned with the specificity of such spatial relations of commodity consumption. For example, Schivelbusch (1977) analyses the ways in which the development of new modes of transportation (such as the railway), of the circulation of commodities (such as through the department store), and of representation (such as the cinema) have produced a new mode of perception – what he calls 'panoramic perception' (see Doane, 1989a).

Doane's own work on the 'economy of desire' employs Benjamin's arguments to look at the relationship between femininity, the commodity form and the screen image. Building on her previous reworking of theories of voyeurism and fetishism, in which she highlighted the significance of spatial relations to sexual difference and the visual pleasures of the cinema, Doane combines these concerns with an important move to locate these questions historically in the emergence of American consumer culture. Analysing the construction of the female spectator as consumer in this context, Doane argues that:

> in her attempt to bring the things of the screen closer, to approximate the bodily image of the star and to possess the space in which she dwells, the female spectator experiences the intensity of the image as lure and exemplifies the perception proper to the consumer.
>
> (Doane, 1989a: 32)

My disagreements with some of Doane's conclusions about the inseparability of feminine subjectivity from processes of objectification in this context have been thoroughly discussed elsewhere (see Chapter 6). Despite these differences, however, Doane's concerns with the specificities of time and space and their significance to female spectatorship nevertheless inform my own interest in such questions.

The notion of a 'cinematic mode of perception', then, is being used here to suggest that the relations of looking are historically produced within specific spatial locations. This is a gendered mode of perception in so far as the female spectator is required to negotiate her dual role as subject and object within the cinema. As I argued at the beginning of this chapter, the centrality of being an image to cultural definitions of femininity can be seen to produce a specificity to the female spectator's required negotiation of self and ideal other. In an attempt to transform the universalistic psychic determinism of object relations theory discussed above, then, I am arguing for the importance of analysing changes in the cinematic mode of perception, and thus in the relationship between the subject and the object, the self and the other, and between image and identity in different historical periods.

At its most generalised, this shift is from a spectator/star relationship based upon distance to one based upon proximity. Thus the psychic mechanisms of projection and introjection differ in their significance to processes of female spectatorship across this historical shift. As I shall demonstrate, processes of projection are more significant in the cinematic mode of perception based upon distance; whereas processes of introjection are more significant in the cinematic mode of perception based upon proximity. This is not to deny that both processes occur across the 1940s and 1950s; indeed, I have suggested that they occur in multiple and simultaneous forms of spectator/star relations (see Chapter 5). Rather, the argument here concerns shifts in the *significance* of different psychic regimes within specific cultural and historical locations. Instead of accepting the claim that female spectatorship is determined by early psychic structures which are universal and unchanging, my argument foregrounds the possibility of identifying changes in modes of perception which link the psychic to broader historical transformations. Thus, forms of projection and introjection are differently organised and have changing significances to spectator/star relations as a result of social and cultural transformations.

Temporal specificities

Throughout this study I have referred to 'the 1940s' and 'the 1950s' to delineate the temporal focus of my interest. The division of this period into two decades functions as a convenient shorthand, and further signals a possible line of distinction between the two time-periods. However, spectators' memories of Hollywood stars cut across this temporal categorisation disrupting any neat conceptualisation of decades as signposts of beginnings and ends. Indeed, the distinctions which emerge as more meaningful to my respondents are those of 'wartime' (1939–45), 'postwar' (1945–53) and 'consumer boom' (1953 onwards). In what follows, then, as well as using this rather loose shorthand of decadal distinction, I shall refer, where possible, to the more specific periodisation.

Drawing conclusions from the ethnographic material analysed in the previous chapters of this book, my argument is based upon highlighting a significant shift in the cinematic mode of perception for female spectators in Britain at this time. Hollywood stars in wartime and postwar Britain are represented through discourses of difference which maximise the distance between the spectator and the star at a number of symbolic levels. Not only is this difference structured through the notion of Hollywood glamour as an impossible ideal in the austere Britain of the 1940s, but also 'Americanness' at this time continues to hold the fascination of otherness. Economic and geographical distance from stars thus combine in the cultural recognition of their difference from spectators. Thus 'distance' represents the symbolic spatial location of the female spectator in relation to Hollywood stars in wartime and postwar Britain.

Conversely, as consumerism expands in Britain in the mid to late 1950s, Hollywood stars increasingly signify proximity to their female fans through the possibility of similarity through commodity consumption. This is compounded by the increasing 'Americanisation' of British culture during the

1950s and the gradual transformation of the significance of geographical and cultural differences so prevalent previously. Thus the spatial relations governing spectators and Hollywood stars shift from those of distance to those of proximity through the expansion of consumer markets and the impact of American culture on Britain in the mid to late 1950s.

To illustrate these somewhat over-generalised claims further I shall refer back to the ethnographic chapters in more detail to highlight instances of this shift in the material analysed in this study. The memories of stars in wartime Britain, for example, are primarily those connected with the processes of escapism and utopianism. Spectators remember 'losing' themselves in the star, forgetting their problems of wartime deprivation and transcending the dreariness of life outside the cinema. America is remembered as representing life 'on another planet' and Hollywood stars as mythical figures from a fairy-tale land (see Chapter 4).

Hollywood stars are repeatedly remembered during this period in terms of their differences from female spectators. One significant difference is articulated through the differences of wealth, luxury and glamour which contrast with the deprivation and drabness of the lives of the spectators. This is frequently expressed through a second difference – that of national identity. In all three of the ethnographic chapters in this book the importance of definitions of Americanness to the appeal of Hollywood stars is striking. The national differences clearly contributed to the pleasures of being 'transported' to another world, a fantasy world of glamour and plenty. 'Glamour' itself is used as a notion to demarcate the difference between *British* femininity and *American* femininity. Indeed, the distinction between 'stars' (Hollywood) and 'actors' (British cinema) is articulated through precisely such a distinction.

Hollywood stars in wartime and postwar Britain, then, remained idols on the screen to be worshipped from afar, be it in the form of Barbara Stanwyck who 'shone in diaphanous creations' or of Bette Davis and Joan Crawford who signified intensity and rebellion. Female spectators may have imagined transformations of the self, or approximated their ideals in the spirit of 'make do and mend' (see Chapter 5), but few possibilities existed beyond this. Admired from a distance, resonant with enigma and mystique, Hollywood stars signified unattainable otherness which precisely constituted their appeal in Britain at this time. The distance between the self and the ideal here remains insurmountable. Furthermore, it is constructed as desirably so. To keep the star at such a distance is to maintain the appeal of stars as icons, as goddesses, as dreams, as ideals. As such, Hollwyood stars can thus be positioned as objects of worship, adoration and devotion – indeed they may be seen to possess precisely the qualities of 'aura', in the original religious sense of 'luminous radiance', which distinguishes a person as special and different (see Chapters 5 and 6). Thus, memories of Hollywood stars might be seen as iconic not only in terms of the forms they take, but also because of their 'auratic' qualities which maintain their iconic status.

The psychic mechanism of projection, the idealisation of the object external to self, thus takes on a particular significance here. Spectators are required to maintain the distance between self and other within this particular historical and national location. The star remains the distant object on the screen onto whom the conscious and unconscious wishes and feelings of the spectators are projected. Thus projection can be seen to be the psychic structuring foregrounded within the mode of cinematic spectatorship organised around distance.

With the expansion of consumer markets in Britain during the 1950s, especially those aimed at women, however, this positioning of Hollywood stars as distant idols is gradually, if unevenly, transformed. Spectators' memories of stars suggest an increasingly interactive relationship between self-image and star ideals with the opening up of multiple possibilities of becoming more like the screen ideal through the purchase of commodities associated with particular stars. Mimetic self-transformations become an imaginable possibility through consumption – be it the suits or blonde hair of Marilyn Monroe, or the styles, fabrics and colours associated with Doris Day. These masquerades of stardom–femininity are embodiments of desirable qualities which bring the desirable object closer to the self. The cinematic mode of perception here is one which is based more on a relationship of proximity between spectator and star than on distance.

This transformation extends to the meaning of cinematic space itself. Like other forms of imaginative space, such as play (see Kristeva, 1980), the therapeutic relationship (see Winnicott, 1974), and producing and consuming the arts (see Green, 1978), the cinema offers a 'potential space' for the interaction and production of subjectivities.[11] Potential space in this sense suggests the space where the potential self is recognised in an other and possibly then, in part, incorporated into the self. This negotiation between self and ideal has been analysed throughout this book in terms of pleasures between femininities – a much neglected dimension of cinematic spectatorship within film studies. Rather than dismissing these processes as 'self-love' or 'narcissicism', I have argued that there may be homoerotic pleasures embedded within such imagined intimacies with feminine ideals (see Chapter 5 for a fuller discussion of homoeroticism).

The cinema can thus be seen to function as the space for potential identities, offering the female spectator an array of possible options. This has, of course, always been one of the pleasures of the cinema for spectators and in this sense is no different from the 1940s. However, the meaning of *potential space* is transformed within the context of the increasing availability of commodities to female spectators in Britain at this time.

Spatial locations

Discourses of national difference between Britain and America are integral to these historical changes in the cinematic mode of perception. 'Glamour' itself is perceived as part of *American* femininity, in contrast to *British* femininity. The splitting of femininity into the 'good' and the 'bad' object through discourses of national identity is significant here: British and American stars, for example, are seen to present a choice between opposing femininities. American femininity is frequently constructed as more desirable, be it in relation to clothes, glamour or sexuality. The expansion of consumerism in Britain during the 1950s is inextricably bound up with the increasing familiarity with American culture in Britain at this time. No longer seen as 'another planet', America, its culture and its stars increasingly became part of the everyday experience of British female spectators through the availability of new consumer commodities.

Introjection here takes on a new significance in the context of shifting national boundaries and identities. The making of the desirable other as a part of oneself becomes increasingly possible through forms of commodity consumption. The threat to the fixity of national boundaries here accounts for both the hostility to, and the eager embracing of, American culture and Hollywood stars through consumption. No longer at a safe distance on the screen, Hollywood stars can be 'introjected' by spectators in new ways in 1950s Britain. With the expansion of particular consumer markets, connections to Hollywood stars can be achieved through the taking in of 'Americanness' by female spectators in Britain at this time.

Thus, the distance, between America and Britain and between star and spectator, is gradually transformed to proximity through the expansion of consumer markets. The mechanism of introjection, the absorption of the qualities of the good other into the self, can be seen as increasingly significant to processes of female spectatorship produced within the cinematic mode of perception based upon proximity in Britain at this time. The expansion of consumer markets in Britain and their close connection to Hollywood stars through particular commodities (styles, brands, outfits and so on), then, privilege certain psychic patternings in accordance with broader cultural transformations.

What, then, are the implications of such a shift for the analysis of the place of the female spectator within patriarchal culture? One interpretation of this cultural connection between spectators and stars through commodity purchase might be to see this shift as an intensification of forms of female objectification.[12] Consumption would thus be condemned as encouraging women to work on their bodies, producing themselves as desirable objects for men. However, as I argued in Chapter 6, the consumption practices of the female spectator are not entirely recuperable by patriarchal culture in this way. Paradoxically, whilst commodity consumption for female spectators in mid to late 1950s Britain concerns producing oneself as a desirable object, it also offers an escape from what is perceived as the drudgery of domesticity and motherhood which increasingly comes to define femininity at this time. Thus, consumption may signify an assertion of self in opposition to the self-sacrifice associated with marriage and motherhood in 1950s Britain.

Similarly, the 'Americanisation' of British culture during the postwar and consumer-boom years also has uneven and contradictory significance. Whilst Americanisation might on the one hand be seen to contribute to the encouragement of forms of female objectification through consumption, such forms of consumption, linked to appearance, which became increasingly possible for many women in the consumer boom, could be seen as rejection of what was perceived as dull British domesticity.

Anxiety about the fixity of this particular national boundary involves the repeated articulation of judgements about appropriate femininity and female sexuality. My argument extends that concern with the impact of American culture on Britain during the 1950s in terms of changing class identities and challenges to bourgeois notions of respectability and taste (Hebdige, 1988) to analyse its impact on discourses of femininity. Female spectators' memories of Hollywood stars suggest the use of *American* femininity to rebel against what they perceived as restrictive *British* norms. In rejecting the previous generation's definitions of acceptable femininities, American femininity offered the chance to rework the Hollywood images on the screen. What is repeatedly articulated is the desire to avoid the typically bourgeois image of respectability and asexuality.

In contrast to this, many female spectators perceived glamorous femininity associated with American culture through Hollywood as a form of self-assertion against the expectations of self-sacrifice. Thus, the 'Americanisation' of British culture, characterised within discourses at that time as 'commercial', 'brash' and 'lacking in moral value', is important in terms of its connection not only to working-class culture, but also to definitions of femininity. Thus, whilst it could be claimed that this Americanisation of femininity through commodity consumption in 1950s Britain contributed to the sexual objectification of women within patriarchal culture, such an analysis ignores the ways in which this process also facilitated the production of particular forms of feminine subjectivity largely unavailable to women in Britain previously. The production of a feminine self in relation to Americanness signified 'autonomy', 'individuality' and 'independence' to many female spectators in Britain at this time.

What I have argued, then, is that there is a shift in the cinematic mode of perception which structured the relations between Hollywood stars and female spectators in 1940s and 1950s Britain. This shift can be characterised as one in which the mode of perception based upon distance is gradually, but increasingly, transformed into a mode of perception based upon proximity. Thus, the processes of projection and introjection change in terms of their significance for the female spectator in Britain at this time. This is not to argue that the shift is smooth, complete or neatly divisible into the two decades in question. Indeed, what I have outlined above is the argument at its most schematic and generalised. The transformations discussed here remain uneven, partial and always in process. As I have stated, female spectatorship involves both projective and introjective processes; however their symbolic meaning is transformed by these broader changes taking place within British culture at this time.

These general shifts outlined above, then, need to be qualified in a number of important ways. First, the shift in historical modes of perception is clearly not a uniform process. Some examples in this study show that stars are remembered through consumption in the early 1940s, such as Lauren Bacall's outfit in *To Have and Have Not* which was copied by one respondent (see p. 190). Similarly, devotion to the star is not a form of spectatorship restricted to the 1940s, as the example of one respondent's memory of Doris Day demonstrates (see p. 81). Neither is it the case that modes of perception based upon distance and upon proximity are mutually exclusive. Indeed, spectator/star relations typically combine the two, as shown in the numerous examples of the complexities of spectators' memories of stars in terms of both similarity and difference (see Chapter 5). Furthermore, the mechanisms of projection and introjection are not straightforwardly separable and both remain important to female spectatorship across the two decades.

It is thus crucial that the generalisations in this final chapter do not deny the complexities of the multiple meanings of female spectatorship analysed so far in this study. When I refer to a shift in the cinematic mode of perception, I am not suggesting that there was a total sea-change in the ways that female spectators related to Hollywood stars. Such a claim would undermine the significance of the diversity of spectatorships highlighted in this study. However, there is nevertheless an uneven and overlapping transformation in the forms of spectatorship within the context of the Americanisation of British culture and the expansion of consumer markets in Britain. Thus, Hollywood stars, for example, are read differently in the context of the increasing availability of consumer goods associated with them.

Most marked in the contrast between the beginning of the 1940s and the end of the 1950s, this shift occurs unevenly and with an unequal impact on different groups of women at this time. The respondents in this study are all white and thus what I have produced is a study of white fantasy. The memories of Hollywood are those of white women and their relationship to white ideals. Their fantasies of becoming are based upon a sense of possible inclusion within white ideals of glamour and sexuality. The shift from distance to proximity is one which suggests forms of recognition between femininities, and imagined possibilities of self-tranformation in order to resemble physically one's star ideal. The physicality of the signs of femininity are important in this respect. Bodily proximity to star ideals is offered through forms of self-transformation and commodity consumption. Given that the body is a key site for the inscription of ethnicity, the recognition of sameness in terms of ethnicity intensifies the possibility of proximity. Whiteness is thus an important dimension in the construction of the female as consumer through fantasies of bodily proximity through consumption.

The unequal access among female spectators to consumer goods in 1950s Britain is another important factor in assessing the significance of the changing modes of perception to different women in Britain at this time. As I discussed in Chapter 6, far from experiencing the possible proximity to one's ideal through consumption, many spectators remembered the frustrations and envy of not achieving such similarity with their favourite stars. Surrounded by new fashions on the screen and now in the shops, many female spectators remember the painful restrictions of economic inequalities throughout the 1950s (see Steedman, 1986).

Such exclusion from white ideals of femininity and unequal access to consumption further emphasise the unevenness of this overall transformation. Female spectators clearly have different sets of relationships to these overall changes, depending on questions of ethnicity and economic privilege. My argument, then, is not based upon an assumption that all female spectators at this time had an unlimited facility to purchase any number of the outfits they had seen and desired on the Hollywood screen. Indeed, such a luxury remains the privilege of a small minority. Rather, I am suggesting that the widespread presence of such goods in British shops and thus the imagined possibility of purchase transforms the symbolic meaning of Hollywood stars from distant objects of desire from another world to more familiar and everyday signs of femininity replicable through consumption.

The psychic regimes of projection and introjection discussed earlier, then, both inform processes of female spectatorship in Hollywood cinema. However, when considered within specific temporal and spatial locations their significance to the cultural meanings of femininity varies importantly. Such variations have been difficult to consider within the psychoanalytic theories which posit a model of the isolated ahistorical female spectator. Countering the universalistic tendencies of much cine-psychoanalysis, then, I have argued for a model of female spectatorship which takes into account changing cultural discourses within particular national and historical locations.

WHEN STARS WERE REALLY STARS

The shift in the cinematic mode of perception I have identified here is important to a sense of nostalgia which pervades the memories of Hollywood and its female stars in this study. Such desire might be seen as nostalgic in so far as it expresses a longing for a lost time which it is impossible to retrieve.[13] As I discussed in Chapter 3, respondents' memories of Hollywood in this study are characterised by a longing for a past which is characterised by a particular way of relating to stars. Whilst, on the one hand, respondents articulated memories of the desire to close the gap between themselves and their ideal, they also expressed regret at the loss of the distance which had characterised the 'specialness' of Hollywood stars. The increasing proximity of Hollywood stars is understood as a loss of their previous status as gods and idols. Indeed, this change is, to some extent, perceived as a loss of the phenomenon of stardom itself. Thus, whilst many of these spectators remember the pleasures of transforming their identities to become more like their ideals, they frequently contradict this through their overwhelming nostalgia for a time when stars remained on their pedestals.[14]

The nostalgia of the female spectators in this study is for several 'lost objects': not only for another time when star status was maintained through difference and distance, but also for former selves, or imagined selves. Remembering the 1940s and 1950s involves reconstructing younger and probably more 'glamorous' images of the self. Even where a sense of success does form part of the memory of the feminine self-image of the past, loss and disappointment will almost inevitably accompany such reconstructions. As I argue in Chapter 3, this sense of loss is bound up with the extent to which femininity is culturally constructed as an unattainable visual image of desirability: an image which is youthful and thus necessarily transient.

This sense of loss works differently in relation to the projective and introjective processes of female spectatorship. Although projection may evoke loss in the sense that the fantasy of 'becoming' the desired part of the ideal other on the screen can only be temporary, the spectator and the ideal nevertheless remain ultimately separate and invulnerable to comparison. Introjection, on the other hand, promises a more permanent transformation through the incorporation of aspects of the ideal other into the self. However, such introjective processes of female spectatorship, which intensified during the 1950s through commodity consumption, involve a sense of loss because of the mismatch between self and ideal image necessarily resulting from the evaluative comparison. Integrating a part of the feminine ideal into the self never produces the pleasing, successful replication which is desired. Thus, nostalgia for the time when stars were kept at an insurmountable distance may be preferable to the sense of failure and disappointment associated with the period that followed which promised impossible feminine transformations.

Memories of Hollywood stars in 1940s and 1950s Britain, then, evoke a nostalgic desire for a lost past, for the specific spectator/star relationships which characterised it, and for the imagined former identities and self-images of that time. In the shift from a cinematic mode of perception based upon distance and difference to that based upon proximity and similarity female spectators increasingly found femininity to be a lost possibility and look back with nostalgic desire to a time and place 'when stars were really stars'. As one respondent writes:

> in those eras we were more inclined to put stars on a pedestal. They were so far removed from everyday lives, they were magical. These days stars are so ordinary – the magic has gone. Hollywood will never be the same again!
>
> (Kathleen Sines)

APPENDIX 1
Letter published in *Woman's Realm* and *Woman's Weekly*

Dear *Woman's Realm/Woman's Weekly*,
I would appreciate it if you would publish the following letter in your magazine.

'Were you a keen cinema-goer in the 1940s and 1950s? Who was your favourite film star and for what reason?

I am doing research at Birmingham University into cinema audiences during this period and would like to hear from any readers who were fans of Hollywood stars such as Bette Davis, Katharine Hepburn, Barbara Stanwyck, Doris Day, Marilyn Monroe, Jane Wyman or any other favourites.

Please write to me care of this magazine for a more detailed question-naire, or simply write to me about the stars you liked or disliked.'

I look forward to hearing from you.

Yours,

Jackie Stacey

APPENDIX 2
Questionnaire

QUESTIONNAIRE ON BRITISH CINEMA AUDIENCES AND HOLLYWOOD STARS IN THE 1940s AND 1950s

Thank you very much indeed for your response to my letter in *Woman's Weekly/Woman's Realm*. This questionnaire is a follow-up to the information you sent me in your replies. I would be very grateful if you could complete it and return it to me.

This survey is part of a research project on cinema audiences I am conducting at Birmingham University. I am interested in your experiences and memories of female film stars from Hollywood in the 1940s and 1950s, especially the reasons for your preferences for particular stars. I realise that this covers quite a long period of time, and have therefore tried to allow you to indicate as many variations and changes as possible. If you have any difficulty remembering this far back, don't worry – just try to give as much detail in your answers as possible.

This questionnaire is divided into four sections: A: *Your picture-going background*, B: *Stars*, C: *Fan clubs and film magazines*, and C: *Details about you*. The section on stars, and in particular question 19, is the most important one for my research. Some of the questions are open-ended, asking you to put your answers in your own words; the others require you to circle whichever answer seems most appropriate to you. This information will remain confidential, unless you agree otherwise in the final section of the questionnaire.

Please return this to me by 15 October if possible. I very much appreciate your time and trouble in contributing to this research project.

Jackie Stacey
University of Birmingham
August 1989

Section A: Your picture-going background

In this section I'm interested in some background information on your picture-going habits in the 1940s and 1950s. Please answer the questions in this section in relation to the time when you went to the cinema most frequently.

1 In which years did you go to the cinema most frequently in the 1940s and 1950s?

2 At the time you went most frequently, did you go on average:
    a. less than once a month
    b. once a month
    c. twice a month
    d. once a week
    e. twice or three times a week
    f. more than this (please specify)
    g. I can't remember

3 What age were you when you went to the cinema most frequently?

4 How much of the money that you spent on leisure did you spend on the cinema each week?
    a. all of it
    b. more than half of it
    c. less than half of it
    d. I can't remember

5 Did you usually go the cinema alone?
    a. yes
    b. no
If no, who did you usually go with?

6 What was your main reason for your choice of film? Choose one of the following:
    a. because of the star
    b. because of the type of film
    c. because of the reviews
    d. whatever was on
    e. other (please specify)
    f. I can't remember

7 Did you have any other leisure activities during this period?
    a. yes
    b. no
If yes, did you enjoy going to the cinema:
    a. a lot more than any other leisure activity
    b. equally with other leisure activities

c. less than other leisure activities
Please give reasons for your answer.

8 What did you particularly enjoy about going to the pictures?

9 How did the war affect the place that cinema had in your life?

10 Which types of film did you enjoy most? Please number the following options (1, 2, 3, etc.) in order of preference.
    a. romance
    b. thrillers
    c. comedy
    d. musicals
    e. westerns
    f. melodrama
    g. other (please specify)

11 Which types of female characters did you like seeing most, and why?

12 Did you ever see the same film several times?
    a. yes
    b. no
If yes, which films and why.

13 Describe your favourite cinema experience of:
    the 1940s:

    the 1950s:

[This could be a scene from a film, your favourite star in a particular role, an event at the cinema, or a particular evening out, or something else that you particularly remember. Please continue your answer to question 13 on a separate sheet if necessary.]

Section B: Stars

This section concerns the most important part of my research. I'm particularly interested in your answer to question 19, so I'd appreciate as full an answer as possible here.

I want to find out which film stars you liked in particular, and what you liked about them. Most of the questions are about *Hollywood* stars, since they are the main focus of my research. In case you preferred British stars, there are a few questions about them at the end of this section.

I'm also interested in whether your preferences changed or not during the 1940s and 1950s, so I'll ask you about them separately, so that you can be as specific as possible. If you were only a fan in one of these decades, just answer the questions relating to those years.

14 Please list your ten favourite female Hollywood stars of the 1940s in order of preference. [Don't worry if you run out before 10.]

    1.
    2.
    3.
    4.
    5.
    6.
    7.
    8.
    9.
    10.

15 Would your list for the 1950s be different from the one for the 1940s?

    a. yes
    b. no

If yes, please list below, in order of preference, your ten favourite female Hollywood stars of the 1950s.

    1.
    2.
    3.
    4.
    5.
    6.
    7.
    8.
    9.
    10.

16 Which female stars did you prefer?

    a. Hollywood
    b. British
    c. I had no preference
    d. I wasn't aware of the difference
    e. I can't remember

If you had a stong preference for either Hollywood or British stars, please say why.

If your preferences changed during the 1940s and 1950s, please say when and why.

17 If some of your favourite female stars in the 1940s were British, please list them here, in order of preference.

18 If some of your favourite female stars in the 1950s were British, please list them here, in order of preference.

Question 19

19 I am interested in finding out about what appealed to you in particular about Hollywood stars. Please write about your favourite female Hollywoood star from the 1940s, and then your favourite from the 1950s, explaining what you liked about them and what they meant to you: what made these stars more appealing than others? [Please answer this question as extensively as possible, continuing on a separate sheet if necessary, since the answer to this question is particularly important for my research.]

20 If your favourite female stars of either the 1940s or of the 1950s were British, please write about what you liked about them here, *in addition* to your answer to question 19. [Please continue on a separate sheet if necessary.]

21 Did you talk about your favourite female stars with anyone else (e.g. family, friends or colleagues)?
     a. yes
     b. no
If yes, please say who. Please indicate the kinds of things you talked about if you can remember.

22 Did you prefer female stars who were like or unlike women in everyday life? Please say why.

23 Did you prefer female stars who were like you in some way?
     a. yes
     b. no
If yes, please say why. If no, please say why not.

24 Were there any female stars you disliked enough for you to avoid seeing their films?
     a. yes
     b. no
If yes, who were they, and why did you dislike them?

25 Has your interest in particular stars continued?
     a. yes
     b. no
If yes, which ones. If no, why not?

26 Is there anything else that you would like to add about Hollywood stars in the 1940s and 1950s? If so, please give details here.

Section C: Fan clubs and film magazines

In this section of the questionnaire, you are asked to write about other aspects of being a keen picture-goer in the 1940s and 1950s.

27 How did you get information about the stars, their films, and their lives, other than through the films they appeared in?

28 Were you a member of any fan clubs during this time?

      a. yes
      b. no

If no, please go on to question 31. If yes, please give details:
Name/s of the star/s:

Dates of membership:

Was this/were these US or GB based club/s?

Address/es (even if outdated, this would be useful):

If you are still a member of any of these fan clubs, please give current addresses.

29 In the 1940s and 1950s, what did the fan clubs send you (e.g. photos, letters, news-sheets etc.)?

30 What did you enjoy most about belonging to a fan club?

31 Did you ever write to a film star or studio?

      a. yes
      b. no

If yes:
Who did you write to?

What kind of response did you want?

Did you get this response?

32 Did you buy any film magazines such as *Picturegoer*, *Kinematograph Weekly*, or *Photoplay*, or film annuals such as *Preview*, *Film Review* etc. during this period?

      a. yes
      b. no

If yes:
Which ones did you buy?

How often did you buy it/them?

For how many years did you buy it/them?

33 What was your main reason for buying this/these film magazine/s or annuals?

APPENDIX 3

Readers' profiles by age and class: *Woman's Realm* and *Woman's Weekly*

Chat (1,662,000 = 7.1%)

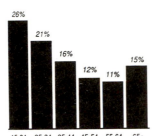

Me (1,405,000 = 6%)

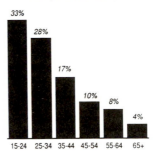

Woman (2,680,000 = 11.5%)

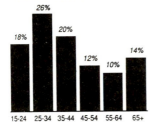

Woman's Own (3,720,000 = 15.9%)

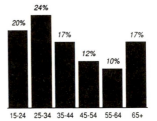

Woman's Realm (1,488,000 = 6.4%)

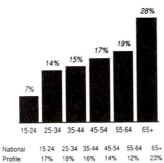

Woman's Weekly (2,408,000 = 10.3%)

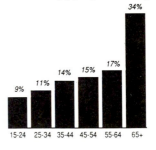

National Profile:	15-24	25-34	35-44	45-54	55-64	65+
	17%	18%	16%	14%	12%	23%

Source: NRS Jan-Jun 1991 Universe: 23,393,700 Women

Figure A3.1 Readership profile by age of IPC women's weeklies (women)
Reproduced with kind permission of IPC Magazines

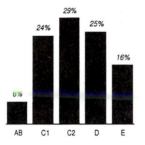

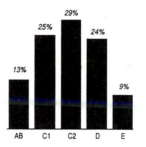

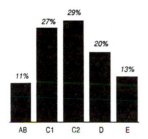

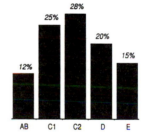

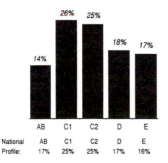

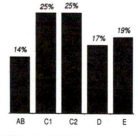

National   AB   C1   C2   D   E
Profile: 17%   25%   25%   17% 16%

Source: NRS Jan-Jun 1991 Universe: 23,393,700 Women

Figure A3.2 Readership profile by class of IPC women's weeklies (women)
Reproduced with kind permission of IPC Magazines

253

KEY TO CLASS CATEGORIES IN READERS' PROFILES

Class:

A   Upper middle class. Professional, managerial, higher administrative work.

B   Middle class. Intermediate management and professional work.

C1 Lower middle class. Supervisory, clerical, junior professional, administrative work.

C2 Skilled working-class manual work.

D   Working class. Semi-skilled manual work.

E   Lowest level of state provision. Widows, casual workers, lowest grade work. Subsistence existence.

Source: Information Pack, IPC Magazines, Ltd, London, September 1991, pages 3 and 4.

NOTES

1 HOW DO I LOOK?

1 See Pollock (1988: 122) quoted in Pearce (1991: 14, 15).
2 The question of whiteness and its importance to the appeal of Hollywood stars has only been touched upon in this book. However, in feminist and cultural theory more generally, it is taking on increasing significance. For some exploratory analysis of the question of whiteness in relation to the category 'woman', see Helen (charles) 1992; for a discussion of whiteness in the cinema, see Richard Dyer (1988).
3 For work on gender and genre, see E. Ann Kaplan (1978); Christine Gledhill (1987); and Jackie Byars (1991).
4 Several recent edited collections have begun to fill this gap, including Christine Gledhill (1991) and Jeremy Butler (1991).
5 The problem of reflectionism is part of the debate about 'positive images' within feminist film criticism. For an example of this debate see Linda Artel and Susan Wengraf's 'Positive images: screening women's films' and Diane Waldman's 'There's more to positive image than meets the eye' in Patricia Erens (1990). See also Charlotte Brunsdon's (1986b) contextualisation of this debate.
6 There are exceptions to this absence which include Richard Dyer's (1986) analysis of gay men's readings of Judy Garland, and Helen Taylor's (1989) analysis of female fans' readings of Vivien Leigh's 'Scarlett O'Hara' in *Gone With The Wind*. See also Lisa Lewis (1992) for a collection on fan culture more generally.
7 The term 'ethnographic' is being used here within the conventions of cultural studies approaches to audiences. This usage refers to an alternative to the analysis of media texts. An 'ethnographic' method in this context would typically analyse what audiences say about the media using sources such as interviews, letters and questionnaires. It should be noted that this usage is very different from the anthropological meaning of ethnography which involves participant observation over a substantial period of time.
8 For a discussion of the relationship between feminist researchers and female spectators, see Helen Taylor (1989) and Ien Ang (1985).
9 See Richard Dyer's (1986) analysis of the 'whiteness' of Marilyn Monroe's star image in the 1950s.
10 For a comprehensive account of the social history of women's changing roles at this time, see Penny Summerfield in Gail Braybon and Penny Summerfield (1987).
11 See E. Ann Kaplan (1978), Christine Gledhill (1987, 1991) and Jackie Byars (1991).

12 For a discussion of the question of method in film studies see Jackie Stacey (1993).

13 For an analysis of the question of desire between women in Hollywood cinema, see Jackie Stacey (1987a).

14 In total thirteen men filled in the questionnaire out of a total of 238 respondents.

15 The class categorisation of women is notoriously problematic because of the ways in which married women have traditionally been defined in relation to their husband's position in the labour market.

2 FROM THE MALE GAZE TO THE FEMALE SPECTATOR

1 See, for example, Jackie Byars (1991); Patricia Erens (1990) and E. Deidre Pribram (1988).

2 The early work of Christian Metz, *Film Language: A Semiotics of the Cinema* (1974), established the field of cinema semiotics in which films were studied in terms of codes and textual systems. He later moved beyond his earlier formalism and introduced psychoanalytic theories of the subject into his study of cinematic signification in *Psychoanalysis and Cinema* (1982). Stephen Heath's influential articles 'Film and system: terms of analysis' (1975) and 'Difference' (1978), both published in *Screen*, foregrounded psychoanalytic questions within film theory.

3 This rather monolithic model of a film as a closed system of meaning is typical of film theory, and indeed, cultural theory, in the 1970s, which was strongly influenced by the work of Althusser and Saussure. The work of Louis Althusser in particular foregrounded the importance of ideology within Marxist critiques of capitalism. In his influential essay 'Ideology and ideological state apparatuses' (1971), Althusser not only ascribed ideological state apparatuses, such as the Church, the law and the media, more power in securing the reproduction of capitalism than had previously been the case within Marxist thinking, but also stressed the importance of ideology in producing subjectivities. In his argument that subjects are 'interpellated' by ideology he gave ideology and, indeed, language an inescapably determining power in society. Studies in structural linguistics also influenced Marxist cultural criticism in the 1970s and 1980s. In particular, Ferdinand de Saussure's work on language as a sign system in his *Course in General Linguistics* (1974) was adopted by many film theorists who applied this structuralist approach to film texts.

4 For a discussion of the relevance of Marxist critiques of realism to feminist film criticism, see Christine Gledhill, in E. Ann Kaplan (1978). See also Terry Lovell (1980).

5 Point-of-view shots are so-called when the camera takes the actual position of the character who is looking; shot/reverse-shot refers to an editing pattern which alternates between two characters in dialogue. Each of these techniques can be used to position the spectator to look (and desire) from the point of view of the male character in the film (see Bordwell and Thompson, 1979).

6 See Freud (1905, 1925, 1931, 1933); for the feminist debates about psychoanalysis, see Juliet Mitchell (1975); Jane Gallop (1982); Juliet Mitchell and Jacqueline Rose (1982); Janet Sayers (1986); Teresa Brennan (1989).

7 Scopophilia is the psychoanalytic term for erotic pleasure in looking.

8 See Mary Ann Doane (1987); E. Deidre Pribram (1988); Tania Modleski (1988); and Lorraine Gamman and Margaret Marshment (1988).

9 As well as the question of the absence of the female spectator in Mulvey's

original attack on visual pleasure (Mulvey, 1975), the other major absence is the pleasure of the male figure as erotic object: see Richard Dyer (1982), Steve Neale (1983) and Andy Medhurst (1985). See also Miriam Hansen (1986).

10 The term 'enunciator' refers to the 'person who possesses the right to speak within the film and the source [instance] towards which the series of representations is logically channelled back' (Raymond Bellour, 1977: 94).

11 See Jackie Stacey (1987a).

12 For a discussion of the history of the term 'empiricism' see Raymond Williams (1976: 98–101). I discuss the overly loose usage of this term in film theory in Chapter 3.

13 The Althusserian model of the spectator refers to a rather rigid textual determinism which was in part derived from Althusser's theories of ideology and subjectivity in which the subject is denied any agency, but rather seen to be totally interpellated by ideology. See note 3.

14 Although E. Ann Kaplan is herself dismissive of audiences as a useful source for the analysis of such a 'socialising urge' (see Kaplan, 1987).

15 'The politics of location' is a shorthand term used to refer to some fundamental changes within feminism during the 1980s and 1990s; typically it is associated with an emphasis on specificity, rather than generality. It has emerged from both a political challenge made by black feminism to the oppressive generalisations made by white feminists, and a postmodernist/feminist theoretical disenchantment with universal theories in favour of theories located historically, culturally and geographically. (See Rich, 1986; Spivak, 1985, 1987; Nicholson, 1990; and hooks, 1991.)

16 For further discussion of the question of differences between women see Elizabeth V. Spelman's *Inessential Woman: Problems of Exclusion in Feminist Thought* (1990) and Caroline Ramazanoglu's *Feminism and the Contradictions of Oppression* (1989).

17 See, for example, Andrea Weiss (1992), Antonia Lant (1991), and Trinh T. Minh-ha (1989), whose book is not about the cinema, but raises questions of relevance to all forms of representation.

18 As I discuss in Chapter 1, the term 'ethnographic studies' is being used here in the rather loose sense of the term meaning studies which deal with audiences' accounts of the media rather than text-based analyses. This is rather different from the anthropological meaning which refers to in-depth interview, or participant observation.

19 For example, John Fiske uses interviews with fans of Madonna to argue against the passive model of the consumption of popular culture. His analysis suggests that Madonna's own redefinition of female sexuality and the ways in which these are taken up by her fans can be seen as instances of resistance to patriarchal definitions of sexuality and gender. (See Fiske, 1989.)

20 For example, Tania Modleski's *Loving with a Vengeance* (1982) is an interesting example of this dilemma. There is a striking shift from the psychoanalytic textual analysis of the latent meanings of literary forms popular with female readers (the Gothic novel and the Harlequin Romance), which pays little attention to the context of reading practices, to the analysis of daytime soap operas, in which the psychoanalytic framework is less prominent and the social context of women's viewing practices is foregrounded. Thus psychoanalysis is again most successfully employed in studies which assume a universal female subject and ignore the social context of cultural consumption.

See Chapter 3 of this book for a discussion of audience research and the question of the unconscious.

21 In particular Modleski challenges the Marxist critics Horkheimer, Adorno and Marcuse, who, she argues, made 'contempt for mass art a politically progressive attitude' (Modleski, 1982: 26).

22 Here the term 'hysterical' is used by Modleski to refer to the psychoanalytic classification of female patients. In one case, for example, the patient had an early:

> 'habit of daydreaming' to escape from her 'monotonous family life' [which] prepared the way for the extreme hysteria she was to develop. Eventually, she began to experience a kind of 'double conscience', as Breuer calls it, which, among other symptoms, was manifested in a need to tell stories about herself in the third person and in a feeling that even when she was at her most 'insane', 'a clear-sighted and calm observer sat . . . in a corner of her brain and looked on at all the mad business'. This kind of duality exists . . . at the very core of romances, particularly in the relation between an 'informed' reader and a necessarily innocent heroine.
>
> (Modleski, 1982: 32)

23 See Bourdieu (1980, and also 1984). For a rather different conceptualisation of 'recognition' and its importance to the formation of the subject see Jessica Benjamin (1990) which is discussed in Chapter 5 of this book.

24 For a discussion of the relationship between 'feminist critics' and the 'ordinary women' whose pleasures in popular culture they study, see Charlotte Brunsdon's paper 'Pedagogies of the feminine' delivered at the *Screen* Studies Conference, Glasgow University, June 1991. This paper is printed in *Screen* 32, 4.

25 For a discussion of the absence of methodological debate in film theory, see Jackie Stacey (1993).

3   THE LOST AUDIENCE

1 Most notably: Dorothy Hobson (1982), Tania Modleski (1982), Janice Radway (1984), Ien Ang (1985) and Ann Gray (1992).

2 Although not based upon audience studies, both Miriam Hansen's recent book and Angela Partington's work investigate questions of cinema history and spectatorship (see Partington, 1991, and Hansen, 1991).

3 See Janet Staiger's recent book on the question of cinema history and methodology (Staiger, 1992). See also Thumin (1992).

4 See, for example, Philip Corrigan (1983), Thomas Elsaesser (1984), Janet Staiger (1986) and Mary Ann Doane (1989a).

5 See Brunsdon (1991) and Stacey (1993).

6 The Mass Observation Archive is part of the library at Sussex University. It is a unique resource which holds files on many aspects of British 'everyday life' which date back to the 1930s. Mass Observation was started in the 1930s as a means of producing an 'anthropology of our own people' (Richards and Sheridan, 1987). According to Richards and Sheridan, the links between cinema and Mass Observation can be traced back to the founders of the project. Continuing the tradition of British documentary film with a political purpose, such as that of John Grierson or Humphrey Jennings in the 1930s, the founders of Mass Observation declared:

> [it] does not set out in quest of truth or facts for their own sake, or for the sake of an intellectual minority, but aims at exposing them in simple terms to all observers, so that their environment may be understood, and

thus constantly transformed. Whatever the political methods called upon to effect the transformation, the knowledge of what has to be transformed is indispensable. The foisting on the mass of ideals developed by men apart from it, irrespective of its capacities, causes mass misery, intellectual despair and international shambles.

(Quoted in Richards and Sheridan, 1987: 2–3)

Thus Mass Observation was conceived not only as 'Anthropology at Home', but also as anthropology with a political purpose, highlighting the circumstances of people's everyday lives in Britain, much as a documentary of the period would have done.

7 The first major Mass Observation project on the cinema was part of 'The Worktown project' in Bolton in 1937; cinema-going was one of the many activities documented in this study of life in a British industrial town. In the 1930s, there were no fewer than forty-seven cinemas within a five mile radius of Bolton, twenty-eight of which were within the boundaries of the borough (Richards and Sheridan, 1987: 3). The cinemas in Bolton gave Mass Observation support for their audience research, and a number of studies were done on cinema-going habits of audiences of the three major cinemas.

The results of these studies can now be found in *Mass Observation at the Movies* (Richards and Sheridan, 1987), which was not available when I began my research. Statistical details have been collated from the Mass Observation Archive files detailing how often people went to the cinema, whether they preferred British or American films, what they would have liked to see more and less of in films, as well as individual comments by members of the audience on their particular tastes and habits. This information is broken down by class and gender difference in order to analyse some of the differences in cinema-going habits between different groups of people in the audience: for example, the most working-class of the three cinemas studied had the highest proportion of young regular attenders, and a slightly higher proportion of women than men preferred British films (Richards and Sheridan, 1987: 33–4).

8 In addition to the Worktown project, Mass Observation carried out several reports and surveys on the cinema in wartime Britain. The Mass Observation work on cinema-going in wartime Britain is extensive; it includes reports on topics such as 'Report on audience preference in film themes', 'Notes on the effect of the war on the film industry' and 'The film and family life'.

9 See File 1871, 2464, Mass Observation Archive.

10 See Janet Thumin (1991, 1992).

11 The work of Antonia Lant (1991) is an exception to this.

12 Recent publications on stars which have filled this gap to some extent include Gledhill (1991) and Butler (1991).

13 Andrew Tudor (1974) points to the fact that there is intense same-sex attachment between spectators and film stars, but does not explore the explanations for this phenomenon.

14 I am grateful to Jane Gaines for pointing out to me the problem of the 'authenticity' of the letters sent to editors of film weeklies.

15 In its film and television periodical holdings, the archive held fifty magazines which fitted such a description. Some of these were not the kind of magazine I sought at all: for example *Film Festival* (1947–51) which dealt with the Edinburgh Festival, *Film User* (1948–71), a technical journal, or *The Circle* (1948–57), a trade journal. Some contained interesting material, but only limited editions were available: *British Film Review* (1948) contained material on British and American stars, *Film Weekly* (1928–39) contained a small letters

page as did *Cinegram Preview* (1939). Others included letters from readers but either these were very short, as in *Screen Review* (1948), or their letters, such as in *Photoplay* (1951), were signed with initials which made identifying the gender of their writers impossible.

16 The term 'discourse' is used here to refer to the way in which cultural meanings are organised and limited within particular boundaries at specific historical conjunctures. Although 'discourse' has a more general currency within linguistics, its use here, as in much cultural studies work, is derived from Foucault's work (1970, 1971, 1979).

17 I am indebted to Phil Levy and David Clarke of the Department of Information Studies at the University of Sheffield for their guidance and advice on the structure and question formulation in the questionnaire compiled for this research.

18 See, for example, Popular Memory Group, 'Popular memory: theory, politics and method', in Centre for Contemporary Cultural Studies (1982) and Frigga Haugg (1986).

19 See Sheila Jeffreys (1990) for a feminist critique of the so-called sexual revolution of the 1960s.

20 Christopher Norris made a useful distinction between history as narrative and history as fiction in his paper 'Deconstruction vs. postmodernism' at the Literary Studies in a Postmodern World Conference, held at Lancaster University on 4 May 1991.

21 See Walkerdine (1986), discussed in Chapter 2.

4 HOLLYWOOD CINEMA – THE GREAT ESCAPE

1 For a useful collection of the 'facts and figures' of cinema-going in Britain, see Pirelli (1983).

2 See Philip Corrigan (1983).

3 There is some sociological work on the concept of 'escapism' (see Katz and Foulkes, 1962).

4 The exclusively textual emphasis of much film studies work on the pleasures of spectatorship has meant that such questions have been ignored (see Chapter 2). Some attention has been paid to the whole cinema-going experience within film history (see for example Corrigan, 1983).

5 For a discussion of the history of cinema architecture, see Alloway (1961) and Furnham (1972).

6 For an analysis of the relationship between mass culture and femininity, see Tania Modleski (1986a), and between the cinema in particular and femininity, see Miriam Hansen (1991), Heide Schlüpman (1980), Andreas Huyssen (1986).

7 This association of British stars with 'acting' and Hollywood stars with 'glamour' was a recurrent theme in the letters pages of *Picturegoer* during the 1940s and 1950s (see Chapter 3).

8 For a discussion of feminist uses of object relations theory, see Sayers (1986).

9 See Gomery (1986) and Balio (1976) on the studio system; see also Part 1 in Gledhill's *Stardom: Industry of Desire* (1991) for analysis of stars and the studio system.

10 For an analysis of the impact of Americanness on postwar British culture, see 'Towards a cartography of taste', in Hebdige (1988).

11 For a discussion of idols and teenage hero worship, see Frith (1989).

5 FEMININE FASCINATIONS

1 For a discussion of female same-sex fascination and teenage 'crushes' see Gill Frith (1989).
2 See Janice Radway (1986) and see also Chapter 2 for a discussion of women and romance reading.
3 See Richard Dyer (1979: 168–72).
4 For an analysis of the relation between 1950s Hollywood melodrama and other forms of cultural consumption, see Angela Partington's 'Melodrama's gendered audience', in Sarah Franklin *et al.* (1991). See also Jane Gaines (1989).
5 For a critique of the concept of identification see Martin Barker (1989). I am grateful for Martin Barker's correspondence in response to an earlier version of this chapter in Christine Gledhill (1991). He questions my employment of the term 'identification' at all, given its conservative roots in mass cultural critiques of the media, and the implicit suggestion that it is a single, unified and universal process. The answer to this criticism would constitute another chapter altogether; suffice it to say here that the term is focused upon because of its centrality to both the ethnographic material I received and the feminist debates about spectatorship I seek to address. I hope the way I have explored identificatory relations emphasises their plurality: my argument throughout the book, and especially in Chapter 7, demonstrates the historical shifts in these relations between stars and spectators and thus challenges the universality of former psychoanalytic conceptualisations of identification.
6 In particular, Benjamin draws on the work of Mahler *et al.* (1975).
7 Ien Ang (1985) also uses the concept of 'recognition' to analyse the pleasures of popular culture, but she draws upon the work of Pierre Bourdieu (1984) rather than a psychoanalytic approach. See Chapter 2 for discussion of Ang's arguments about recognition.
8 Benjamin's account of the feminine equivalent to these processes in boy–father relations is more problematic, typical of psychoanalytic accounts which have endlessly wrestled to answer the 'riddles of femininity'. The girl's desire for recognition in the father will be less straightforward, since his identification with her will be weaker, and hers with him will be riddled with contradictions because of their 'difference'. However, Benjamin argues that girls also seek identification with the father who represents separation and the outside world. Indeed her interpretation of what has been classically referred to as 'penis envy' would be precisely such a desire. But their desire is generally denied, and mutual identification between daughter and father is unlikely to be fulfilled. Thus 'unprotected by the phallic sign of gender difference, unsupported by an alternative relationship, they relinquish their entitlement to desire. . . . They grow to idealize the man who has what they can never possess – power and desire' (Benjamin, 1990: 109).

Within the conventional patriarchal ordering the only desire open to women is envy and submission:

> the girl's identification with the father is typically refused, her love commonly tainted by envy and submission. We know that on the level of daily life, when desire goes unanswered, envy takes its place. Envy is often a signal of thwarted identification. The longing for the missing phallus, the envy that has been attributed to women, is really the longing for just such a homoerotic bond as boys may achieve, just such an identificatory love. This is why there are so many stories of women's love

being directed towards a hero such as she herself would be – the wish for disciplehood, serving an idol, submission to an ideal.

(Benjamin, 1990: 111)

See also Chapter 6 for an analysis of female spectators' envy in the context of consumption.

9 See the example of 'adoration' discussed earlier in this chapter.
10 Teresa de Lauretis (1991) suggests that the 'deeroticisation of desire' is the implication of my earlier arguments in relation to this question. See Chapter 2 for a discussion of her critique.
11 See Jackie Stacey (1987a), Valerie Traub (1991) and Merle Storr (1992) for discussions of the specificities of the pleasures of same-sex desire.

6 WITH STARS IN THEIR EYES

1 See Daniel Miller (1987) for an analysis of material culture and consumption.
2 For an analysis of the relationship between cinema and other cultural industries, see Angela Partington (1991).
3 The connection between shopping and matinées at the cinema for women is also represented within films: see for example *Brief Encounter* (1945, David Lean) in which the weekly shopping trip of the female protagonist, 'Laura' (Celia Johnson), is routinely combined with a matinée screening.
4 See Foucault (1971 and 1979) for his analysis of the ways in which the forms of subjectivity produced by discourse have also been forms of subjection and control. For a discussion of the relevance of his work to feminism, see Diamond and Quinby (1988).
5 See Chapter 4 for a discussion of the problems with Bourdieu's analysis of the pleasures of consumption in terms of gender.
6 'The intimacy which is knowledge' is a phrase borrowed from Gill Frith's study of female friendship in literature, originally formulated in Virginia Woolf's *To the Lighthouse* (see Frith, 1989).
7 See Marx (1976) on commodity fetishism, and Freud's 'Fetishism' (1963).
8 Much psychoanalytic theory has restricted analysis of desire to that produced by sexual difference and has ignored questions of same-sex desire, reading it within a rigidly dichotomous framework of sexual difference. See Merle Storr (1992), Valerie Traub (1991) and the discussion at the end of Chapter 5.
9 According to Lacan, the mirror phase necessitates the fundamental division between subject and object in all subjectivities (see Lacan, 1977); the argument made here, however, depends upon a consideration of the historical and gendered specificity of such a division.
10 The celebration of pleasure in popular culture is frequently criticised as a naive populism which has been identified with certain tendencies in cultural studies. For a discussion of these debates within the context of feminism, see Chapter 2.
11 Janet Thumin is at present studying the gendered discourses of broadcasting programming in 1950s Britain. For an analysis of the gendered cinema audience at this time see Thumin (1991 and 1992).

7 RELOCATING FEMALE SPECTATORSHIP

1 It has been argued that such a distinction has been somewhat eroded by recent changes in gender and consumer culture. In some work on gender and consumption, it has been argued that in the 1980s and 1990s we have witnessed an

increasing 'feminisation' of men's bodies. The 1980s, for example, saw the introduction of magazines for men about style, image and clothes. This genre of magazine had traditionally been reserved for women whilst magazines for men had tended to be either 'hobby magazines' or pornography. Similarly, it has been argued that the proliferation of cosmetic products and of different styles of clothes aimed at men in the last ten years has extended the role of being an object of the gaze to include masculinity. Thus, it could be argued that it is not only femininity which requires the reproduction of oneself as an image for others. Indeed, work in film studies, such as Dyer (1982), Neale (1983) and Hansen (1991), has demonstrated clearly that the male body on the screen can also be read as the object of the erotic gaze of the cinema spectator.

2 See Valerie Walkerdine's work on spectatorship and masculinity (Walkerdine, 1986).

3 Barry Norman (January 1993, BBC 1) quoted the troubling statistic that roles for female characters over forty make up only 9 per cent of roles in feature films.

4 See, in particular, the work of Stuart Hall (1986), Jacqueline Rose (1982, 1986) and Jeffrey Weeks (1985).

5 See Graham Dawson's discussion of masculine hero narratives in the 1950s in Dawson (1990).

6 See Susannah Radstone's work on nostalgia and memory (1993).

7 There have, however, been some recent feminist publications on stars, such as Christine Gledhill's (1991).

8 See, for example, Nancy Chodorow (1978) and Juliet Mitchell's recent collection of Melanie Klein's work (1986). It is also worth noting that much feminist therapy and work published in that field tends to use object relations theory.

9 See Chapter 5 and see also Jessica Benjamin's theory of recognition as central to the formation of subjectivity (Benjamin, 1990).

10 For a discussion of Walter Benjamin's work, see Andrew Benjamin (1989), Eugene Lunn (1985) and Celia Lury (1993).

11 Elizabeth Wright references the following writers on different forms of imaginative space such as play, Kristeva (1980); the therapeutic relationship, Winnicott (1974); and consuming the arts, Green (1978).

12 See Sheila Jeffreys (1990).

13 See Radstone (forthcoming) for a discussion of the place of nostalgia in postmodern culture.

14 The decline of the star system is typically attributed to the break-up of the Hollywood studio system and general changes in the organisation of film production, exhibition and distribution, as well as to the reorganisation of leisure, such as the effects of the introduction of television. Changes in the spectator/star relationship at the level of consumption have rarely been considered a relevant factor. What I would suggest, however, is that this change in the status of stars may well have contributed to the breakdown of the star system. What is perceived as stardom 'proper' is lost during the 1950s for many spectators who remember the increasing proximity of Hollywood stars with regret and look back with nostalgic desire to their previous status of distant idols.

I am grateful to John Caughie for raising this point in response to my paper given at the John Logie Baird Centre Seminar in Glasgow, 1990. For further references to the decline of the star system, see Gomery (1986), Balio (1976).

BIBLIOGRAPHY

Allen, Jeanne (1980) 'The film viewer as consumer', *Quarterly Review of Film Studies* 5, 4: 481–99.

Allen, Robert C. (1990) 'From exhibition to reception: reflections on the audience in film history', *Screen* 31, 4: 347–56.

Alloway, Lawrence (1961) 'Architecture and the modern cinema', *The Listener* 22 June: 1085–6.

Althusser, Louis (1971) 'Ideology and ideological state apparatuses', in *Lenin and Philosophy and Other Essays*, London: New Left Books.

Ang, Ien (1985) *Watching Dallas: Soap Opera and the Melodramatic Imagination*, London: Methuen.

Angelou, Maya (1984) *I Know Why The Caged Bird Sings*, London: Virago.

Artel, Linda and Wengrath, Susan (1990) 'Positive images: screening women's films', in Erens, Patricia (ed.) *Issues in Feminist Film Criticism*, Bloomington and Indianapolis: Indiana University Press.

Atwell, D. (1981) *Cathedrals of the Movies*, London: Heinemann.

Austin, Bruce A. (1989) *Immediate Seating: A Look at Movie Audiences*, California: Wadsworth.

Balio, Tino (ed.) (1976) *The American Film Industry*, Madison: University of Wisconsin Press.

Barker, Martin (1989) *Comics: Ideology, Power and the Critics*, Manchester: Manchester University Press.

Beechey, Veronica (1987) *Unequal Work*, London: Verso.

Bellour, Raymond (1977) 'Hitchcock the enunciator', *Camera Obscura* 2: 66–91.

—— (1979) 'Psychosis, neurosis, perversion', *Camera Obscura* 3/4: 105–6.

Benjamin, Andrew, (ed.) (1989) *The Problems of Modernity: Adorno and Benjamin*, London: Routledge.

Benjamin, Jessica (1990) *The Bonds of Love: Psychoanalysis, Feminism and the Problem of Domination*, London: Virago.

Benjamin, Walter (1970) *Illuminations*, London: Fontana.

Berger, John (1972) *Ways of Seeing*, Harmondsworth: Penguin.

Bergstrom, Janet (1979) 'Enunciation and sexual difference', *Camera Obscura* 3/4: 33–69.

Bernstein, Sydney (1947) 'The Bernstein report', FR 2464, Mass Observation Archive, Sussex University.

Betterton, Rosemary (1985) 'How do women look? The female nude in the work of Suzanne Valadon', *Feminist Review* 19: 3–24.

Bhabha, Homi K. (ed.) (1990) *Nation and Narration*, London: Routledge.

Birmingham Feminist History Group (1979) 'Feminism as femininity in the nineteen-fifties?', *Feminist Review* 3: 48–65.

Biskind, Peter (1983) *Seeing is Believing: How Hollywood Taught Us To Stop Worrying and Love The Fifties*, London: Pluto Press.

Bobo, Jacqueline (1988) '*The Color Purple*: black women as cultural readers', in Pribram, E. Deidre (ed.) *Female Spectators: Looking at Film and Television*, London: Verso.

Bordwell, David and Thompson, Kristin (1979) *Film Art: An Introduction*, New York: Alfred A. Knopf.

Bourdieu, Pierre (1980) 'The aristocracy of culture', *Media, Culture and Society* 2, 3: 225–54.

—— (1984) *Distinction: A Social Critique of the Judgement of Taste* (trans. by Richard Nice), London: Routledge & Kegan Paul.

Bowlby, Rachel (1985) *Just Looking: Consumer Culture in Dreiser, Gissing and Zola*, London: Methuen.

Box, Kathleen (1946) 'The cinema and the public', FR 2429, Mass Observation Archive, Sussex University.

Box, Kathleen and Moss, Louis (1943) *The Cinema Audience* (Wartime social survey), FR 1871, Mass Observation Archive, Sussex University.

Braybon, Gail and Summerfield, Penny (1987) *Out of the Cage: Women's Experiences in Two World Wars*, London: Pandora.

Brennan, Teresa (ed.) (1989) *Between Feminism and Psychoanalysis*, London: Routledge.

Bruno, Giuliana (1989) untitled entry, *Camera Obscura* 20/21: 28–40.

Brunsdon, Charlotte (1981) '*Crossroads*: notes on soap opera', in *Screen* 22, 4: 32–7.

—— (1986a) 'Women watching TV', paper presented at the Women and Electronic Mass Media Conference, Copenhagen.

—— (1986b) *Films for Women*, London: British Film Institute.

—— (1989) 'Text and audience', in Seiter, Ellen, Borchers, Hans, Kreutzner, Gabriele and Warth, Eva-Maria (eds) *Remote Control: Television, Audiences and Cultural Power*, London: Routledge.

—— (1991) 'Pedagogies of the feminine: feminist teaching and women's genres', *Screen* 32, 4: 364–81.

Brunsdon, Charlotte and Morley, David (1978) *Everyday Television: 'Nationwide'*, BFI Television Monograph, London: British Film Institute.

Burgin, Victor, Donald, James and Kaplan, Cora (eds) (1986) *Formations of Fantasy*, London: Methuen.

Butler, Jeremy (ed.) (1991) *Star Texts: Image and Performance in Film and Television*, Detroit: Wayne State University Press.

Byars, Jackie (1991) *All That Hollywood Allows: Rereading Gender in 1950s Melodrama*, London: Routledge.

Campbell, Colin (1987) *The Romantic Ethic and the Spirit of Modern Consumerism*, Oxford: Basil Blackwell.

Centre for Contemporary Cultural Studies, University Of Birmingham (1982) *Making Histories*, London: Hutchinson.

(charles) Helen (1992) 'Whiteness: the relevance of politically colouring the "non"', in Hinds, Hilary, Phoenix, Ann and Stacey, Jackie (eds) *Working Out: New Directions for Women's Studies*, London: Falmer.

Chodorow, Nancy (1978) *The Reproduction of Mothering: Psychoanalysis and the Sociology of Gender*, Berkeley: University of California Press.

Citron, Michelle, Lesage, Julia, Mayne, Judith, Rich, B. Ruby and Taylor, Anna Marie (1978) 'Women and film: a discussion of feminist aesthetics', *New German Critique* 13: 83–107.

Corrigan, Philip (1983) 'Film entertainment as ideology and pleasure: a preliminary approach to a history of audiences', in Curran, James and Porter, Vincent (eds) *British Cinema History*, London: Weidenfeld & Nicolson.

Coward, Rosalind (1984) *Female Desire: Women's Sexuality Today*, London: Paladin.

Cowie, Elizabeth (1978) 'Woman as sign', *m/f* 1: 49–63.

—— (1984) 'Fantasia', *m/f* 9: 71–104.

—— (1985) 'Strategems of identification', paper given at Sexual Difference Conference, University of Southampton, July.

—— (1989) untitled entry, *Camera Obscura* 20/21: 127–32.

Creed, Barbara (1989) untitled entry, *Camera Obscura* 20/21: 132–7.

Curran, James and Porter, Vincent (eds) (1983) *British Cinema History*, London: Weidenfeld.

Dawson, A. (1948) 'British and American motion picture wage rates compared', *Hollywood Quarterly* 3, 3.

Dawson, Graham (1990) 'Soldier heroes and adventure narratives: case studies in English masculine identities from the Victorian empire to post-imperial Britain', unpublished PhD Thesis, Dept. of Cultural Studies, University of Birmingham.

Debord, Guy (1977) *Society of the Spectacle*, Detroit: Black and Red.

de Lauretis, Teresa (1984) *Alice Doesn't: Feminism, Semiotics, Cinema*, London: Macmillan.

—— (1987) *Technologies of Gender: Essays on Theory Film and Fiction*, Bloomington: Indiana University Press.

—— (1991) 'Film and the visible', in Bad Object Choices (eds) *How Do I Look?: Queer Film and Video*, Seattle: Bay Press.

Diamond, Irene and Quinby, Lee (eds) (1988) *Foucault and Feminism: Reflections on Resistance*, Boston, MA: Northeastern University Press.

Doane, Mary Ann (1981–2) '*Caught* and *Rebecca*: the inscription of femininity as absence', *Enclitic* 6, 1/2, Fall/Spring: 75–89.

—— (1982) 'Film and the masquerade: theorising the female spectator', *Screen* 23, 3/4: 74–87.

—— (1987) *The Desire to Desire: The Woman's Film of the 1940's*, Bloomington and Indianapolis: Indiana University Press.

—— (1989a) 'The economy of desire: the commodity form in/of the cinema', *Quarterly Review of Film and Video* 11: 23–33.

—— (1989b) untitled entry, *Camera Obscura* 20/21: 142–7.

Doane, Mary Ann, Mellencamp, Patricia and Williams, Linda (eds) (1984) *Re-Visions: Essays in Feminist Film Criticism*, Frederick, MD: American Film Institute and University Press of America.

Dorner, Jane (1975) *Fashion in the Forties and Fifties*, London: Ian Allen.

Dyer, Richard (1979) *Stars*, London: British Film Institute.

—— (1982) 'Don't look now – the male pin-up', *Screen* 23, 3/4: 61–73.

—— (1985) 'Entertainment and utopia', in Nichols, Bill (ed.) *Movies and Methods: Volume II*, Berkeley, Los Angeles, London: University of California Press: 220–32.

—— (1986) *Heavenly Bodies: Film Stars and Society*, Basingstoke: Macmillan.

—— (1988) 'White', *Screen* 29, 4: 44–65.

Eckert, Charles (1978) 'The Carole Lombard in Macy's window', *Quarterly Review of Film Studies* 3, 1: 1–21.

Ellis, John (1982) *Visible Fictions: Cinema, Television, Video*, London: Routledge & Kegan Paul.

Elsaesser, Thomas (1984) 'Film history and visual pleasure: Weimar cinema', in Mellencamp, Patricia and Rosen, Philip (eds) *Cinema Histories, Cinema Practices*, American Film Institute Monograph Series, 4, Frederick, MD: University Publications of America.

England, Len (1944) 'The film and the family', FR 2120, Mass Observation Archive, Sussex University. (Also reprinted in Richards and Sheridan (eds) (1987).)

Erens, Patricia (ed.) (1990) *Issues in Feminist Film Criticism*, Bloomington: Indiana University Press.

Evans, Caroline and Thornton, Minna (1989) *Women and Fashion: A New Look*, London: Quartet.

Ewen, Elizabeth (1980) 'City lights: immigrant women and the rise of the movies', *Signs* 5, 3, supplement: 45–66.

Ewen, Stuart (1976) *Captains of Consciousness: Advertising and the Social Roots of Consumer Culture*, New York: McGraw-Hill Books.

Ewen, Stuart and Ewen, Elizabeth (1982) *Channels of Desire: Mass Images and the Shaping of American Consciousness*, New York: McGraw-Hill Books.

Feuer, Jane (1986) 'Dynasty', paper presented at International Television Studies Conference, London.

Finch, Janet and Summerfield, Penny (1991) 'Social reconstruction and the emergence of companionate marriage 1945–59', in Clark, David (ed.) *Marriage, Domestic Life and Social Change: Writings for Jacqueline Burgoyne (1944–88)*, London: Routledge: 7–32.

Fiske, John (1989) *Reading the Popular*, London: Unwin Hyman.

Flinn, Carol (1989) untitled entry, *Camera Obscura* 20/21: 151–5.

Flitterman, Sandy (1981) 'Women, desire and the look: feminism and the enunciative apparatus in cinema', in Caughie, John (ed.) *Theories of Authorship: A Reader*, London: British Film Institute/Routledge & Kegan Paul.

Foucault, Michel (1970) *The Order of Things: An Archaeology of the Human Sciences*, London: Tavistock.

—— (1971) *Madness and Civilisation: A History of Insanity in the Age of Reason*, London: Tavistock.

—— (1979) *The History of Sexuality, Volume 1: An Introduction* (trans. by Robert Hurley), London: Allen Lane.

Franklin, Sarah, Lury, Celia and Stacey, Jackie (eds) (1991) *Off-Centre: Feminism and Cultural Studies*, London: HarperCollins Academic (now Routledge).

French, Brandon (1978) *On The Verge of Revolt – Women in American Films of the 50s*, New York: Frederick Ungar Publishing Co.

Freud, Sigmund (1905) 'Three essays on the theory of sexuality', in *Standard Edition* 7: 123–246, London: Hogarth Press.

—— (1920) 'The psychogenesis of a case of homosexuality in a woman', in *Standard Edition* 18: 147–72, London: Hogarth Press.

—— (1925) 'Some physical consequences of the anatomical distinction between the sexes', in *Standard Edition* 19: 243–58, London: Hogarth Press.

—— (1931) 'Female sexuality', in *Standard Edition* 21: 225–46, London: Hogarth Press.

—— (1933) 'On femininity', in *Standard Edition* 22: 112–35, London: Hogarth Press.

—— (1963) 'Fetishism', in Rieff, Philip (ed.) *Sexuality and the Psychology of Love*, New York: Collier Books.

Friedberg, Anne (1982) 'Identification and the star: a refusal of difference', in *Star Signs: Papers from a Weekend Workshop*, London: British Film Institute.

Frith, Gillian (1989) 'The intimacy which is knowledge: female friendship in the novels of women writers', unpublished PhD thesis, Department of English and Comparative Literature, University of Warwick.

Fryer, Peter (1984) *Staying Power: The History of Black People in Britain*, London: Pluto Press.

Furnham, David (1972) 'Garden of dreams', *New Society* 10 August: 297–8.

Gaines, Jane (1986) 'War, women and lipstick: fan mags in the forties', *Heresies* 18: 42–7.

—— (1989) 'The Queen Christina tie-ups: convergence of show windows and screen', *Quarterly Review of Film and Video* 11: 35–60.

Gaines, Jane and Herzog, Charlotte (eds) (1990) *Fabrications: Costume and the Female Body*, London: Routledge.

Gallop, Jane (1982) *The Daughter's Seduction: Feminism and Psychoanalysis*, London: Macmillan.

Gamman, Lorraine and Marshment, Margaret (eds) (1988) *The Female Gaze: Women as Viewers of Popular Culture*, London: The Women's Press.

Gledhill, Christine (1978) '"Klute": a contemporary film noir and feminist criticism', in E. A. Kaplan (ed.) *Women in Film Noir*, London: British Film Institute.

—— (1984) 'Developments in feminist film criticism', in Doane, Mary Ann, Mellencamp, Patricia and Williams, Linda (eds) *Re-Visions: Essays in Feminist Film Criticism*, Frederick, MD: American Film Institute and University Press of America.

—— (ed.) (1987) *Home is Where The Heart Is: Studies in Melodrama and The Woman's Film*, London: British Film Institute.

—— (1988) 'Pleasurable negotiations', in Pribram, E. Deidre (ed.) *Female Spectators: Looking at Film and Television*, London: Verso.

—— (ed.) (1991) *Stardom: Industry of Desire*, London: Routledge.

Gomery, Douglas (1986) *The Hollywood Studio System*, Basingstoke: Macmillan.

Gray, Ann (1987) 'Behind closed doors: video recorders in the home', in Baehr, Helen and Dyer, Gillian (eds) *Boxed In: Women and Television*, London: Pandora.

—— (1992) *Video Playtime: The Gendering of a Leisure Technology*, London: Routledge.

Green, André (1978) 'Potential space in psychoanalysis: the objects in the setting', in Gronick, Simon G. and Barkin, Leonard (eds) *Transitional Objects and Phenomena*, New York and London: Jason Aronson.

Grieg, Don (1987) 'The sexual differentiation of the Hitchcock text', *Screen* 28, 1, Winter: 28–48.

Hall, Stuart (1980) 'Encoding/decoding', in Hall, Stuart, Hobson, Dorothy, Lowe, Andrew and Willis, Paul (eds) *Culture, Media, Language*, Birmingham: Centre for Contemporary Cultural Studies, University of Birmingham.

—— (1986) 'New ethnicities', in *Black Film, British Cinema*, ICA Document no. 7, London: ICA..

Handel, Leo (1950) *Hollywood Looks at its Audience*, Urbana, IL: University of Illinois Press.

Hansen, Miriam (1986) 'Pleasure, ambivalence, identification: Valentino and female spectatorship', *Cinema Journal* 25, 4.

—— (1989) untitled entry, *Camera Obscura* 20/21: 169–75.

—— (1991) *Babel and Babylon: Spectatorship in American Silent Film*, Cambridge, MA: Harvard University Press.

Haskell, Molly (1973) *From Reverence to Rape: The Treatment of Women in the Movies*, New York: Holt, Rinehart & Winston.

Haugg, Frigga (ed.) (1986) *Female Sexualisation*, London: Verso.

Heath, Stephen (1975) 'Film and system: terms of analysis', *Screen* 16, 1 and 2: 7–77 and 91–113.

—— (1978) 'Difference', *Screen* 19, 3: 51–112.

Hebdige, Dick (1988) 'Towards a cartography of taste 1935–1962', in *Hiding in the Light: On Images and Things*, London: Comedia.

Heron, Liz (ed.) (1985) *Truth, Dare or Promise: Girls Growing Up in the Fifties*, London: Virago.

Hobson, Dorothy (1982) *'Crossroads': The Drama of a Soap Opera*, London: Methuen.

Hoggart, Richard (1958) *The Uses of Literacy*, Harmondsworth: Penguin.

hooks, bell (1991) *Yearning: Race, Gender and Cultural Politics*, London: Turnaround Press.

Hopkins, Harry (1963) *The New Look*, London: Secker & Warberg.

Huyssen, Andreas (1986) 'Mass culture as woman: modernism's other', in Modleski, Tania (ed.) *Studies In Entertainment: Critical Approaches to Mass Culture*: 188–208, Bloomington and Indianapolis University Press.

Irigaray, Luce (1985) *This Sex Which is Not One* (trans. by Catherine Porter with Carolyn Burke), Ithaca, NY: Cornell University Press.

Jarvie, I. C. (1970) *Towards a Sociology of the Cinema*, London: Routledge & Kegan Paul.

Jeffreys, Sheila (1990) *Anti-Climax*, London: The Women's Press.

Kaplan, E. Ann (ed.) (1978) *Women in Film Noir*, London: British Film Institute.

—— (1983) *Women and Film: Both Sides of the Camera*, London: Methuen.

—— (1984) 'Is the gaze male?', in Snitow, Ann, Stansell, Christine and Thompson, Sharon (eds) *Desire: The Politics of Sexuality*, London: Virago.

—— (1987) *Rocking Around the Clock: Music Television, Postmodernism and Cultural Consumption*, London: Methuen.

—— (1989) untitled entry, *Camera Obscura* 20/21: 194–9.

Katz, Elihu and Foulkes, David (1962) 'On the use of the mass media as "escape": clarification of a concept', *Public Opinion Quarterly* 26: 377–88.

Katz, Elihu and Liebes, Tamar (1985) 'Mutual aid in the decoding of *Dallas*', in Drummond, Philip and Patterson, Richard (eds) *Television in Transition*, London: British Film Institute.

Kay, Karyn and Peary, Gerald (1977) *Women and the Cinema: A Critical Anthology*, New York: Dutton.

Kindem, Gorham (ed.) (1982) *The American Movie Industry: The Business of Motion Pictures*, Carbondale: Southern Illinois University Press.

Kristeva, Julia (1980) *Desire In Language*, New York: Colombia University Press.

Kuhn, Annette (1982) *Women's Pictures: Feminism and Cinema*, London: Routledge & Kegan Paul.

—— (1984) 'Women's genres', *Screen* 25, 1: 18–28.

—— (1989) untitled entry, *Camera Obscura* 20/21: 213–17.

Kuhn, Annette (ed.) with Radstone, Susannah (1990) *The Women's Companion to International Film*, London: Virago.

Lacan, Jacques (1977) 'The mirror stage as formative of the I as revealed in psychoanalytic experience', in *Ecrits* (trans. by Alan Sheridan), London: Tavistock.

Lant, Antonia (1991) *Blackout: Reinventing Women for Wartime British Cinema*, Princeton, NJ: Princeton University Press.

La Place, Maria (1987) 'Producing and consuming the woman's film: discursive struggle in *Now, Voyager*', in Gledhill, Christine (ed.) *Home Is Where The Heart Is: Studies in Melodrama and The Woman's Film*, London: British Film Insitute.

Laplanche, Jean and Pontalis, Jean-Bertrand (1968) 'Fantasy and the origins of sexuality', reprinted in Burgin, Victor, Donald, James and Kaplan, Cora (eds) (1986) *Formations of Fantasy*, London: Methuen.

Lewis, Lisa (ed.) (1992) *The Adoring Audience: Fan Culture and Popular Media*, London: Routledge.

Lewis, Peter (1978) *The Fifties*, London: Heinemann.

Lovell, Terry (1980) *Pictures of Reality: Aesthetics, Politics and Pleasures*, London: British Film Institute.

Lunn, Eugene (1985) *Marxism and Modernism: An Historical Study of Lukacs, Brecht, Benjamin and Adorno*, London: Verso.

Lury, Celia (1993) *Cultural Rights: Technology, Legality and Personality*, London: Routledge.

MacCabe, Colin (ed.) (1986) *High Theory, Low Culture: Analysing Popular Television and Film*, Manchester: Manchester University Press.

MacKinnon, Catherine (1982) 'Feminism, Marxism, method and the state: an agenda for theory', *Signs* 7, 3: 515–44.

Mahler, Margaret, Pine, Fred and Bergman, Anni (1975) *The Psychological Birth of the Human Infant: Symbiosis and Individuation*, London: Hutchinson.

Marks, Elaine and de Courtivron, Isabelle (1981) *New French Feminisms*, Brighton: Harvester.

Martin, Emily (1987) *The Woman in the Body: A Cultural Analysis of Reproduction*, Boston, MA: Beacon Press.

Marx, Karl (1976) 'The fetishism of the commodity and its secret', in *Capital: A Critique of Political Economy* (trans. by Ben Fowkes), vol. 1, book 1, chapter 1, section 4, Harmondsworth: Penguin.

Mayne, Judith (1982) 'Immigrants and spectators', *Wide Angle* 5, 2: 32–41.

Medhurst, Andy (1985) 'Can chaps be pin-ups?', *Ten 8* no. 17.

Merck, Mandy (1987) 'Introduction: difference and its discontents', *Screen* 28, 1, Winter: 2–10.

Metz, Christian (1974) *Film Language: A Semiotics of the Cinema* (trans. by Michael Taylor), New York: Oxford University Press.

—— (1975) 'The imaginary signifier', *Screen* 16, 2, Summer: 14–76.

—— (1982) *Psychoanalysis and Cinema: The Imaginary Signifier* (trans. by Celia Britton *et al.*), London: Macmillan.

Miller, Daniel (1987) *Material Culture and Mass Consumption*, Oxford: Basil Blackwell.

Minns, Raynes (1980) *Bombers and Mash: The Domestic Front 1939–45*, London: Virago.

Mitchell, Juliet (1975) *Psychoanalysis and Feminism*, Harmondsworth: Penguin.

—— (ed.) (1986) *The Selected Works of Melanie Klein*, London: Penguin.

Mitchell, Juliet and Rose, Jacqueline (1982) *Feminine Sexuality: Jacques Lacan and the École Freudienne*, London: Macmillan.

Modleski, Tania (1982) *Loving With a Vengeance: Mass-Produced Fantasies for Women*, London: Methuen.

—— (1986a) 'Femininity as mas[s]querade: a feminist approach to mass culture', in MacCabe, Colin (ed.) *High Theory, Low Culture: Analysing Popular Television and Film*, Manchester: Manchester University Press.

—— (1986b) 'Introduction', in Modleski, Tania (ed.) *Studies in Entertainment*, Bloomington: Indiana University Press.

—— (1988) *The Women Who Knew Too Much: Hitchcock and Feminist Theory*, London: Methuen.

Monaco, James (1977) *How To Read a Film: The Art, Technology, Language, History and Theory of Film and Media*, New York: Oxford University Press.

Morley, David (1980) *The 'Nationwide' Audience: Structure and Decoding*, London: British Film Insitute.

—— (1986) *Family Television: Cultural Power and Domestic Leisure*, London: Comedia.

—— (1989) 'Changing paradigms in audience studies', in Seiter, Ellen, Borchers, Hans, Kreutzner, Gabriele and Warth, Eva-Maria (eds) *Remote Control: Television, Audiences and Cultural Power*, London: Routledge.

—— (1991) 'Where the global meets the local: notes from the sitting room', *Screen* 32, 1: 1–15.

Morris, Meaghan (1988) 'Banality in cultural studies', *Block* 14.

Mulvey, Laura (1975) 'Visual pleasure and narrative cinema', *Screen* 16, 3: 6–18.

—— (1981) 'Afterthoughts on "visual pleasure and narrative cinema" inspired by *Duel in the Sun*', *Framework* 6, 15/16/17: 12–15.

—— (1989) *Visual and Other Pleasures*, Basingstoke: Macmillan.

Muscio, Giuliana (1989) 'Mass images of consumption', *Quarterly Review of Film and Video*, 11: 121–5.

Nava, Mica (1992) *Changing Cultures*, London: Sage.

Neale, Steve (1980) *Genre*, London: British Film Institute.

—— (1983) 'Masculinity as spectacle', *Screen* 24, 6: 2–17.

Nichols, Bill (ed.) (1985) *Movies and Methods: Volume II*, Berkeley, Los Angeles and London: University of California Press.

Nicholson, Linda (ed.) (1990) *Feminism/Postmodernism*, London: Routledge.

Partington, Angela (1990) 'Consumption practices as the production and articulation of differences: rethinking working-class femininity in 1950s Britain', unpublished PhD Thesis, University of Birmingham.

—— (1991) 'Melodrama's gendered audience', in Franklin, Sarah, Lury, Celia and Stacey, Jackie (eds) *Off Centre: Feminism and Cultural Studies*, London: Harper Collins/Routledge.

Pearce, Lynne (1991) *Woman/Image/Text: Readings in Pre-Raphaelite Art and Literature*, Brighton: Harvester Wheatsheaf.

Penley, Constance (1984) paper given at *m/f* Conference, London.

—— (1985) 'Feminism, film theory and the bachelor machines', *m/f* 10.

—— (1989) untitled entry, *Camera Obscura* 20/21: 256–60.

Perkins, Victor (1972) *Film as Film: Understanding and Judging Movies*, Harmondsworth: Penguin.

Petro, Patrice (1989) untitled entry, *Camera Obscura* 20/21: 260–3.

Pirelli, Patricia (1983) 'Statistical survey of the British film industry', in Curran, James and Porter, Vincent (eds) *British Cinema History*, London: Weidenfeld & Nicolson: 372–82.

Pollock, Griselda (1988) *Vision and Difference: Femininity, Feminism and the History of Art*, London: Routledge.

Popular Memory Group (n.d.) 'Popular Memory', unpublished papers, Birmingham: Centre for Contemporary Cultural Studies, University of Birmingham.

Pribram, E. Deidre (1988) *Female Spectators: Looking at Film and Television*, London: Verso.

Radstone, Susannah (1993) 'Remembering Medea: the uses of nostalgia', *Critical Quarterly* 35/3.

—— (forthcoming) 'Gender and nostalgia', in Florence, Penny and Reynolds, Dee (eds) *Media/Subject/Gender: Feminist Positions and Redefinitions*, Manchester: Manchester University Press.

Radway, Janice (1984) *Reading the Romance: Women, Patriarchy and Popular Literature*, Chapel Hill, London: University of North Carolina Press.

—— (1986) 'Identifying ideological seams: mass culture, analytical method and political practice', *Communication* 9: 93–123.

—— (1988) 'Reception study: ethnography and the problems of dispersed audiences and nomadic subjects', *Cultural Studies* 2, 3: 359–76.

Ramazanoglu, Caroline (1989) *Feminism and the Contradictions of Oppression*, London: Routledge.

Rich, Adrienne (1986) 'Notes toward a politics of location', in *Blood, Bread and Poetry: Selected Prose 1979–1985*, New York and London: W. W. Norton.

Richards, Jeffrey and Sheridan, Dorothy (eds) (1987) *Mass Observation at the Movies*, London: Routledge & Kegan Paul.

Riviere, Joan (1986) [1929] 'Womanliness as a masquerade', in Burgin, Victor, Donald, James and Kaplan, Cora (eds) *Formations of Fantasy*, London: Methuen.

Roach, Jacqui and Felix, Petal (1988) 'Black looks', in Gamman, Lorraine and Marshment, Margaret (eds) *The Female Gaze: Women as Viewers of Popular Culture*, London: The Women's Press: 130–42.

Rodowick, David (1982) 'The difficulty of difference', *Wide Angle* 5, 1: 4–15.

Rose, Jacqueline (1976–7) 'Paranoia and the film system', *Screen* 17, 4: 85–104.

—— (1982) 'Introduction', in Mitchell, Juliet and Rose, Jacqueline (eds) *Feminine Sexuality: Jacques Lacan and the École Freudienne*, London: Macmillan.

—— (1986) *Sexuality in the Field of Vision*, London: Verso.

—— (1989) untitled entry, *Camera Obscura* 20/21: 274–9.

Rosen, Marjorie (1973) *Popcorn Venus: Women, Movies and the American Dream*, New York: Coward, McCann & Geoghegan.

Runnymede Trust and the Radical Statistics Race Group, The (1980) *Britain's Black Population*, London: Heinemann Educational Books.

Saussure, Ferdinand de (1974) *Course in General Linguistics*, London: Fontana.

Sayers, Janet (1986) *Sexual Contradictions: Psychology, Psychoanalysis and Feminism*, London: Tavistock Publications.

Schivelbusch, Wolfgang (1977) *The Railway Journey: Trains and Travel in the Nineteenth Century* (trans. by Anselm Hollo), New York: Urizen Books.

Schlüpman, Heide (1980) 'Kinosucht', *Frauen und Film* no. 33: 45–52.

Seiter, Ellen, Borchers, Hans, Kreutzner, Gabriele and Warth, Eva-Maria (1989) 'Introduction', in Seiter, Ellen, Borchers, Hans, Kreutzner, Gabriele and Warth, Eva-Maria (eds) *Remote Control: Television, Audiences and Cultural Power*, London: Routledge.

—— (1989) 'Don't treat us like we're so stupid and naïve: towards an ethnography of soap opera viewers', in Seiter, Ellen, Borchers, Hans, Kreutzner, Gabriele and Warth, Eva-Maria (eds) *Remote Control: Television, Audiences and Cultural Power*, London: Routledge.

Sherman, Cindy (1991) *Cindy Sherman 1991*, exhibition catalogue, Basel, Kunsthalle, London: Whitechapel Art Gallery.

Sinfield, Alan (1989) *Literature, Politics and Culture in Postwar Britain*, Oxford: Basil Blackwell.

Spelman, Elizabeth V. (1990) *Inessential Woman: Problems of Exclusion in Feminist Thought*, London: The Women's Press.

Spivak, Gayatri C. (1985) 'Strategies of vigilance', *Block* 5: 5–9.

—— (1987) *In Other Worlds: Essays in Cultural Politics*, London: Methuen.

Stacey, Jackie (1987a) 'Desperately seeking difference', *Screen* 28, 1: 48–62.

—— (1987b) 'The invisible difference', *Homosexuality: Which Homosexuality Conference Papers*, Amsterdam: Free University Press.

—— (1990) 'Romance', in Kuhn, Annette (ed.) with Radstone, Susannah, *The Women's Companion to International Film*, London: Virago.

—— (1993) 'Textual obsessions: method, memory and researching female spectatorship', *Screen* 34, 3.

Staiger, Janet (1986) '*The Handmaiden of Villainy*: methods and problems in studying the historical reception of film', *Wide Angle* 8, 1: 19–28.

—— (1992) *Interpreting Films: Studies in the Historical Reception of American Cinema*, Princeton, NJ: Princeton University Press.

Steedman, Carolyn (1986) *Landscape for a Good Woman: A Story of Two Lives*, London: Virago.

Storr, Merle (1992) 'Psychoanalysis and lesbian desire: the trouble with female homosexuals', paper at the Activating Theory Conference, York University, to be published in Bristow, Joe, and Wilson, Angie (eds) (forthcoming).

Studlar, Gaylyn (1989) Untitled entry in *Camera Obscura* 20/21: 300–4.

Swann, Paul (1987) *The Hollywood Feature Film in Postwar Britain*, Kent: Croom Helm.

Taylor, Helen (1989) *Scarlett's Women: 'Gone with the Wind' and its Female Fans*, London: Virago.

Thumin, Janet (1991) 'The "popular": cash and culture in the postwar British cinema industry', *Screen* 32, 3: 245–71.

—— (1992) *Celluloid Sisters: Women and Popular Cinema*, London: Macmillan.

Traub, Valerie (1991) 'The ambiguities of "lesbian" viewing pleasure: the (dis)articulations of *Black Widow*', in Epstein, Julia and Straub, Kristina (eds) *Body Guards: The Cultural Politics of Gender Ambiguity*, London: Routledge: 305–28.

Trinh T. Minh-ha (1989) *Woman, Native, Other: Writing, Postcoloniality and Feminism*, Bloomington: Indiana University Press.

Tudor, Andrew (1974) *Image and Influence: Studies in the Sociology of Film*, London: George Allen & Unwin.

Walby, Sylvia (1986) *Patriarchy at Work: Patriarchal and Capitalist Relations in Employment*, Oxford: Polity Press.

—— (1990) *Theorizing Patriarchy*, Oxford: Basil Blackwell.

Waldman, Diane (1990) 'There's more to a positive image than meets the eye', in Erens, Patricia (ed.) *Issues in Feminist Film Criticism*, Bloomington: Indiana University Press.

Walkerdine, Valerie (1986) 'Video replay: families, films and fantasy', in Burgin, Victor, Donald, James and Kaplan, Cora (eds) *Formations of Fantasy*, London: Methuen.

Weeks, Jeffrey (1985) *Sexuality and Its Discontents*, London: Routledge & Kegan Paul.

Weiss, Andrea (1992) *Vampires and Violets: Lesbians in the Cinema*, London: Jonathan Cape.

Williams, Linda (1989) untitled entry, *Camera Obscura* 20/21: 332–6.

Williams, Raymond (1965) *The Long Revolution*, Harmondsworth: Penguin.

—— (1976) *Keywords*, London: Fontana.

—— (1977) *Marxism and Literature*, Oxford: Oxford University Press.

Williamson, Judith (1978) *Decoding Advertisements: Ideology and Meaning in Advertising*, London: Marion Boyars.

—— (1986a) 'The problems of being popular', *New Socialist*, September: 14–15.

—— (1986b) *Consuming Passions: The Dynamics of Popular Culture*, London: Marion Boyars.

Wilson, Elizabeth (1980) *Only Halfway to Paradise: Women in Postwar Britain: 1945–1968*, London: Tavistock.

Winnicott, D. W. (1974) *Playing and Reality*, Harmondsworth: Penguin.

Winship, Janice (1981) 'Woman becomes an "individual" – femininity and consumption in women's magazines 1954–69', *Stencilled Occasional Paper* 65, Birmingham: Centre for Contemporary Cultural Studies, University of Birmingham.

Wright, Elizabeth (1984) *Psychoanalytic Criticism: Theory in Practice*, London: Methuen.

INDEX

(Page numbers in bold type indicate illustrations.)

white feminists 257n15
whiteness 13, 255n2
Williams, Esther 161
Williams, Linda 19, 133
Williams, Mary 116, 121
Williams, Raymond 35
Williamson, Judith 8, 9, 46
Wilson, Elizabeth 222
Wilson, Mary 110, 160, 200, 209
Winnicott, D. W. 236
Winship, Janice 8, 185–6, 187, 218
woman 133; as image 10, 21
Woman 60, 221; *see also* women's
   magazines
woman's film, the 9, 85
Woman's Realm 16, 60, 62, 87, 88,
   243; *see also* women's magazines

Woman's Weekly 16, 60, 62, 87, 88,
   243; *see also* women's magazines
women: black 62; class categorisation
   of 256n15; and commodities 8, 184,
   186–7; as consumers 177; in the
   Second World War 102–4; and
   television viewing practices 40;
   young 110; white 62, 239; *see also*
   soap opera(s)
women's magazines 221–2
Worktown Project 51, 259ns7/8
worship 138, 142–3
Wright, Elizabeth 131, 228, 229, 230
Wright, Sheila 152
Wyman, Jane 60, 168, 203, 216, 243

Young, Loretta 52, 160, 209